Taking Brand Initiative

Taking Brand Initiative

How Companies Can Align Strategy, Culture, and Identity Through Corporate Branding

Mary Jo Hatch, Majken Schultz

Foreword by Wally Olins

JOSSEY-BASS
A Wiley Imprint
www.josseybass.com

Published by Jossey-Bass
A Wiley Imprint
989 Market Street, San Francisco, CA 94103-1741—www.josseybass.com

Readers should be aware that Internet Web sites offered as citations and/or sources for further
information may have changed or disappeared between the time this was written and when it
is read.

Limit of Liability/Disclaimer of Warranty: While the publisher and author have used their
best efforts in preparing this book, they make no representations or warranties with respect
to the accuracy or completeness of the contents of this book and specifically disclaim any
implied warranties of merchantability or fitness for a particular purpose. No warranty may
be created or extended by sales representatives or written sales materials. The advice and
strategies contained herein may not be suitable for your situation. You should consult with a
professional where appropriate. Neither the publisher nor author shall be liable for any loss
of profit or any other commercial damages, including but not limited to special, incidental,
consequential, or other damages.

Jossey-Bass books and products are available through most bookstores. To contact Jossey-Bass
directly call our Customer Care Department within the U.S. at 800-956-7739, outside the
U.S. at 317-572-3986, or fax 317-572-4002.

Jossey-Bass also publishes its books in a variety of electronic formats. Some content that
appears in print may not be available in electronic books.

Library of Congress Cataloging-in-Publication Data

Hatch, Mary Jo.
    Taking brand initiative : how companies can align strategy, culture, and identity through
corporate branding / Mary Jo Hatch, Majken Schultz.—1st ed.
        p. cm.
    Includes bibliographical references and index.
    ISBN 978-0-7879-9830-1 (cloth)
    1. Corporate image.   2. Corporate culture.   3. Branding (Marketing)
I. Schultz, Majken.   II. Title.
    HD59.2.H38 2008
    658.8'27—dc22

                                                                2007049669

Printed in the United States of America
FIRST EDITION
HB Printing   10 9 8 7 6 5 4 3 2 1

Contents

For our daughters, Jennifer Cron and Julie Junge-Jensen

Foreword

I have a little story to tell.

Many, many years ago when Britain still had a flourishing industrial base, my then company Wolff Olins was appointed by the chairman of one of the largest machine tool companies to create what we were starting to call a corporate identity programme.

Our client was about to launch a new range of CAD CAM machines—that is, computer-aided design and manufacturing equipment. We were told that CAD CAM was going to sweep the world and that the new machines being designed by our client's company were state of the art. So he desperately wanted them to be first to market. Breakthrough in design, relatively easy to operate, superb global backup and service. That was the intention.

The new corporate identity was to relaunch the company. Our programme was to be thorough and rigorous. The identity was to be launched first internally, to the workforce, and then to the importers and the newly formed global dealer network, and finally externally, to customers, potential customers, and the technical press worldwide. With the benefit of the new machines and our new identity our client's company was to turn itself from a lowish-profile, respected, conservative, rather traditional organisation into a high-profile world leader.

We were thrilled. Wolff Olins was small and we saw this as our big chance. At the time, the early 1970s, this type of corporate identity activity was new. We were young and very excited. Our client would make a huge impact in the world and we would too.

We could see this job as a breakthrough for the corporate identity business and for our own company.

We had been appointed after a competitive pitch, and we were working directly with the chairman, a charming, determined, and forceful man totally committed to the project.

We did our homework very carefully. We carried out interviews amongst competitors, suppliers, and customers. We learnt that our client's company was well respected in the outside world, but regarded as a bit conservative—even old-fashioned.

We also learned that the machine tool business as a whole was changing fast. Computers were the new thing. The company that initiated CAD CAM on a grand scale had a chance of cleaning up in world markets.

Then we did the internal interviews. With very few exceptions we were told that although the new machines were superb conceptually, they were nothing like ready to launch. There were very many features of the detailed design that needed to be cleaned up; the machines were difficult and expensive to make and new small faults kept emerging. It also became clear that the proposed global service network was badly trained, understaffed, and didn't understand how the machines could most effectively be utilised in different industrial situations. In other words, we were told that the company was just not ready.

On top of all that, it was clear to us that there was deep discomfort within the organisation. The culture of the business was traditional, cautious, and low-profile. People at all levels were terrified of what they were being pushed into. Phrases like "putting all your eggs in one basket," said with a negative shake of the head, became familiar to us.

We went back and told all this to the chairman—our client. He discounted all of it. He told us not to worry about what we had heard; this was all traditional corporate caution, even pessimism, typical of the old style of the company, which had to be broken. Above all he was deeply concerned about the competition getting out there first and losing prime mover position.

Although we were doubtful, we wanted to believe him. We went back and did more interviews with the shop floor and most of the management, with similar results. They didn't like it. They weren't comfortable. They were anxious. But the chairman remained absolutely firm—launch in six months. At meetings between the chairman and his top managers, which we attended, doubts were raised, but in a muffled, implicit sort of way. Nobody spoke up as they did when they were with us or alone with each other because they were intimidated. There was clearly a tacit agreement amongst managers not to rock the boat. We found the rift between the top management and chairman disturbing, but when we spoke to him about what we had heard he evidently thought we were exaggerating.

Anyway despite our fears we went ahead. We wanted to believe that it would be OK. We prepared the newly refreshed brand; shortened the name, redesigned the logo with new colours, new typography—the works. It was, though I say it with hindsight, a brilliant piece of work, well planned and well executed. And we launched.

What happened? It was a disaster from which the company never truly recovered. We had helped to turn a decently performing, low-profile, medium-sized company into a badly performing high-profile company. The machines weren't ready. Deliveries were late. The products didn't perform. Service was slow and inadequate.

A couple of years later the company went into receivership.

Why do I tell this story?

Because through that experience I learned a lesson that I never forgot, an experience that Hatch and Schultz carefully lay out page by page in this very thoughtful, thorough, intelligent, insightful book. Get it right. And get your team behind you. Get the inside and the outside working together. Don't kid yourself. Develop a brand based around real performance—not hype.

Schultz and Hatch have a lot of experience. What they write about really happens. They recognise that brands need a mix of functional and emotional content. That the whole company has to believe in what it is doing, but that even then things can and often do go wrong.

They believe you should not try to quantify the unquantifiable. For example, they are sceptical about attributing a financial value to a brand on the basis of theoretical and complex econometric measurements. So am I.

I enthusiastically endorse the authors' approach. Hatch and Schultz know what they are talking about. This is a very worthwhile book.

Wally Olins
Goring-on-Thames
December 2007

Wally Olins is the co-founder and former chairman of Wolff Olins and currently the chairman of Saffron Brand Consultants. One of the world's most experienced practitioners of corporate identity and branding, he has been consulting with leading companies, regions, and institutions all over the world and is the author of numerous renowned books and articles on corporate identity and branding. Olins is a visiting fellow at Said Business School in Oxford and adjunct professor at Lancaster University and Copenhagen Business School. Learn more from www.wallyolins.com.

Preface

This book was inspired by a joint venture between the authors and corporate branding leaders from some of the world's most well-branded companies. Corporate brand managers from the LEGO Group, Nissan, Novo Nordisk, Johnson & Johnson, ING Group, Telefónica, SONY, and Boeing all participated. Known as the Corporate Brand Initiative (CBI), this undertaking involved regular meetings on both sides of the Atlantic to focus on defining and refining the field of brand management by sharing issues and challenges as they arose. CBI was supported by the Copenhagen Business School and the University of Virginia, with funding from the LEGO Group.

We created CBI in partnership with this particular group of managers because we felt that they sat at the forefront of corporate branding as an exciting new business practice. Being in the vanguard meant that the participants had few role models to follow, and CBI was a means for them to build an intellectual foundation for their work and to help one another develop processes and practices that would benefit their firms.

In part, participants agreed to join CBI to explore the value of organization theory in their world and to help educate students about corporate brand management. Members included a COO and functional executives from Marketing, Communication, and Human Resources, all of whom operated across multiple functions in their organizations to produce corporate brand thinking and influence decision making company-wide. This book documents the knowledge that CBI produced.

Acknowledgments

We have many people to acknowledge for their indispensable help with this project. Those involved in CBI include Simon Boege, Francesco Ciccolella, Stefan Gerond, Esther Trujillo Gimenez, Erich Joachimstahler, Iben Eiby Johannesen, Philip Mirvis, George Overstreet, Mark Perry, Alberto Andreu Pinillos, Caty Price, Owen K. Rankin, James Rubin, Mike Rulis, Kåre Schultz, Julie Staudenmier, Anne Toulouse, Frank Banke Troelsen, and Denise Yohn. In addition, CEOs Jørgen Vig Knudstorp and Kjeld Kirk Kristiansen, both of the LEGO Group, and Peter Ingwersen of Noir were more than generous with their time in sharing their experience and knowledge with us.

We thank Philip Mirvis, Lee Bolman, and Kåre Schultz for much good advice on early drafts of the book; Phil in particular played many roles, he was our sounding board, adviser, devil's advocate, and writing coach. Several others were instrumental in helping us refine some of the case stories. Deserving thanks in this regard are Nick Adams, Doug Childs, Charlotte Ersbøll, Andrea Higham, Iben Eiby Johannesen, Esben Karmark, Tom Lassiter, Mark Perry, James Rubin, Mike Rulis, and Paul Vinnogradov.

Wally Olins and Edgar Schein have been our mentors over many years and continue to be sources of inspiration to our work on corporate branding and organizational culture respectively. Our study of Wolff-Olins, the corporate identity and branding firm Wally co-founded, seeded our early writings on corporate branding and we learned a great deal working with Wally's many colleagues there, particularly Hans Arnold, Doug Hamilton, Jonathan Knowles, Paul Vinnogradov, John Williamson, Charles Wright, and Pamela Wooley. We also thank David Aaker, Yun Mi Antorini, John Balmer, David Bickerton, Lesley de Chernatony, Rosa Chung, Gary Davies, Charles Fombrun, Andrea Higham, Nikolas Ind, Esben Karmark, Simon Knox, Martin Kornberger, Stan Maklin, Kasper Ulf Nielsen, Niels Christian Nielsen, James O'Rourke, Davide Ravasi, Cees Van Riel, Violina Rindova, and

Nikolas Trad, with whom we have enjoyed many scintillating conversations regarding branding matters over the years.

The team at Jossey-Bass, especially Neal Maillet, Jessie Mandle, Carolyn Carlstroem, Kasi Miller, Rob Brandt, Andrea Flint, and Hilary Powers, were indispensable in getting this book into print. Finally, we thank Skype, without which this book would have been significantly more costly and altogether less fun to write.

Mary Jo Hatch
Ipswich, Massachusetts

Majken Schultz
Copenhagen, Denmark
December 2007

Introduction

A corporate brand is one of the most important strategic assets a business can have. In our globalizing world, companies that manage their corporate brands effectively gain advantages of market entry, penetration, and differentiation over their competitors in ways that help them integrate their wide-ranging activities. But no brand does this perfectly forever—the environment they face changes constantly, with ever-shifting patterns of competition and fluctuations in stakeholder support.

Alongside the growing importance of corporate brand in the midst of change comes the need for a different sort of brand management. No longer do marketing departments rule the domain of branding. Instead, responsibility radiates out from the very top of the company to every nook and cranny in the organization and, beyond even this, into the web of stakeholders that make up the enterprise. As a consequence of these changes, current ways of thinking about corporate branding are in need of an overhaul.

For the past several years we have worked alongside executives as they dealt with a range of challenging business issues. Nissan needed to reinvent itself as a strong niche player to correct past sins of copying archrival Toyota instead of forging its own identity. As a medium-sized company from a small country, Novo Nordisk needed to make a broad enough gesture to get noticed on the global stage. Telefónica, a huge bureaucracy trying to reinvent itself following privatization, was flailing about as it acquired the also newly privatized telephone companies of several Latin American countries while juggling the shift from landline to mobile services. Boeing was struggling to redefine itself after its acquisition of McDonald Douglas and to recover from contracting scandals. Johnson & Johnson, rated among the world's top corporate brands, needed to establish itself in China. And the LEGO Group was in the throes of a financial meltdown, the result of not knowing how best to respond to the shifting play patterns of kids who are growing older and ditching traditional toys for electronic games and other gizmos.

What brought these managers together was the recognition that they were all facing corporate branding problems. Through the Corporate Brand Initiative (CBI), a three-year collaborative self-study that produced the frameworks presented in this book, we were able to track these managers as they became experts in handling corporate brands, not in the restrictive sense of logo design and consistency of message but in the sense of drawing on all the people who make up their enterprises.

As the CBI managers learned from each other, so we learned from them how each stakeholder plays an important role in defining the meaning and creating the value of the brand that connects the stakeholders to the enterprise. Together we developed and learned to use the brand management techniques described in this book. In the process, we developed a diagnostic model for assessing how well companies manage their corporate brands through alignment of their strategic visions, organizational cultures, and stakeholder images, along with a theory of organizational identity dynamics that underpins the model.

In Part One, we guide you through the basics of what makes corporate brands work—and why they sometimes don't. Our examples show what corporate branding in the wider domain of the enterprise means, how corporate branding as we see it differs from what marketers and economists describe, and how the managers we studied shifted their practices as they began to employ these new ways of thinking in their companies.

Part Two examines the variety of management practices and processes involved in the execution of full-scale corporate branding. We begin by describing the varying roles leaders play in branding over the life of the organization. Then we shift attention to how employees serve and are served by the corporate brand they help build through their everyday work activities and the organizational culture they create. Finally, we explain how brands can become part of the stakeholder communities through which they live without jeopardizing the delicate relationships that sustain them.

Part Three concludes by pulling all the threads of corporate branding together. There we show you how the LEGO Group found its way back from the brink of disaster by learning to align its vision, culture, and images through corporate branding. To show you how to do the same for your corporate brand, the final chapter translates the knowledge presented in this book into concrete steps. It includes reflections on where the field of corporate branding is headed, how best to prepare yourself to manage your corporate brand, and the dilemmas branding presents as well as advice for how to confront them based on our studies of the CBI companies and others that have built strong corporate brands.

The pages of this book include plenty of examples of brand executives using the ideas we offer to execute brand strategy. The examples are meant to inspire you to try similar things in your organization, but beware of imposing any of these ideas as a ready-made solution. The corporate brand management practices that are right for your company will need to come from the unique values and meanings that you and your enterprise alone can provide. The VCI Alignment Model and the organizational identity dynamics conversation that underpin it all are designed to set the stage for your success. Once you have mastered these tools, you should be ready to lead your corporate branding effort now and into the future.

Taking Brand Initiative

Part One

THE BASICS

1

WHAT IS CORPORATE BRANDING?

Before British Airways was privatized in 1987, and for some time thereafter, people in Britain joked that "BA," the company's familiar acronym, really stood for "Bloody Awful."[1] The joke reflected what were then widely shared images of the airline as operationally incompetent and as indifferent to customers. However, by the early 1990s conditions at BA had improved considerably. Through severe downsizing and corporate-wide customer service training, Colin Marshall, who was CEO at the time, turned a stodgy, military-style bureaucracy into a profitable, respected, and highly competitive enterprise.

The change took shape after lengthy preparations that included repositioning the company around the idea of "the world's favorite airline." The word *favorite* symbolized the new attention to customers that was to characterize the company's transition to private enterprise. Over the years, BA conducted dozens of change programs aimed at developing a service-minded culture. These programs considerably improved BA's image with its customers, allowing the airline to overcome its former reputation for incompetence and indifference.

Even as BA's reputation for service improved, however, it faced new pressures from the ever-demanding, rapidly globalizing marketplace the airline industry serves. By the mid-1990s, marketing research showed that BA's customer base was shifting: only 40 percent of its passengers were British, and these numbers were falling. An alliance frenzy in the airline industry created another pressure. Along with incessant talk about globalization throughout the business world, and under the then new leadership of CEO Robert Ayling, BA made its move.

The first step was to address BA's strategic vision of being "the world's favorite airline." Ayling and his managers did not see the need for an entirely new vision; instead, they shifted the emphasis from being the "world's *favorite* airline" to being the "*world's* favorite airline." Although this in itself may not seem like a major change, implementing this transition led BA to realize it needed to address its market in a less rigidly national tone of voice. To engage its global market more fully, BA decided to incorporate a diversity of national origins and styles into a bold new visual identity for its corporate brand.

The most immediate and controversial aspect of the new visual identity—the tail fins of its fleet of aircraft—were to be decorated with patterns taken from contemporary, original folk art that BA commissioned from artists around the world. A different design was planned for each airplane, making the fleet into a flying art gallery that visually celebrated the world's diversity while it carried BA's message around the globe. To further avoid nationalistic associations, the British flag that had long marked the planes as BA's property was replaced by a design called a "speedmark."

The speedmark, which looks like a twisted ribbon that is blue on one side and red on the other, was conceived as a contemporary symbol that retained the colors of the Union Jack without actually displaying the national flag. According to a company spokesperson at the time, the new airplane livery was "a creative expression of a company, which, both in the letter and the spirit, regards the whole world as its customer."[2]

Using work from artists in different countries to decorate the tail fins of an airline fleet was a radically new way to express strategic vision. In place of a single symbol, style, or color palette, BA's tail-fin displays embraced and emphasized diversity. This idea carried over into other areas of communication. For example, the annual report for 1996–97 was illustrated, both on the cover and throughout, with photographs of BA staff from many ethnic backgrounds. The same message was implied in television commercials that showed people on different continents being reunited with family members from overseas.

But trouble was already brewing. The new look of the repainted fleet did not run very deep in the organization. It didn't even run deep in the airplanes themselves, where British accents, manners, styles of dress, and other expressions of traditional Britishness continued to reign. For example, members of BA staff were expected to maneuver large and heavy traditional metal tea and coffee pots. This was awkward, clumsy, and hazardous, but conformed to a notion of old-world style and correctness promoted by traditionalists as synonymous with being British. Thus there was built-in dissonance between the revamped exteriors of the airplanes, with their message of inclusive diversity, and the interior—where an aggressively deferential service culture, along with the silver tea service, symbolically signaled the continued dominance of traditional Britishness within the company culture. Strategy and culture were at odds, both symbolically and attitudinally.

The pervasive culture of traditional Britishness within BA presented some immediate problems for the airline. For many who reside outside Britain, BA's cultural traditions were a reminder that Britain was once a formidable colonial power. In June 1997, CEO Ayling acknowledged this when he told the *Yorkshire Post:* "We want to show a modern Britain rather than an imperial Britain." But it was not necessarily associations with colonization that were objectionable. Apparently the passengers targeted by the airline's desire to secure a global image simply did not appreciate the British style of service. In July 1997, the *Financial Times* reported that Ayling had told shareholders "there were elements of 'Britishness' that were standing in the way," and he was quoted as saying, "We are seen to be slightly aloof."[3]

Meanwhile, at home, the new designs provoked anger and hostility from traditionalists. To the delight of the news media that captured her gesture on videotape, Margaret "Maggie" Thatcher, former British Prime Minister and arch conservative, twisted her handkerchief around the tail fin of a model BA airplane to hide one of the new designs. This clip was seen repeatedly throughout Britain for many months, rallying conservative business class passengers around demands that the Union Jack not be removed from BA's planes.

At the time, Britain was engaged in an extended political debate over the values of Britishness, and the new Labour Party and its recently elected Prime Minister, Tony Blair, showed much interest in finding fresh ways of articulating those values. This concern, to use a popular media catchphrase of the day, involved rebranding Britain as "Cool Britannia." It is likely that this political discussion influenced strategic thinking inside BA. However, while BA's vision seemed to lie with a New Britain, resistance by the Old Britain continued.

Pressure to conform to traditional British style does not fully describe the resistance to change that BA experienced during this period. Immediately following the launch of the new look for the fleet, the U.K. cabin crew union held a seventy-two-hour strike over a new pay scheme and the outsourcing of catering services. Part of BA's effort to be globally competitive involved substantial cost reductions aimed at competing with U.S. rivals. But cost reductions are always difficult internally, and the reaction of the cabin crews at the precise moment of the launch showed that employees were not positively engaged by the new vision nor fully involved in the campaign to promote it. The strikers emphasized the contradictions found between cutting costs internally while spending millions on corporate rebranding.

While the multiracial and multicultural nature of BA has remained an important theme of its communications, the radicalism of its new look came to be regarded by the company as less than successful. This evaluation led to announcements in 1998 that the full series of tail fin designs would never be implemented. Although reasons for this decision were not spelled out clearly, Ayling suggested that resistance among the lucrative and conservative British business class passengers caused BA to cut back on its tail-fin program. The media and many employees at the time believed that the costs of the program were simply too high. Regardless of the logic used, BA, it seems, lost its corporate nerve. It also lost Bob Ayling, who in early 2000 was replaced as CEO by Rod Eddington.

Under Eddington's leadership, BA remained concerned to communicate a sense of belonging to the world and being made up of representatives from many different parts of it. The retreat from repainting the tail fins did not alter the corporation's resolve to have a global image, and for many years the look of BA remained caught between traditionalism and the global diversity of those planes whose tail fins still sported colorful and non-British images. Until the company was again able to afford repainting its fleet, the aircraft that sported the folk-art tail fins stood as testimony to BA's mismanagement of its rebranding effort.

Although today all BA airplanes again wear identical livery, the company, now under the leadership of its youngest CEO ever, William "Willie" Walsh, shows no clear signs of having overcome its problems with connecting its global vision to its many internal and external stakeholders. In fact, BA seems so bogged down in other crises at the moment that *Guardian* reporter Jane Martinson referred to the company as "the world's once-favourite airline."[4]

Where Corporate Brands Differ from Product Brands

BA's rebranding problems were complicated. Before taking a more disciplined look at what went wrong, it's worth considering what a corporate brand is—and is not. First and foremost, branding an enterprise is not the same thing as branding a product. And, although corporate and product brands share some similarities, assumptions about product branding can sometimes leave the wrong impression of what corporate branding entails.

It can be easy to confuse corporate with product brands due to similarities in their use of imagery. For example, Nike's swoosh and the golden crest on a packet of Marlboros are both graphic symbols bound together with a familiar name and associated with various emotions, ideas, and memories. And both have become significant in popular culture, partly as the result of all manner of marketing, communication, and sales efforts. Yet these similarities mask important differences. Nike is a corporate brand that symbolically integrates the wide-ranging activities of an enterprise that not only provides consumers with sporting goods but also influences how sports are played and shapes the identities of those who play them. Marlboro, even given its global iconic stature and enormous equity, is but one of many products in the Philip Morris empire.

The concept of *brand architecture,* which explains how multiple product brands owned by a single company relate to one another, helps some people understand the relationship between a product and a corporate brand. For example, product brands may operate independently, the way Procter & Gamble's stable of product brands do (Tide, Ivory, Pampers, Crest, Duracell, Gillette, and so on), or be grouped into brand families like General Motors' Chevrolet, Buick, Pontiac, GMC Truck, Saturn, Hummer, Saab, and Cadillac.

But notice that the GMC Truck brand incorporates the General Motors acronym (GM). In this sense the GMC Truck brand is like Nestlé KitKat or Apple iPod. These are all cases of endorsed product brands, where the company name adds weight to the product brand, or in some rare cases, the other way around (for example, the cachet Jaguar and Aston Martin briefly lent to the Ford brand). Endorsement begins to reveal the company behind the brand, but not until a company brands all of its products under one name using a singular style like Virgin, BMW, or McDonald's is there potential for a corporate brand.

We say *potential* because unity of logo, name, and house style is only one aspect of a corporate brand. Corporate branding involves a great deal more. Points of difference include the scope and scale of the branding effort, where the brand identity originates, the audience targeted, the placement of responsibility for the

Table 1.1. How Corporate and Product Brands Differ.

	Product Brand	*Corporate Brand*
Scope and scale	One product or service, or a group of closely related products	The entire enterprise, which includes the corporation and all its stakeholders
Origins of brand identity	Advertisers' imagination informed by market research	The company's heritage, the values and beliefs that members of the enterprise hold in common
Target audience	Customers	Multiple stakeholders (includes employees and managers as well as customers, investors, NGOs, partners, and politicians)
Responsibility	Product brand manager and staff, Advertising and Sales departments	CEO or executive team, typically from Marketing, Corporate Communication, Human Resources, Strategy, and sometimes Design or Development departments
Planning horizon	Life of product	Life of company

brand's performance, and the extent of the planning horizon (see Table 1.1).[5]

Product brands typically lavish all their attention on customers and consumers, whereas corporate brands address all the company's stakeholders—not only customers and consumers but also investors, suppliers, distributors, partners, governments, and local, national, and international community groups, as well as employees—in other words, the entire enterprise.

In short, branding the enterprise means involving everyone who is important to the company. The leaders of BA, for example, thought about the changing demographics of the company's customer base but failed to consider how the British public would respond to its brand renewal effort, or even how its own employees might react. In effect, BA treated its brand like a marketing problem when it was really an enterprise problem.

Another difference between product and corporate brands is that product brands gain market share through short-lived advertising campaigns invented by marketers. Sometimes these are effective and memorable (for example, the Budweiser frogs), but corporate brands express enduring ambitions and the values and beliefs of all connected with the enterprise. This is how they embody the interests and earn lasting trust among their stakeholders. BA would have been well advised to think about the past (the company's iconic role in the British heritage) and to relate that past to its future, rather than jettisoning it in favor of the image of a New Britain that Tony Blair's government was promoting at the time. A corporate brand cannot focus only on the future; it must connect with what it has meant to its stakeholders throughout its history. Unlike a product brand, which lives and dies with its product, a corporate brand accompanies the firm for life.

Thus a corporate brand targets all stakeholders, inside and out. It influences organizational activities from top to bottom, and it infuses everything the company is, says, and does, now and forever. Heading up such an enterprise-wide and potentially integrative effort must be company leaders. The top team is not there to provide window-dressing; its members individually and collectively make the corporate brand focal within the organization's culture and inspire creative thinking that keeps the brand alive for all stakeholders. Under Colin Marshall, BA had this kind of leadership, but lost it when Robert Ayling failed to grasp the difference between product and corporate branding. Ayling's missteps led to a failure of such proportions that the BA brand has yet to fully recover its lost ground.

When Corporate Brands Work

Whenever you encounter a successful corporate brand, standing behind that brand you will find coherence between what the company's top managers want to accomplish in the future (their strategic *vision*), what has always been known or believed by company employees (lodged in its *culture*), and what its external stakeholders expect or desire from the company (their *images* of it). The basic principle of the Vision-Culture-Image (VCI) Alignment Model—that the greater the coherence of vision, culture, and images, the stronger the brand—is the central message of this book (see Figure 1.1).

Figure 1.1. The VCI Alignment Model.

Conversely, misalignments (or gaps) between vision, culture, and images indicate an underperforming corporate brand (see Figure 1.2).

Think of strategic vision, organizational culture, and stakeholder images as pieces of a jigsaw puzzle. Spread out on the table, the pieces are incoherent. Put into place, they form an integrated, expressive, and satisfying whole that builds strong corporate reputations while integrating organizational behavior behind delivery of the brand promise to all the stakeholders who make up the enterprise. If you are wondering whether your corporate brand

Figure 1.2. VCI misalignment causes gaps between vision, culture, and images.

Figure 1.3. Questions to ask yourself about the VCI alignment of your corporate brand.

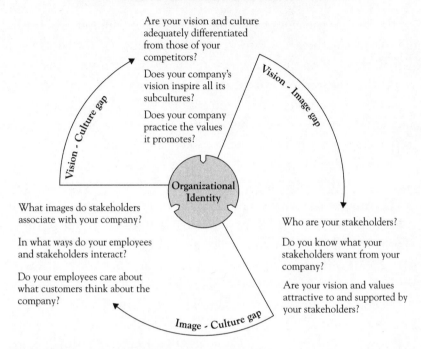

Are your vision and culture adequately differentiated from those of your competitors?

Does your company's vision inspire all its subcultures?

Does your company practice the values it promotes?

What images do stakeholders associate with your company?

In what ways do your employees and stakeholders interact?

Do your employees care about what customers think about the company?

Who are your stakeholders?

Do you know what your stakeholders want from your company?

Are your vision and values attractive to and supported by your stakeholders?

Source: Based on M. J. Hatch and M. Schultz, "Are the Strategic Stars Aligned for Your Corporate Brand?" *Harvard Business Review,* February 2001, pp. 128–134.

suffers from any VCI misalignments, answering the questions in Figure 1.3 should give you some initial indications.

If they are to be worthy of their stakeholders' enduring trust, corporate brands need to be managed effectively throughout the life of the company, not just during brand launch. And when you consider what needs to be managed—alignment in all the interfaces between corporate vision, organizational culture, and stakeholder images—it is clear why corporate brands come to be valued as strategic assets. The combination of vision, culture, and images represents in one way or another everything the organization is, says, and does.

How British Airways Failed
Its Corporate Brand

At the time of the launch of their first repainted aircraft, BA leaders surely felt they had done everything right: their vision was global, their culture was service-oriented, and their image as "the world's favorite airline" was ready for expansion to "the undisputed leader in world travel." Yet, even though BA had vision, culture, and desired image in good shape, these three essential elements of its corporate rebranding program lacked alignment.

First, BA's culture did not support its vision. Instead, employees, who were being subjected to another round of cost cutting at the time of the new brand launch, interpreted the expenditure of £60 million on tail-fin painting as a breach of faith. They expressed their anger with a strike symbolically timed to coincide with the unveiling of the first repainted tail fins, making public the rift between employees and their leaders.

Second, the images key stakeholders associated with BA were not in line with the airline's new global vision. BA's move to implement its global vision was met with formidable resistance on the part of British conservatives, who constituted the bulk of BA's lucrative business class passenger pool. For these passengers, on whom BA still depends for the greater part of its revenue stream, BA was an icon of British culture—and they were not ready to share it with the world.

And finally, BA experienced misalignment of its culture and the global expectations the company encouraged its key stakeholders to hold. This gap was symbolized by the juxtaposition of its global ambition and the British look and feel of its service. As the tail-fin program proceeded, it became obvious to passengers, if not to employees, that the airline might be global on the outside, but inside it was still terribly British. From the traditional silver tea service down to the properly stodgy uniforms of the cabin crew, little about the culture encountered inside the airplanes (or the company!) matched the global expectations encouraged by the proud display on the tail fins.

Figure 1.4. What happened when British Airways did not align its vision, culture, and images.

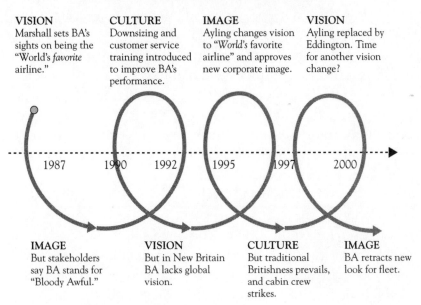

VISION
Marshall sets BA's sights on being the "World's *favorite* airline."

CULTURE
Downsizing and customer service training introduced to improve BA's performance.

IMAGE
Ayling changes vision to "*World's* favorite airline" and approves new corporate image.

VISION
Ayling replaced by Eddington. Time for another vision change?

1987   1990   1992   1995   1997   2000

IMAGE
But stakeholders say BA stands for "Bloody Awful."

VISION
But in New Britain BA lacks global vision.

CULTURE
But traditional Britishness prevails, and cabin crew strikes.

IMAGE
BA retracts new look for fleet.

Although British Airways managed the elements of its corporate brand effectively, the company did not align them with one another. The elements BA put into place at different points in time are listed above the time line. Below the line are some of the problems BA's inattention to alignment caused.

Source: Based on M. J. Hatch and M. Schultz, "Bringing the Corporation into Corporate Branding," *European Journal of Marketing*, 2003, *37*(7/8), 1041–1064.

By doing things so badly during the period of its global brand launch, BA demonstrated the importance of aligning vision, culture, and images. The lesson the BA example teaches is that the *alignment* of vision, culture, and images determines the success of a corporate branding effort, not the elements themselves. Figure 1.4 traces the multiple upheavals BA endured and relates them to continuing misalignments in vision, culture, and images.

Why Southwest Gets Corporate Branding Right

BA continually failed to align its vision, culture, and images (VCI), thereby undermining its corporate brand. But are there success stories to support the principle of VCI alignment? We believe that although no company enjoys permanent immunity from misalignment, Southwest Airlines represents one that comes close. Even though it, too, has faced misalignment recently, this company gets VCI alignment in its bones.

By now everyone has heard how, as a small regional carrier, Southwest had to fight tooth and nail to get its tiny fleet of airplanes into the sky. But once in the air, by offering its passengers a cheap and efficient means of enjoying short-haul, low-cost, no-frills air transportation, it grew into one of the world's most valuable airlines, with a market capitalization almost as large as all other U.S. airlines combined.

Southwest built its brand on the back of a strong and productive relationship between management, workers, and unions. This relationship forged the airline's corporate culture, whose central belief is that if you take good care of your employees, they will take good care of your customers. What may be only an urban myth about Southwest nonetheless demonstrates the lengths to which the company's managers uphold this belief. The story tells of a customer who was abusive to an employee, and the company informed the guilty passenger by letter that their business would no longer be welcomed at Southwest! Can you imagine in this age of the-customer-is-always-right, a company siding with an employee over an instance of disrespect? Even if this never really happened, it is the sort of thing that stakeholders inside the company and out believe Southwest Airlines would do, and it represents a true corporate brand in action.

How did Southwest develop customer loyalty at the same time that it enjoyed levels of enthusiastic employee commitment few companies before it ever achieved? As a new generation of managers takes over from beloved founder and longtime CEO Herb Kelleher, the story of this airline's rise to fame and fortune is worth examination. In all the ways BA failed to integrate its vision with its organizational culture and stakeholder images, Southwest has for the most part succeeded.

Let's start with culture. As carriers of culture, leaders cannot do much better than Kelleher has. Working tirelessly over his many years as Southwest's CEO, Kelleher was legendary for the hours put in as he traveled around the country visiting and working alongside his employees, sharing menial tasks, and partying with them after hours. As the result of his example, and of the concern taken to ensure cultural compatibility in recruiting, Southwest has become the prototypical work hard–play hard culture. And, as often as possible, work *is* play at this airline. People never take themselves too seriously except where getting the job done is concerned. Southwest's laid-back style is celebrated inside the company and out in story after story like the ones about the ways in which mundane aspects of air travel are handled, from the way flight crews joke with their passengers about the limited amount of space under the seat in front of them to the sincere playfulness with which service staff provide Southwest's signature no-frills peanuts.

Supported by a business model that delivers low-cost operations, Southwest offers its customers a seductive cocktail of modest prices and an entertaining service experience. Once the airline got off the ground, word of Southwest's unconventional approach to air travel spread quickly. Soon curious travelers became devoted passengers and the foundation for a strong corporate brand was laid in the alignment between employees who enjoyed delivering service and customers who clamored for the services those employees delivered. Internally, Southwest shared the benefits of its early success through a generous stock option program and the promise of secure employment. As Southwest succeeded, so did its hardworking and good-natured employees.

As Kelleher neared retirement, Southwest chose the people who would take his place from among the airline's many devoted managers. The culture was not threatened in the least by the advancement of people who had, for the most part, learned to manage at Kelleher's side, and the transition at first went smoothly.

Then 9/11 hit the airline industry hard, and, with so few passengers traveling over an extended period, keeping Southwest profitable severely challenged everyone in the company.

True to its cultural heritage, Southwest furloughed no one in the aftermath of 9/11, preferring to downsize its cash reserves rather than its employee base. Kelleher's long-established practice of saving for a rainy day paid off, allowing the company not just to weather this storm but to continue growing even while the same conditions forced its competitors to cut back. Many grateful employees chipped in, returning a portion of their paychecks to help keep their company going. When all was said and done, Southwest dominated the domestic U.S. air travel market. The strategy forged from Kelleher's leadership principles paid off and kept the image of the organization strong, not just among customers but also among investors and the public.

So long as the investors included company employees, things ran smoothly. But twenty-five years of continuous growth meant that some of Southwest's newer employees enjoyed fewer benefits of stock ownership than did those who had been there from the start. As the company's profits rose without their participation, a rift appeared between the company's original vision (as employee benefactor) and the reality employees experienced daily as members of a low-cost airline culture. Salaries, which had by now equaled or surpassed those of other airlines that had forced wage cuts on their employees, were not keeping up with the expectations set by Southwest's celebrated record of continuous profitability.

With continued good brand management, the divide between employees (especially managers) who shared in Southwest's good fortune and those who now contribute to it without the same high levels of profit sharing will lead the airline to reassess its employment practices, allowing the organization to return to its envied position based in alignment of the interests of its internal and external stakeholders with the strategic vision for the company's future. But no matter what can be said in criticism of this company today, for a very long time its brand rested on one of the best foundations of VCI alignment ever seen, and this enviable heritage can never be taken away.

What makes alignment of vision, culture, and images so essential to corporate brand building? What value does VCI alignment bring to the company? How do you know when you have misalignment? How does VCI alignment fit in with all the other business issues a company must confront? In Chapters Three and Four we present the background necessary to answer these questions. Then, in Part Two, we show how our CBI companies and other firms have tackled a variety of common business problems in VCI-aligning ways that built both better brands and stronger companies. But first, Chapter Two provides a further explanation of why corporate brands are valuable and brings consideration of symbolism front and center.

2

THE VALUE OF BRANDS

Before there was a Swoosh, Nike co-founder Bill Bowerman used one of his wife's kitchen appliances to create the company's first innovation—the famous waffle sole running shoe. In collaboration with Phil Knight, Bowerman used his sole as the foundation for what is now a globally recognized corporate brand. But even as a steady stream of product innovations marked the difference between Nike and its competitors, the Swoosh arose to symbolically rally employees and customers around Nike's cause. The Nike name, as you may recall, was chosen to invoke associations with the Greek goddess of victory (the Swoosh is one of her wings). The emphasis on victory gains additional symbolism from the company via ads and slogans such as the popular tagline "Just Do It."

Corporate brands like Nike's represent the way a company differs from its competitors, but they also welcome investors, potential employees, and customers into the enterprise and make them feel like they belong. Differentiation and the benefits of belonging that corporate branding brings are the root sources of brand value. The most successful corporate brands simultaneously communicate belonging and differentiation and other ideas as well, and do all this while engaging multiple audiences. It is the symbolism of powerful brands that allows them to do this sophisticated communicative work, and in this chapter we outline why differentiation and belonging demand a symbolic approach to branding—and what taking a symbolic approach means. We also discuss how the methods of symbolic research complement the more familiar techniques of brand valuation and brand equity management that the disciplines of economics, marketing research, and consumer behavior provide.

Two Benefits of Branding: Differentiation and Belonging

Most companies rely on their corporate brands to perform the strategic function of *positioning*, that is, discovering or creating points of differentiation vis-à-vis competitors. But corporate brands are also designed to attract customers and appeal to other stakeholders, reminding people why they belong to or should join the community of interests that swirls around the brand. For example, although (or perhaps because!) the emotional tone set by the Apple brand repels some people, it attracts others who feel that what they share is distinctive, and this fosters a sense of belonging to a like-minded community. It is this tissue of differentiating associations supported by communal feelings that we regard as the corporate brand. Clearly differentiation and belonging are related.

Sociological and psychological evidence shows that successful corporate differentiation derives from the sense of belonging that brand symbolism enables in its users. Marketing researcher Douglas Atkin explained how this works.[1] Based on the sociological theory that human difference (or alienation) drives people to seek similar others and avoid those who do not share their interests, Atkin reasoned that brand symbolism helps people to identify others with similar values or interests (the basis of belonging) while at the same time differentiating them from people with dissimilar interests. Thus differentiation and belonging represent two sides of the same coin when it comes to branding.

How does a company manage the interplay between belonging and differentiation in the context of its many stakeholders? Take the case of BMW. This corporate brand welcomes employees, customers, and other stakeholders into its extended family and also differentiates BMW from competitors who simply make cars. Rated one of the most attractive employers in the United States (one MBA survey ranked it fourth in 2005),[2] BMW has a strong employer brand. However, instead of boasting, the career page on the BMW Web site states: "If you love mobility in all its many guises and want to get ahead, then the BMW Group is just the place for you." The theme of mobility that threads through the Web site links recruitment efforts to the organization's familiar brand slogan: "The Ultimate Driving Machine." This coherence creates alignment between the attitudes new employees bring to the company and the images of BMW other stakeholders hold.

Once recruited, BMW employees are encouraged to connect with their customers and make them part of the family. For instance, some years ago BMW convinced its dealers to organize service representatives into teams to which BMW owners were assigned to expedite their car maintenance and repairs. This reorganization resulted in customers' recognizing their service team representatives and feeling their automotive needs were being given personal attention. It also gave team representatives the chance to get to know their customers via repeat visits, adding a personal dimension to their work and making their workplace feel more like a community.

BMW's example shows how changing the interaction between customers and dealers can shift the boundary that separates insiders from outsiders, in this case by treating customers like insiders. But BMW does not stop there. This company also recognizes that a host of fan-originated brand communities support the company by sharing information and enthusiasm for the brand. In fact, the BMW network of brand enthusiasts has grown into the largest among the premium car brands, with community events like the annual Bimmerfest in the United States that attract thousands of current and potential brand-loyal customers every year.

To see how drawing a customer into the inner circle of belonging works from the perspective of the consumer, consider this story told by one of the authors, who initially had a negative image of the BMW brand. Mary Jo Hatch writes:

> Returning to the United States after living in Europe for nearly a decade, I was determined not to be swayed by the new trends in lifestyle advertising that were all the rage here. My ambition was to own a car that was fun to drive, something to which I had become accustomed while living overseas. My standards were not all that high, I told myself, having happily driven a Ford Escort for the past five years, albeit one built in Germany.
>
> After test-driving numerous cars, I concluded that U.S.-built cars were universally unacceptable. Sloppy steering, poor acceleration, and inadequate brakes added up to disappointment for my European-inflected tastes. My boyfriend got me to drive an Audi, but it did nothing to impress me. The Audi salesman, however, after listening to my complaints, offered to put me in a used BMW he had sitting on his lot. I resisted the very idea of a "Bimmer" because I had negative images of BMW drivers: conservative, snobbish, unoriginal. But he insisted I at least try it out, and one short—and fast—drive down a twisty road converted me.
>
> I shopped around and finally settled on a little silver number with all the fixings that a BMW executive had driven for a year. Laying down twice as much money as I had ever imagined spending on a car, I was even more stunned when the manager of the dealership came into the finance office where I was signing my life away and asked, "Is this your first BMW?" Surely it was obvious that it was. Beaming broadly, he stretched out his hand, proudly announcing in a loud voice, "Welcome to the BMW family!" My skin crawled a little, but I managed a weak smile and shook his hand. As I drove off the lot in my new car, the question "What have I done?" rang in my head. I was convinced the Bimmer was not me.
>
> Yet over the following weeks and months my question was answered in surprising ways. First my boyfriend expressed shock over my purchasing this expensive car with so little apparent dissonance

after having such a negative image of BMW drivers. He drove a Jeep. Perhaps, I told myself, the purchase was worth it based on shock value alone. Then total strangers started approaching me in parking lots to comment on my car and express their admiration of it. My dealer treated me like an old friend whenever my BMW needed maintenance. And not to be overlooked was the genuinely immersive experience of operating the ultimate driving machine. I started to feel like the car was a physical part of me, and the long drives to visit my boyfriend became sources of pleasure as opposed to the wasted time they otherwise might have seemed.

But the pièce de résistance came with the totally unexpected respect I received from children. One, a colleague's son who had never seen the car or me before, called me "cool" because of it— high praise from a pre-teen to an adult who is practically a stranger. Puzzled, I asked him how he knew what car I drove. He silently pointed to my car key, emblazoned with BMW's distinctive logo! Who I was in the eyes of others had become colored by my Bimmer, and I recognized that I had truly become part of the BMW family in spite of my firm intention not to succumb.

Now an avid fan, I surf the BMW Web site regularly, having enjoyed particularly those innovative short films produced by some of the world's most daring film makers. Each features an ultimate driving experience in the ultimate driving machine, to which I respond as if I were the brand. Who knows, maybe a visit to the factory is in order? Perhaps I will wear my "Ultimate Driving Machine" T-shirt, the one my salesman gave me after his boss welcomed me into the family. . . .

Successful corporate brands like the one BMW built mark boundaries and claim territories that indicate inclusion and exclusion, and this creates the dual benefits of differentiation and belonging. This marking and claiming of territories, alongside the ability to express values and style, involves brands in the daily meaning-making activities of the individuals who form an enterprise. Recognition of their involvement in everyday life leads to what may be the most significant thing we can say about brands: brand meanings are produced by and distributed among the people they touch. Therefore it is through personal acts of meaning making—known to those who study these matters as *symbolism*—that corporate brands gain the power that enhances their firm's market value.

Without giving people the ability to express and symbolize cultural and personal values, brands would have no economic value. Nonetheless the symbolic value of brands is often underemphasized, and this can make it difficult to get the full picture of corporate branding. To understand how and why symbolism affects economic value requires a detour through the world of symbols into brand valuation techniques and back again.

Brands Are Symbols

Although they may not be approaching branding from the symbolic perspective, almost everyone equates a brand with the symbols that carry its meaning. For example, the American Marketing Association defined *brand* as "a name, term, symbol, or design, or combination of these, which is intended to identify goods or services of one seller or group of sellers and to differentiate them from those of competitors."[3] This definition sometimes leads people to focus exclusively on the tangible aspects of branding—the sound of the name, the color and shape of the logo, or the look and feel of products and of retail outlets and other company facilities—all of which contribute to the brand but do not complete it. The meanings invested in brand symbols give brands economic value, and grasping this requires appreciating how interpretation affects branding—this is the symbolic perspective.

A *symbol* is any object, word, or action that stands for something else. A corporate brand is represented by not just one symbol (say a logo or a name) but a constellation of symbols. Take the case of Japanese car brand Nissan.[4] The large, shiny aluminum badge that adorns every vehicle Nissan produces under its name is but one symbol of this maverick, power-obsessed brand

Figure 2.1. Part of Nissan's constellation of brand symbols.

The Nissan Badge

Nissan Dealer Showroom

Source: Copyright © Nissan (2007). Nissan and the Nissan logo are registered trademarks of Nissan.

(see Figure 2.1). When you visit a Nissan dealer's showroom you are wrapped in an experience that expresses the merger of technology, bold design, and thoughtfulness. You feel as if you have been transported inside the brand. Nissan's newer products reflect this same design sense and interconnect with the badge and the showroom to form a constellation of symbols. Then, when you take an Altima out for a test spin, or drive your new Xterra home from the shiny Nissan dealership, you weave the brand's symbols into your life and give them your own meanings. It is in this sense that the meanings of brand symbols are provided by all those who engage with the brand.

Atkin claims that symbols work best when they are part of meaning systems in which various symbols are connected and support each other. It is much easier for a competitor to copy your logo or aesthetic style than to copy the relationships among your house style, product designs, service delivery systems, employee characteristics, leadership style, and management practices, or the quality of the many relationships (sometimes called touch-points) you have with your stakeholders. Compared with product brands, corporate brands open onto a much larger pool of interconnected symbols located throughout the enterprise and interpreted by all of the company's employees and other stakeholders. Reproducing such a complex distributed system of valued meaning is practically impossible. This is why highly evolved corporate brands provide a measure of security against copycatting even though their success almost always attracts those who will try.

The constellation of corporate brand symbols, to the extent it can be designed, is designed to express what the organization stands for and represents how it will act now and in the future. For this reason, some companies regard their corporate brand to be as binding as their officers' signatures and refer to the promise their brand makes. Johnson & Johnson (J&J) takes this commitment so seriously that it calls its corporate brand a "trustmark." But you should remain alert to the role interpretation plays in determining what brands mean, and this requires giving consideration to those who ultimately determine that meaning—stakeholders.

Marketing expert Sidney J. Levy was one of the first to describe the role meaning plays in the human response to brands and their symbolism. He said: "People buy things not only for what they can do, but also for what they mean."[5] To elaborate this telling point a little:

- We don't buy products only for what they ARE: a car as a means of transportation or a watch as a way to measure time.

- We don't buy products only for what they HAVE: a car with five seats and a 200 HP engine or a watch with 99.999 percent precision.

- We buy products for what they MEAN: a Volvo (safety) or a BMW (driving pleasure), a Swatch (informal, youthful) or a Rolex (lavish luxury).

Although Levy made his point using product brands, his focus on symbols and meaning applies to corporate brands too. Strong brands don't just pass meaning directly to stakeholders, they inspire them to *make* meaning using the brand's symbolism. Stakeholders each do this in their own unique way, often using the common pool of brand symbols as material for constructing their identity and the identities of others (for example, "Meg and I are Apple people"). Thus stakeholders collectively weave the tapestry of meanings that form the brand in and around their own identities. According to Wally Olins, who pioneered corporate identity, a corporate brand combines:[6]

- Names, symbols, and experiences
- A central idea or set of ideas
- Qualities, emotions, attitudes, and style

A corporate brand gives interpreters symbols to represent their own ideas, feelings, or experiences while associating them with the company the brand represents. For example, stakeholders uniquely associate brand names and other brand symbols and experiences with the enterprise and these associations facilitate the sense of belonging and differentiation that defines the brand. The central idea attracts or repels internal and external stakeholders to the prospect of being identified with the organization, thus setting up the conditions for inclusion and exclusion, while emotions, attitudes, and even the brand's style give the brand motivational force. Then, when individual stakeholders link their identities and emotional and aesthetic responses to brand symbols in communicative ways, they create a symbolic community within which the brand takes shape.[7]

In other words, the brand is symbolically created by acts of interpretation that occur throughout the population of stakeholders who keep it alive by producing, reproducing, and sometimes changing its social and cultural meanings. From the symbolic perspective, until someone has made and communicated meaning with it, a brand does not exist at all!

Taking a symbolic perspective makes it clear that the interpretive work of corporate branding is distributed among an organization's many stakeholders: employees, customers, investors, suppliers, partners, regulatory agencies, special interests, and members of the general public and local communities, as well as managers, executives, and brand designers. Competitors and the media contribute to this interpretive work when they convince stakeholders to engage with or disengage from various brands. Together stakeholders produce webs of meaning that are then invested in and carried by the brand's symbols and that, from an all-inclusive view, help define the identity of the enterprise that they create together. In this way brand symbols stand as a kind of shorthand for what would otherwise entail lengthy and complex explanation.

Consider a national flag—that of Denmark, for example. The Danish flag is a material artifact (a piece of cloth) that bears all the meanings Danes and others associate with it. Loading an artifact with meaning like this transforms it into a symbol. Now notice how even a long-standing symbol like the Danish national flag constantly evolves to absorb any new meanings people give it.

In 2006, for example, a Danish newspaper published editorial cartoons showing the Prophet Muhammad. The cartoons not only violated Islamic prohibitions against making such images but denounced the religion's followers.[8] Offended Muslims made such a stir that the flag's meaning underwent significant change that in turn affected brands that use the flag. For example, Arla, the producer of Lurpak dairy products, whose logo features the Danish flag, became an easy target for boycotts in the Middle East, Pakistan, and Indonesia following publication of the cartoons. Memories of these events will likely be embedded in Arla's flag-bearing brand symbol for many years to come.

Our point is not just that symbolism can be tricky to manage. It can be, but that should not put you off working with stakeholders to build a meaningful brand. As companies like Royal Dutch Shell and Coca-Cola have learned, weathering the storms of scandal depends upon having a strong bond with significant numbers of stakeholders who feel their identities are intertwined with the brand. Brand symbolism not only represents these bonds, it helps to establish and maintain them. What is required to build a strong brand from the meanings upon which they depend is a symbolic approach to branding.

You might be thinking that taking a symbolic approach means forsaking substance. After all, people often say things like: "He didn't mean to offend; his action was only symbolic." On the contrary, the substance of symbolism lies in the richness of meaning that symbols carry. A symbolic act is as much an act as chopping down a tree or visiting your grandmother. In fact these and all other acts carry symbolic significance and hence value. Substance and symbolism go hand in hand.

To better explain what we mean by taking a symbolic approach to corporate branding, it is helpful to contrast it with approaches developed within the fields of economics, finance, and marketing that vary in the extent to which they consider symbolism. In the following section we describe a number of these approaches and show how each of them can be complemented by taking the symbolic perspective on board.

Brand Valuation and Its Limits

What do economists and financiers care about most when they turn their attention to brands? Unsurprisingly, their focus is almost universally on the financial value of brands, and their preferred assessment methods are adapted from asset valuation models. For example, the London-based consulting house Interbrand annually publishes its valuations of the top hundred global brands. Figure 2.2 shows the brand values that have led Interbrand's list, published by *Business Week*, since 2001. You can see from the chart that when you manage a corporate brand well, you can expect big dividends.

Brand valuation models like the one Interbrand uses estimate the value of a brand's contribution to market capitalization or

**Figure 2.2. Asset valuation:
Interbrand's top brands (2001-2006).**

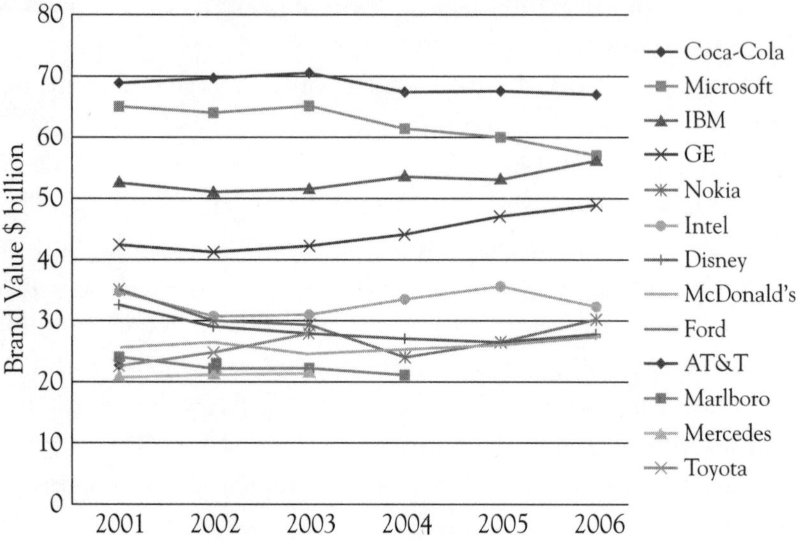

cash flow. In the market capitalization approach, the difference between what a firm's tangible assets are worth and the value of its outstanding shares of stock is computed and then attributed to the firm's "intangible assets," a term that includes its corporate brand along with its product brands, proprietary knowledge, innovation pipeline, and human capital, among other variables. The trouble with asset valuation approaches is that economists cannot reliably isolate the effects of intangible sources of value. Thus they cannot estimate the likely value of investing in any particular intangible.

For product brands, cash flow analysis begins with an estimate of the price premium a branded product or service commands over its generic equivalent. You multiply the premium by your esti-mated sales volume for the length of time you expect this benefit to endure, and discount the resulting figure using the weighted average cost of capital for your business. This can be problematic when you can't find generic comparables to help you estimate your product's premium, or when commoditization negates premium pricing altogether. These drawbacks become even more problematic when cash flow analysis is applied to corporate brand valuation because of the difficulty involved in isolating the portion of cash flow attributable to a corporate brand or the difficulty in weighting investments in product brand marketing against those directed at building and maintaining corporate brand equity.

Over and above the problems already mentioned, both economists and financiers all but ignore the brand's emotional and symbolic effects. For example, a highly valued brand like that of Coca-Cola may influence the firm's weighted average cost of capital due to the influence its strong brand exercises on perceptions of risk. Or, to give other examples, BMW, Apple, and Google have all created brands that make it easier for these companies to recruit talented workers and to motivate their employees. These effects get into territory that is highly subjective, such as the emotional attractions of a workplace or a brand's motivational implications. This territory lies beyond the reach of ordinary economic analyses.

An economist might argue that the subjectivity of the effects just described does not matter because they will show up in objective prices paid for products or for the company's stock. On one level, this is true. However, the emotional and other symbolic effects of branding matter greatly if you want to know how branding works, and thereby how to manage brands effectively. This level of knowledge demands a different sort of reasoning, which has been advanced by proponents of brand equity theory.

Brand Equity Theory

Given the problems associated with asset valuation methods, marketers have instead tried to identify measurable factors that contribute to brand value, or as they term it, brand equity. For example, David Aaker's Brand Equity model proposes five different ways customers and consumers affect a brand's strength and thereby the value it will have in the marketplace: market behavior, awareness, association and differentiation, quality, and loyalty.[9] Market behavior and awareness are rational considerations that can be measured objectively with ease. Market behavior represents the brand's standing with customers using traditional economic measures like market share, price, and distribution, while awareness measures the extent to which a population of consumers claims to know that the brand exists.

The remaining three factors of Aaker's model tap the emotional overtones of a brand, although they are mixed with rational considerations. Take the measures of association and differentiation that Aaker recommends. This category includes perceived brand value (good value for money), brand personality (the extent to which the brand generates interest and excitement), and associations with the brand such as trust and admiration for the organization. Aaker describes quality as a rational dimension of brand performance supplemented by emotional responses to the brand's innovativeness. Finally, willingness to pay a premium price is offered as an objective indicator of the emotional value underpinning brand loyalty, which is moderated by the mostly rational perceptions of product or service performance.

Millward Brown's Brand Pyramid is another popular market research model, not least because this consulting house provides a service that tracks consumer brand responses and determines their distribution across five levels ranging from awareness through loyalty.[10] The top level—bonding—clearly taps the emotional component of consumer behavior, while the lower levels offer rational reasons consumers respond to brands (advantage, performance, and perceived relevance). The bottom of the brand pyramid is anchored by brand awareness or "presence."

In addition to estimating the percentages of consumers who respond to your brand in numerous ways, the models provided by Millward Brown and Aaker have other uses, including incorporating the logic of their market research tools into economic valuation models. For example, Sunil Gupta and Donald Lehman promote a customer-based valuation approach, recommending that firms be allowed to capitalize investments in the projected lifetime purchases of loyal customers, rather than treating these outlays as business expenses.[11] They claim this would bring market and book values of the firm into greater agreement and acknowledge the important contribution brands make to the market capitalization of well-branded firms.

But what, you might ask, can you actually influence using market research methodologies like those just described? Although these models account for the effects of both emotion and reason on consumer behavior, they remain detached from the symbolic meaning brands carry. They supply useful bases for measuring and tracking the effects of brand management efforts, but they cannot explain why these effects occur or tell you how to provoke the reactions that will improve your brand's performance. To answer these questions, marketers turn to consumer behavior research.

Consumer Behavior Research

Those who study consumer behavior are interested in the decision-making processes and choices consumers make when they buy things; What do consumers buy? and How and why do they buy? are typical questions these researchers ask. Most consumer behavior research into branding focuses on matters of human perception, attachment, and trust or alienation. For example, Susan Fournier described the bonds that three women formed with the product brands they routinely used in their homes, such as Contadina tomato sauce and Tide detergent.[12] Her study revealed that these consumers used their favorite brands to create and give meaning to their self-concepts during daily activities including shopping, cooking, and cleaning. Showing how brands are embedded in consumer identities provides evidence of how deep brand meanings can run and the extent to which they rest on the interpretations consumers give to brand symbols.

Intriguingly, Robert Kozinets, another consumer behavior researcher, produced a similar set of findings when he studied

Burning Man gatherings, which occur in the New Mexico desert.[13] Burning Man is an annual community-building event attended by people who are devoted to *resisting* brands. Their resistance takes many forms such as cutting brand labels off clothing and covering brand badges on cars, trucks, and motorcycles. Yet even though their emotional responses to branding can be described as the polar opposite of the enthusiasm Fournier describes, Burning Man participants similarly engaged in acts of self-definition using brand symbolism. Ironically, to participate in their brand obliteration rituals, Burning Man devotees first had to purchase items that carried brands. Thus, like the women Fournier studied, Burning Man participants used brand consumption to define themselves. Still, Kozinets's study goes beyond Fournier's in showing that not just individual but community identities get forged within processes of brand interpretation.

Studies of consumer behavior steeped in the symbolic perspective, like those of Fournier and Kozinets, provide significant insight into the emotional and aesthetic foundations of brand meaning and emphasize the roles meaning and interpretation play in giving brands economic value. However, from the standpoint of explaining *corporate* brands, the difficulty with these studies, as with most other consumer behavior approaches to branding, is that they focus exclusively on consumers. Brand value is created by the relationships an organization forms throughout its enterprise, which includes many other stakeholders in addition to customers. To the extent that symbolism expresses or enhances the values held by all of a brand's stakeholders, economic value is created and sustained. When a brand loses equity, it is a sign that some or all of the meanings that sustain it have been damaged or lost. Understanding how meaning influences brand value demands taking a symbolic approach.

The Symbolic Value of Branding

The symbolic perspective adds consideration of how brands are interpreted, including what brands mean in a variety of spiritual, social, and cultural contexts. Although meaning is implied by some of the earlier brand valuation measures employed, such as Aaker's perceptions of brand personality and trust in a brand, or in the consumer behavior notions of identification with brands, the symbolic dimension of branding remains underutilized in these approaches.

This does not mean that efforts to measure symbolic associations are not being made. The one with which we are most familiar is part of a larger effort to measure and rank corporate reputations conducted by the Reputation Institute (RI). The RI has tracked corporate reputations over the last seven years using its RepTrakPulse tool (see Figure 2.3). Studies using this tool show

Figure 2.3. The Reputation Institute's RepTrak model.

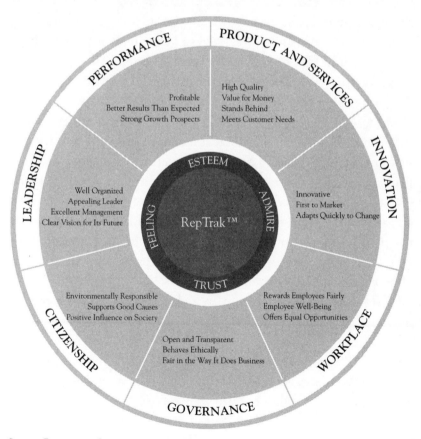

Source: Reputation Institute.

that stakeholders' emotional responses to a brand contribute significantly to its corporate reputation. The RI defined these emotional factors as the feelings, trust, esteem, and admiration that stakeholders develop toward a brand.[14]

Intriguingly, the effects of these factors on corporate reputation were moderated by national attitudes. For instance, Danes who reported a favorable perception of a company's corporate citizenship behavior were significantly more likely to have positive emotional responses to that company's corporate brand, while American brand perceptions were correlated strongly with perceptions of the quality of a firm's products and services. Yet even though the RI has found indicators of the emotional and symbolic effects of corporate branding, these findings still do not explain the interpretive processes by which the meanings of brands are made (or lost). Without this level of knowledge it is difficult to determine how best to manage a corporate brand.

Returning to Sidney Levy's point, when you buy an Apple iPod, it is not just because it is a portable and efficient MP3 player, or because you feel it offers value for money, or trust the company that stands behind the product, or even identify yourself with it or want others to do so. You also buy an iPod because of what it means and how it expresses that meaning on your behalf to those who matter to you. Its meaning may derive from your deep appreciation for intuitive simplicity or from the look and feel of the iPod's sleek styling. Perhaps you believe in creative corporate activity and want to support it, or want to associate with the sort of people who use iPods.

The iPod symbolism is rich enough to express all these meanings and many more besides. Furthermore, the iPod encourages you to connect with other parts of Apple's meaning system, inviting you into the Apple experience where, in highly involving brand stores or Web sites, you can feel like you belong to the Apple community and further differentiate yourself from PC users by buying more products and services—thus forming tighter relationships with the brand. Differentiation and belonging combine to make

Apple a clear example of how brand symbolism grows by virtue of stakeholder interpretation.[15] There are, for example, legions of Mac users and even more iPod fans, all of whom sport the Apple logo on their gear and many of whom also belong to Internet communities that celebrate Apple and its products. Some even tattoo themselves with the Apple logo or shave the brand into their haircuts! By brandishing Apple symbols they include themselves in the inner circle of this brand while, at the same time, those on the outside help them to define what it means to belong, sometimes simply by not joining them.

It is almost by definition that brands have a symbolic nature. The dictionary definition of a symbol is "something that stands for or suggests something else by reason of relationship, convention, or association." For successful corporate brands "something else" becomes "something more," something that adds value for customers, employees, or corporate partners. The added value of symbolism rests on the brand's ability to create or avail itself of a common ground of understanding among its stakeholders, and the opportunity it gives individuals to participate in sustaining or changing that understanding. Symbolic value translates into economic value when stakeholders buy the company's products, hire on, invest in its stock, or lend their support in times of crisis (in whole or in part) because of meanings the brand conveys.

Take the company hats, T-shirts, coffee mugs, and other assorted paraphernalia that employees wear, use, display in their offices, and give away to their friends and family. These branded objects symbolize the employees' relationship to the company, but because they also spread throughout employees' entire social networks and into the larger culture, they acquire additional meanings. In Denmark, for example, the employees of Novo Nordisk, a company that began by providing diabetics with insulin, wear corporate T-shirts to annual events where they meet with diabetics. These events not only connect them to people who suffer from diabetes, they also link them with doctors, nurses, fellow employees, and even the drivers that take them to and fro. And when the events are covered by the media or appear in corporate communications, an entire network of stakeholders joins symbolically in common cause.

Similarly, when a woman sets out to buy an expensive handbag, her choice to buy Prada may have to do with its Milan heritage of up-to-the-minute fashion innovation. But it also may have to do with how the larger culture symbolizes Prada, as so vividly expressed in the book and film *The Devil Wears Prada*. Rather than simply being tempted to revitalize her dress code four times a year, she may be announcing her power and forcefulness as a woman, particularly within the world of fashionable women.

And it also may have to do with the dynamic that allows an airline's symbolic qualities of branding to evoke meanings that permit stakeholders to express themselves and interpret others' brand-embellished expressions. Symbolism is not an alternative to appreciating the instrumental value of companies and products that carry brands; it adds meaning to the mix and thereby allows you to better manage a brand's contribution to corporate equity. This symbolic value not only helps explain the considerable differences between book value and market capitalization for firms with iconic corporate brands like Coca-Cola or Microsoft that routinely lead the pack, it points to different means of studying the sources of that value.

Studying Brand Symbolism and Its Meanings

How do researchers tap the symbolic meaning of brands? Brand ethnography provides the favored method and typically begins with observing how people interact with brands and the products that carry them. It then moves to in-depth interviews to find out what the brands in use mean to those who engage with them. Though in its infancy as a tool for analyzing corporate brands, ethnography offers a means to address what brands mean and ultimately how that meaning is created, maintained, and changed.

The LEGO Group, for example, has steadily increased its use of ethnographic research over the last twenty years, focusing on how children and their parents play with LEGO bricks and how they interact with one another while they play. LEGO researchers talk to children and parents about how it feels to play with LEGO bricks and how playing with them differs from other play experiences. Through observation they can directly study how children engage in play, both alone and with others, at home and in school. Playing alongside children gets them to talk with researchers about what the LEGO brand means to them and what more they would wish from the company that makes their play materials. In 2000 the LEGO Group's ethnographic research revealed that even though older children loved the way LEGO play spurred their imaginations, they felt the company's products had lost their innovative edge and were no longer "cool." The story about how the LEGO Group responded to this information is told in Chapter Eight.

Nissan combines ethnography with psychographics to drive classic market segmentation research. They search for understanding of met and unmet needs in consumers' "ideal" car or truck. Their research reveals nuggets that help define product concepts and characteristics and identify possible areas of innovation that align with Nissan core brand attributes. For example, use of psychographic methods helped Nissan define Infiniti customers as "passionate curators." According to Jane Nakagawa, formerly Nissan NA's director of advanced planning:

> The curator comes from the idea that they curate their lives so they run around the world and basically choose what they like from a global palette of things. They're very smart, knowledgeable, well-educated. They love food and travel . . . and they have incredibly discerning taste. And the coolest thing of all . . . is that they're very benevolent. It's this weird combination of ultra-successful and benevolent. There are a lot of Donald Trumps of the world, but I don't know if I would use Donald Trump and benevolent in the same sentence. . . . [When we presented] a bunch of imagery, the non-passionate curator and

the passionate curator would pick the same picture but they would have completely different readings of it. One was about conquering and control and being on top of the mountain and the other one was exhilaration and freedom.[16]

As an example of one of the most telling differences between passionate and non-passionate curators, Nakagawa explained:

I have this thing about superheroes and superpowers, because I think it's very indicative of culture . . . [so] we always ask, if you could have any superpower, what would it be? And almost everybody said "see into the future." But the reason why was completely different. For passionate curators, as you might imagine: "If I can see into the future, I could heal the world, I could prevent disaster, I could [do] all these incredibly beneficial things." The non-passionate curator [would say something like] "I could read the stock market and make a lot more money.

Having determined the psychographic profile of the Infiniti driver, Nissan then sought out people who fit the profile and visited them in their homes. The visits not only confirmed the accuracy of the profile but added new information, such as that the homes of these customers were of contemporary design with minimal interior clutter. Ethnographic research like this helps design teams refine Nissan vehicles to suit the tastes and lifestyles of targeted consumers.

Although our examples of the corporate use of ethnography in branding are focused on defining the meanings consumers make with product brands, they link to the consumer behavior research mentioned earlier in the chapter. Consumer behavior researchers have already made the connection between product brands and individual identities. All that remains is to extend this insight to corporate brands. To do this requires looking into research on organizational identity, a topic that comes from the discipline of organization theory.

The Need for Organization Theory

Models of brand valuation, studies of consumer behavior, even a look into the symbolic exchange of meaning circulating around brands, all draw from traditional academic disciplines of finance, marketing, consumer psychology, and anthropology. What is missing is the contribution made by organization theory, specifically what it has to say about organizational identity and how stakeholders create that identity in their everyday interactions with the corporate brand.

Applying organizational identity theory specifies the actions you can take to help your organization create, sustain, and enhance crucial stakeholder relationships through corporate brand management. Because these actions help you align strategic vision, organizational culture, and stakeholder images, they also show you new ways to manage the brand relationships upon which a considerable proportion of potential cash flow and market capitalization depend.

3

WHO ARE YOU?

When corporate branding works, it is intimately tied into the organization's identity. Knowing what creates the sense of "we" in your company allows you to authentically tell others what your brand stands for. But knowing who you are also requires intimate knowledge of how stakeholders see you. This is because external images interact with the ways in which employees think about their organization.

In the late 1980s the Port Authority of New York and New Jersey faced significant misalignment of its vision, culture, and images.[1] At that time the growing presence of homeless people in New York City's bus and train terminals was upsetting customers and creating negative public images of the Port Authority, which operates these facilities. At first its managers reasoned defensively that the Port Authority was not in the business of providing social services and so did not need to respond to the homeless. In their minds the problem was the responsibility of the police and social workers, so they trained their security guards to handle the homeless and sought links with city outreach services. Working together they got the homeless collected up and sent somewhere else.

But the problem would not go away. In the interim the Port Authority finished renovations on many of its facilities, a backdrop against which the unwashed and sometimes aggressive homeless stood out. Of course they were as attracted to the pleasant refurbished facilities as everyone else, and the negative publicity their presence invited generated serious concern within the Port Authority. Just when the renovations were expected to bring the organization glory, the Port Authority was getting negative press like never before.

The damage to their image of professionalism, combined with organizational pride and an action-oriented culture, inspired Port Authority officials first to investigate and then to get involved in building drop-in shelters in which the homeless could find comfort when the weather turned severe. As the organization educated itself about the issue, some of its members became advocates for meeting the needs of homeless people and taught others about their plight. Eventually the Port Authority found partners among other city agencies and stepped into the background once leadership started to emerge from these other sources.

According to organizational researchers Jane Dutton and Janet Dukerich, who studied this situation while it was ongoing, it was the identity of the Port Authority that triggered action on the issue of homelessness and ultimately reclaimed the reputation of its brand, so the VCI Alignment Model provides useful insight into this case. Reporters and vocal members of the public offered up images of the Port Authority as cold-hearted and insensitive to the problems of the homeless. These images were misaligned with the Port Authority's cultural values, which include being professional and taking action to solve problems efficiently and effectively. The resulting image-culture gap motivated organization members to reflect on their identity and to act differently as a result of their discomfort with stakeholder images. They hoped their responses to the image-culture gap would cause negative stakeholder images to realign with their positive self-perceptions, but at the same time, their actions fed into organizational dynamics that subsequently changed the organization's identity from that of a professionally detached government agency to that of an involved community member eager to collaborate with other agencies to solve problems the community considered important.

As discussed in Chapter Two, established models of branding based in traditional economics overlook the emotional side of the topic, and marketing models focus too narrowly on customers and consumers. Besides being subject to these criticisms, the models proposed by both economists and marketers emphasize the financial outcomes of branding and say little about the processes that shape and sustain it.

What is it that makes some brands stand out and create value in the eyes of their stakeholders, while others just never get it? Why has Nike been able to "bring inspiration and innovation to every athlete in the world" while Reebok and Adidas constantly play catch-up? And how was the Port Authority of New York and New Jersey able to extract itself from a developing scandal?

Puzzles like these are easily explained when you look at the degree to which organizational identity has been made into the foundation for corporate brand management. This approach overcomes the deficiencies of existing models by revealing the meaning-making processes that define strong brands. When organizations use their identity as the foundation for corporate branding, they enjoy better differentiation and more motivated employees.

Identity Dynamics

You cannot change who you are as an organization overnight through clever advertising campaigns. You may be able to provoke fast changes in the expectations customers hold for your product brands, but convincing employees to deliver on promises that affect how they see themselves is a much bigger challenge. Whether you aspire to change the organizational culture behind your corporate brand or to profit from the unique aspects of your organizational identity, knowing who you are as an organization and how your stakeholders see you is the first step toward successful corporate branding.

Various theories of identity have a lot to say about the relationship between an organization and its external stakeholders: customers, suppliers, investors, partners, communities, regulators, special interests (for example, NGOs), and the general public.

For some historical perspective, we begin with George Herbert Mead, a social psychologist. Mead was among the first to bring social context into the theory of how human identity is formed.[2]

In the 1930s, Mead developed a theory of the process by which humans develop their identities. Starting at infancy, Mead claimed, children encounter feedback as the people they depend upon tell them things about themselves. This feedback produces an embryonic "me"—each individual's understanding of itself based on what others say about it. Mead's theory was inspired, in part, by Charles Horton Cooley's concept of the *looking-glass self*. According to Cooley, just as what you see when you look in the mirror reflects what others see when they look at you; when you look at the images others form of you, you see your social identity.

Mead renamed Cooley's looking-glass self the "me" and argued that its initial formation encourages the child to start thinking about certain characteristics and behaviors as "mine." Eventually ownership of those characteristics and behaviors prompts individuals to accept responsibility for what others think of them, and what Mead designated the "I" arises out of this sense of ownership. The logic is something like this: *Because others say things about "me," "I" must exist, and "I" can respond.*

As the "I" matures it learns how to counterbalance the influence of the "me" such that, throughout an individual's lifetime, the "I" and the "me" converse (see Figure 3.1). It is from this conversation, Mead claimed, that identity arises and is maintained or changed. In this sense identity is dynamic; it occurs as the product of continuous negotiation between the individual and those with whom that individual forms relationships. But be sure to notice the important role played by the choices of which others to maintain relationships with. The "I" potentially has as much influence on the "me" as the other way around. Also notice that, as identity develops over the course of an individual's lifetime, it continuously arcs between the poles of "Who am I?" and "What do others think about me?"

Figure 3.1. Identity is created in the conversation between two aspects of self: the "I" and "me."

The Organizational Identity Conversation

Organizations learn what customers and consumers think about them through information provided by sales representatives and through market research and customer relations programs. To learn what other stakeholders think, companies monitor the media and conduct press clipping analyses; they track their public reputation through opinion surveys; and they engage in numerous interactions with stakeholders via investor, public, government, and community relations activities. This outreach provides immediate payoff by influencing how others see the organization. For example, the desired image of the company can be communicated through advertising, corporate communication, and direct selling. But outreach to stakeholders also provides information about how the company looks to others. This information feeds the organizational "us" in the same way that the looking-glass self creates a "me" for the individual. Stakeholder images provide a mirror in which the organization sees itself reflected in the eyes of others.

Of course any organization from time to time is going to encounter stakeholder images that are disappointing and that it will want to change, like the image of coldhearted indifference the New York and New Jersey Port Authority struggled to overcome. The impulse to alter how others see the organization is the same dynamic at the organization level as that which produces the "I" for the individual in Mead's theory. The organizational "we," however, is quite a bit more complicated than the individual "I" because it is distributed among organizational members. Yet even though each member holds a piece of it, the organizational "we" is not completely fragmented thanks to the interpretive context organizational culture provides. Because people make meaning in a social way, their cultures contribute to the creation of organizational identity. The organizational culture also provides much of the symbolic material from which the most influential corporate brand expressions of "we" are forged.

Although culture involves more than providing the shared experience to which "we" refers, influencing collective identity is one of its prominent functions. Seen in this way, the organizational identity conversation between the "we" and the "us" confronts members of an organizational culture with their stakeholders' feelings and thoughts about them. But the obverse also holds—stakeholders meet the organization's culture in the responses (or lack thereof) they receive from employees when they encounter them. Thus the organizational identity conversation involves members of the organizational culture listening and responding to stakeholders who listen and respond to them, as depicted in Figure 3.2.

As you can see from the two thin black arrows crisscrossing Figure 3.2, information, expectation, and emotion have a two-way flow between culture members and their stakeholders. The flow from stakeholders to the organization produces a sense of

Figure 3.2. The Organizational Identity Dynamics Model.

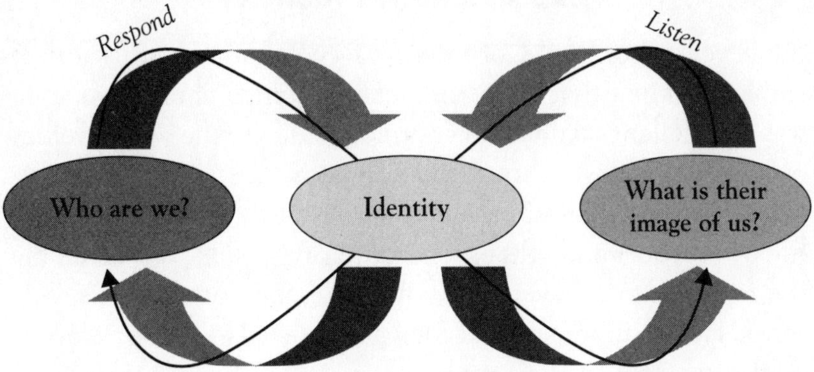

Communication within an effective organizational identity conversation flows in two directions. From the perspective of the organization, one moves from the outside in (right to left) and can be equated with listening. The other moves from the inside out (left to right) and involves responding to what stakeholders have to say about the organization and its brand.

Source: Based on M. J. Hatch and M. Schultz, "The Dynamics of Organizational Identity," *Human Relations,* 2002, 55(8), 989–1017.

what others see in "us." Moving in the opposite direction, organizational self-expression involves making claims about who "we" are or otherwise behaving in ways that indicate self-concept (for example, corporate architecture or styles of dress). When the organizational identity conversation is fully engaged, both sides will listen and respond to what their conversation partner offers.

The identity conversation directly influences VCI alignment because of identity's ability to create or destroy coherence between organizational culture and stakeholder images. The Organizational Identity Dynamics Model demonstrates the fluid state of culture and images in the VCI Alignment Model. We return to the precariousness of the organizational identity conversation when we examine identity dysfunctions at the end of this chapter. First consider how the Organizational Identity Dynamics Model applies to a company that listened and responded to its stakeholder images.

How Intel Grew Corporate Brand Equity by Expressing Its Identity

Some years ago, Intel Corporation faced a difficult situation. Its employees knew that their work making computer processor chips was of excellent quality and enormous value to the world, yet few outside the industry knew the company existed. For example, when answering questions about where they worked at neighborhood barbeques and other social gatherings, employees often met the reply, "Intel? Never heard of it." Disappointed by this widespread lack of awareness, the company decided to use its newfound marketing clout to assert itself.

Having recently discovered that it could push its third-generation processors (known simply as 386s) into the market with advertising, Intel decided to promote itself as a company. Simply placing a sticker that identified the chip maker on the outside of every personal computer containing an Intel processor announced the presence of the company as well as its product. Introducing Intel as a corporate brand meant the company no longer had to market each new generation of processors as a different product brand. Not only did this increase advertising efficiency, it solved the problem created by a court ruling that said product names consisting only of numbers (including Intel's 286 and 386 chips) could not be trademarked.[3]

The corporate branding campaign marked a shift in identity for the company. It no longer simply manufactured processors; it became "the computer inside." Instead of supplying bushels of chips to computer makers, Intel wanted to become synonymous with the computer itself. Of course this required some finesse with its computer assembling and distributing customers, whom it hoped to replace in the hearts and minds of end users. To overcome computer companies' objections, the company truncated the original "Intel: The computer inside" to "intel inside" and offered advertising budget support to any customer that would apply the Intel sticker to its computers and promote the company's products in its advertising.

Intel's strategy had the dual advantage of making co-branding highly attractive and of fighting the rampant commoditization that was reducing everyone's margins. By thus differentiating itself from the otherwise invisible computer processor industry, Intel created significant corporate brand equity for its investors. Today the previously unknown Intel name sits proudly among the most valuable brands in the world and its margins soar above those of the computer makers who use its processors.[4]

The lack of recognition Intel once faced corresponds to a missing stakeholder-to-organization movement in the identity conversation (see Figure 3.3). As a consequence, the company's identity suffered from lack of feedback from the end users of its products. "Intel inside" provoked a conversation with end users and convinced the world to trust a computer displaying the "intel inside" sticker. By expressing itself in a way that shared the internal pride employees felt in their company (anchored in its "we") with external stakeholders, the company provoked an identity conversation that brought stakeholder images (and through it the organizational "us") into alignment with organizational culture and gave Intel a

Figure 3.3. Intel faced a lack of recognition from its stakeholders and suffered from low self-esteem as a result.

Source: Intel and Intel logo are trademarks or registered trademarks of Intel Corporation or its subsidiaries in the United States and other countries.

much-envied position in the global marketplace, not to mention an iconic status within consumer culture.

You should recognize, however, that the story we just told describes only one of many moves in Intel's ongoing organizational identity conversation. For example, the company recently updated its logo by incorporating the circle from the "intel inside" sticker. This change symbolized the company's responsiveness to its customers' overwhelmingly positive support of "intel inside" and now serves as a constant celebration of the success of that historic campaign. It also allowed the company to clean up its branding, which had by this time resulted in several versions of the Intel logo. By creating consistency in the display of its logo, Intel can better establish its corporate brand equity position as something that is unique. As an umbrella brand, all products that Intel makes from now on will carry the Intel logo, complete with the "intel inside" circle that refers to the origin story of Intel's corporate brand.

There is, of course, more to the Intel brand story. In recent years the company found that its Pentium brand enjoyed greater brand equity than that of the Intel name. The company has now decided to de-emphasize the Pentium* name, replacing it on its next generations of processors with the name Core coupled with the Intel brand. Thus the company now promotes Intel Core* Duo and Intel Core 2 chips, but has reduced its support for the Intel Pentium Processor for co-branded advertising of this product. Monitoring brand equity allowed Intel to avoid a serious brand proliferation problem and good brand management caught the potential misalignment this would cause in time to correct it. Intel's story shows that you can never be complacent about your branding. You must remain vigilant even against amazing successes like the Intel Pentium name to make certain they do not damage the equity of your corporate brand.

---

*Intel, Intel Logo, Intel Core, Intel Inside, Intel Inside Logo, Intel Pentium are trademarks of Intel Corporation in the U.S. and other countries.

Figure 3.4. The identity conversation is dynamic; many layers of interpretation build up over time.

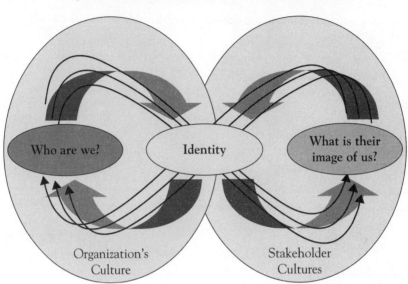

Given that identity conversations continue and change over time, listening and responding build the identity that underpins the corporate brand layer by layer. (Figure 3.4 depicts a few of the many layers involved.) And while you want to avoid the misalignment between organizational culture and stakeholder images that can visit your brand from time to time, there will always be aspects of running your business that change, creating new challenges for your corporate brand.

Dysfunctional Organizational Identities

Companies face many disruptions to their identity conversations, making them occasionally incoherent—or even worse, completely disconnecting their cultural heritage from their stakeholders' images (see Figure 3.5). For example, mergers and acquisitions, internal growth, and changes in leadership can all create at least

Figure 3.5. Severe misalignment creates incoherence among culture, identity, and images.

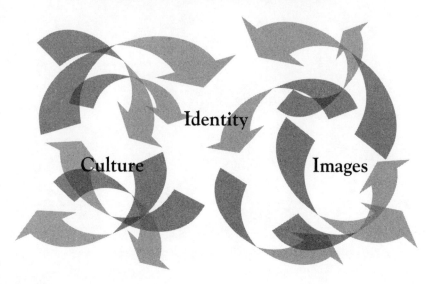

temporary misalignments among vision, culture, and image. For this and the other reasons discussed earlier, the relations between culture and image that shape your organizational identity dynamic must be continuously monitored. Your organization needs to develop and actively manage systems for listening and responding to stakeholders (examples of which are described in Chapter Four and Chapter Seven).

It is important not to overreact to surprises or disappoint-ment by trying to control what stakeholders (including your own employees) think about your company. Persuasion is one thing—manipulation is another. As in any good conversation, you want to leave as much latitude as possible for all the participants to stay interested. This means that you must engage with matters that are of concern to your stakeholders, rather than always and only pre-senting what you want your stakeholders to believe. To illustrate the problem created by overcontrolling your brand message, sup-pose that every time you responded to your conversation partner, you said exactly the same thing:

Other: Hi, I'm Tom, I work as an engineer at Omega.
You: I'm Jen. I work for Alpha, the best computer company
    on earth!
Other: That's interesting, I used to work in the computer industry.
You: Alpha is the best computer company on earth!
Other: Yes, I remember we regarded Alpha as our greatest rival.
You: Alpha is the best computer company on earth!
Other: You seem very happy at Alpha.
You: Alpha is the best computer company on earth!
Other: Why do you keep repeating yourself?
You: Alpha is the best . . .

This one-sided, highly stilted conversation is what many otherwise astute communication experts believe makes a strong corporate brand. But if, for the sake of consistency, you never vary your input to the identity conversation, your "we" will be static and uninteresting, not to mention unresponsive to the changing needs and interests of your stakeholders. Just as exhortations to stay "on message" can lead politicians to lose the trust of their people, blind adherence to brand guidelines and official corporate brand stories drains the life out of a corporate brand. To keep the brand alive you must go to where it lives—deep within your stakeholders' relationships with the company.

In balancing your organization's identity conversation, you must walk a fine line between being overresponsive and underresponsive to stakeholders. If you lose the balance between the "we" and the "us," you risk ending up with a dysfunctional identity that will damage your corporate brand.

This raises the question of how to recognize and repair dysfunctional identity dynamics. The two most common types of dysfunctional identities—hyper-adaptation and narcissism—are illustrated in figure 3.6. This figure shows a breakdown between the right and left sides of the Organizational Identity Dynamics Model. The left side of the figure represents narcissistic companies that talk only to themselves and remain deaf to the voices of their stakeholders. The

Figure 3.6. Two dysfunctions that can befall organizational identity dynamics.

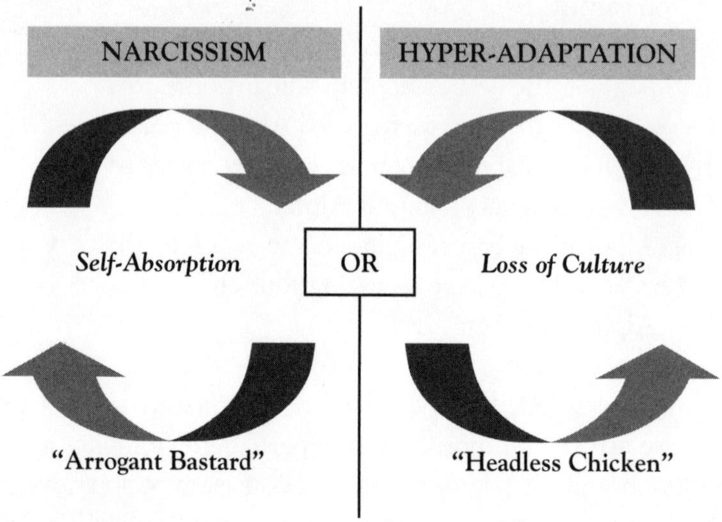

NARCISSISM	HYPER-ADAPTATION

Self-Absorption   OR   Loss of Culture

"Arrogant Bastard"   "Headless Chicken"

To avoid or overcome either of these dysfunctions requires rebalancing the organizational identity conversation so that the organization and its stakeholders are listening and responding to one another.

Source: Based on M. J. Hatch and M. Schultz, "The Dynamics of Organizational Identity," *Human Relations,* 2002, 55(8), 989–1017.

right side of the figure represents hyper-adaptive companies that are so responsive to what others say about them they lose their internal compass. Both cases represent companies whose identity dynamics have become unbalanced by ignoring either the "us" ("what do others think of us?") or the "we" ("who we know ourselves to be?").

Any imbalance in an organization's identity conversation will affect its corporate brand. In the worst cases the disconnect between the "we" and the "us" terminates the conversation, at least for the duration of the problem and quite possibly long after that. Although such damage can be repaired, the longer the conversation is dysfunctional, the graver the risk of permanent damage. To give greater clarity to the corporate branding problems unbalanced organizational identities create, here are illustrations of the two dysfunctions, beginning with hyper-adaptation.

Hyper-Adaptation: The Headless Chicken

Some companies are obsessed with following the latest market trends—most likely out of lack of knowing who they are, fear of losing momentum for their brand in the marketplace, or over-emphasis on growth. Constantly striving to be "cool" or "cutting edge," these companies quickly adopt all the latest gimmicks and fads. When a number of competitors engage in this behavior at once, it produces the big waves of imitation you sometimes see in the marketplace, where all the companies in an industry suddenly move in the same direction.

Remember when all the "cool" cell phones had to have small clamshell designs, in spite of the fact that many prospective customers could barely read the small screens and found it impossible to open the phones when engaged in another activity? In this instance the fickle teenage market combined with the competitive challenges laid down by Samsung (the first to offer the clamshell phones) forced other brands to play catch-up by reworking their central design principles. This not only foreshadowed the "cool hunting" that has driven companies in this industry and others to the equivalent of hyperventilation in product design, it produced lack of differentiation for the cell phone companies that got caught up in changing their identity to fit current fads.

Overreaction to uncool images can create confusion in the internal activities of your company because change without regard for the organization's unique heritage can leave the organization's "we" to wither and dry up. Nonetheless, some companies fall into the trap of changing their identity claims every time they gather new data about one or another of their key stakeholder groups. Desiring to be profitable and knowing the importance of customer opinion, these companies become obsessed with responding to each and every criticism or suggestion they hear. Like adolescents who try to change themselves into whatever others admire, the hyper-adaptive organization has no strong sense of itself to guide its choices.

For quite some time the Danish toy manufacturer LEGO Group's top management endlessly debated how to respond to the latest consumer trends, particularly in the electronic games sector. Internally they used the metaphor of "The Headless Chicken" as a symbol of their hyper-adaptation. Blindly they followed the latest trends knowing full well that their competitors were responding to similar pressures that made their behavior nondifferentiating. This jeopardized the LEGO Group's ability to make its brand communications heard in its noisy marketplace and threatened its previously enviable brand equity position.

AT&T provides another example of hyper-adaptation. Over the course of its long history, the company made many different claims about who it is: from Ma Bell the monopoly to Bell Labs the research company, and from a purveyor of land lines to a supplier of mobile phone services, business solutions, and now Internet access. Its current nondescript slogan "Your world. Delivered" gives the impression that AT&T intends to be anything anyone wants it to be, anytime, anywhere. While this may represent a global vision, it is an incredibly blurry one. The problem can be seen in AT&T's mobile phone business. When AT&T acquired Cingular mobile phones, it rebranded AT&T mobile services under the Cingular name, but within the year re-rebranded them with the AT&T name. This is just one symptom of hyper-adaptation in this company's organizational identity.

Of course, sometimes hyper-adaptation works. Consider the case of pop music star Madonna and her numerous self-reinventions. On the surface it might seem that, at least in the entertainment industry, hyper-adaptation attracts attention that converts to profit. But consider that in Madonna's case the principle of balancing the right and left sides of the Organizational Identity Dynamics Model still applies, in that the pop star plays her hyper-adaptation off against a notoriously profound self-infatuation that even her most ardent admirers readily acknowledge.[5] This points to the other dysfunction of organizational identity dynamics you should look out for—narcissism.

Narcissism: The Arrogant Bastard

Saying you are a customer-driven service company does not *make* you a customer-driven service company. Never checking your internal beliefs about who you are against stakeholder opinions can leave you believing your own propaganda when no one else does. In fact, any time you are oblivious to stakeholder feedback you tempt fate.

Royal Dutch Shell learned this lesson when the company announced its plan to sink the *Brent Spar*, a worn-out oil storage terminal anchored in the North Sea. Its announcement was greeted with cries of outrage from environmentalists led by Greenpeace. When these complaints were ignored, Greenpeace attempted to subvert the company's plan via the arousal of negative public opinion throughout Europe. Instead of discussing the matter with Greenpeace, Shell turned a deaf ear, playing into an already negative public opinion of Shell executives as arrogant and aloof, and the company as uncaring.

On the day Shell began towing its rig east of Scotland to sink it in that part of the North Sea, Greenpeace's tiny but fierce boat *Rainbow Warrior* challenged Shell's much larger ship. Having been alerted by Greenpeace of the likely confrontation, reporters were on hand to film the *Rainbow Warrior* as it bravely darted to and fro in front of the much larger ship. While they were filming, the captain of Shell's vessel, not sure what to do, ordered a water cannon directed at the little boat to shoot a powerful spray at it. The journalists made sure that a clip of the incident appeared on nightly news broadcasts across Europe. This image of Goliath Shell picking on good-hearted little David Greenpeace sparked public outrage that not only convinced large numbers of people to boycott the company's products but also cost Royal Dutch Shell a good portion of its reputation.

The Royal Dutch Shell example depicts the dysfunction that arises when a company restricts its identity conversation to the left side of the Organizational Identity Dynamics Model. Unfortunately, soon after the *Brent Spar* incident, Shell repeated this mistake when it chose not to get involved in the Nigerian government's execution of Ken Sara-Wiwa and several other political activists. Because Shell worked closely with this government in keeping its Nigerian business concerns going, it was perceived as having had an opportunity to intervene. When it chose not to do so, its reputation received another black eye.

Shell's mistakes taught the company to be more responsive to its stakeholders. For example, its communication specialists established an ambitious system for listening to stakeholder feedback. Known as "Tell Shell," this interactive Web site allowed the company to respond immediately to e-mailed messages, and—more important—to relay those messages to the parts of the organization in a position to act on their content. Through the collection and dissemination of stakeholder feedback Shell constantly tracks and responds to stakeholder concerns and uses stakeholder opinion as input into decision making throughout the firm.

Around the same time Shell campaigned worldwide using the slogan "Profits and Principles—Does There Have to Be a Choice?" to tell the world how the company was responding to its multiple stakeholders by engaging in responsible behavior.[6] In spite of these efforts to overcome narcissism, Shell was involved in yet another scandal in 2004. According to media reports, Shell overestimated its oil reserves in Oman by as much as 40 percent and kept this knowledge from its investors and other stakeholders for more than two years. Responsibility for the scandal was first placed on Sir Philip Watts, former head of exploration and development and chairman of the executive board, but the incident soon escalated as angry investors criticized management's outlandish remuneration packages and demanded changes in the company's governance structure to avert future misbehavior.[7]

The oil reserve scandal resulted in a significant drop in the market value of the company and precipitated the firing of Watts, the finance director, and the current head of exploration and development. It also demonstrates how difficult it is to overcome narcissism when it is entrenched in top management. Narcissism arises whenever members of a company infer their identity solely on the basis of how they express themselves to others rather than tempering this with knowledge of how others actually regard them. Although Royal Dutch Shell executives might initially have believed they were impressing outsiders with their rational decisions about sinking *Brent Spar*, and that they were being politically correct by staying out of Nigeria's affairs, their actions were taken without sufficient understanding of how key stakeholders would respond. Similarly, Shell's top managers underestimated their shareholders' role in the enterprise when they chose to cover up their handling of the oil reserve crisis. In all three instances, the company narcissistically believed that others would see it as its people saw themselves, that is, as heroes in Royal Dutch Shell's corporate brand story.

The Painful Lessons Dysfunctional Companies Learn

Sigmund Freud claimed that narcissism is a dysfunctional psychological response to the need to manage self-esteem. Organizational researcher Andrew Brown extended this idea to organizations by defining *organizational narcissism* as a dysfunction of the collective need for self-esteem, a complex consisting of denial, rationalization, self-aggrandizement, egotism, a sense of entitlement, and anxiety.[8] As Brown and Kenneth Starkey explain: "Overprotection of self-esteem from powerful ego defenses reduces an organization's ability *and* desire to search for, interpret, evaluate, and deploy information in ways that influence its dominant routines."[9]

Even worse than a disconnect in the identity conversation, corporate narcissism can lead a company to interfere with its stakeholder images in unethical ways. This situation contributed to the demise of Enron Corporation, rendering its narcissism legendary. The company convinced itself that it had rewritten the rules of business in the oil distribution sector, and that the economic success it enjoyed during its heady years provided good reasons to ignore its critics (because the critics were simply not smart enough to understand Enron's geniuses).

But the company chose to go beyond ignoring criticism and, venturing into despotic behavior, convinced the employers of its financial analysts to silence or fire anyone who suggested that Enron's stock was overvalued. In this way the company kept knowledge of its considerable internal problems to itself while some of its top executives divested billions of dollars of personal stock holdings and stock options. In terms of the Organizational Identity Dynamics Model, Enron didn't just ignore its stakeholders, for a time it managed to put words in their mouths. This narcissism was not just rampant on the left side of the Organizational Identity Dynamics Model, it spilled over onto the right side of the model by manipulating the images held by others.

The lessons of corporate narcissism are many, but prime among them should be this one: *Do not use your corporate power and influence as substitutes for confronting the ways in which others see you.* You must continually monitor and respond to criticism and comment, whether or not you like what you hear. And when you do not like what you hear, it is imperative that you intensify your efforts to understand and appreciate your stakeholders' points of view. If you merely use their feedback defensively, seeking ways to spin your message to *seem* responsive, you put your brand at risk of being found dishonest and subjected to the deservedly punishing responses of those whose trust you have violated.

But what about the lessons of hyper-adaptation? These seem to fly in the face of the advice given to prevent organizational narcissism. For example: Do not sacrifice who you are to every vacillation in the marketplace; use your sense of organizational self and your organizational culture to guide your choices. How is an organization to avoid both narcissism and hyper-adaptation when it seems that avoiding one condition creates the conditions for the other?

Balancing Organizational Identity

Recognizing that corporate branding is a process built on the dynamics of organizational identity is the first step toward managing your corporate brand effectively. The second step is to learn how to influence identity dynamics in ways that align with strategic vision. This step involves recognizing how culture and image need to influence vision, as well as the other way around. Once vision is introduced into the mix, you must stay vigilant. When vision, culture, and images are aligned, your brand will teach you ways to anticipate and innovate, rather than simply react to, the ever-changing demands of your organization's environment. The next chapter focuses on diagnosing and correcting VCI alignment gaps.

4

DIAGNOSING YOUR
CORPORATE BRAND

To manage your corporate brand effectively you need to address the two polar questions of the identity conversation: Who are we? and What is their image of us? But that isn't enough. Brand managers also need to consider a third question: Who do we want to be and how will we be known? The answer to this future-directed question taps into the company's strategic vision. Bringing strategic vision together with the organizational identity conversation yields the elaborated VCI Alignment Model shown in Figure 4.1.

The Role of Strategic Vision

Who do we want to be and how will we be known? Asking that question raises the bar on the challenge of alignment that the organizational identity conversation defines. The need for alignment is not just between culture and images but between each of these and strategic vision. Some years back Jim Collins and Jerry Porras developed what is today one of the most familiar models of strategic vision. The model has four elements: core values, shared purpose, BHAGs (big hairy audacious goals), and vivid description of the desired end state.[1]

In the VCI framework, the elements of the Collins and Porras model map onto organizational culture (core ideology = core values + shared purpose) and strategic vision (envisioned future = BHAGs + vivid description). That is, when organizational culture

Figure 4.1. A healthy organizational identity dynamic sits at the center of a successful corporate branding process.

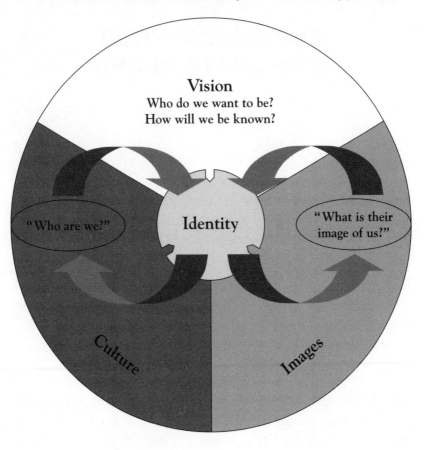

supports top management's envisioned future, strategy will more likely be executed successfully. This is all well and good, but in our view Collins and Porras missed a crucial piece of the puzzle. Without alignment between vision and stakeholder images there is no guarantee that executing a strategic vision will contribute to organizational success. A corporate brand depends on aligning vision, culture, and images.

When Vision Does Not Align with Culture

The misalignment of strategic vision and organizational culture can be seen in a somewhat counterintuitive example provided by a British cell phone service that started life as a late entrant to the market.[2] Hutchison Microtel, which had invested considerable capital in a satellite system, recognized the difficulties its late entry to the mobile phone market created. Its management approached the London offices of corporate identity consultants Wolff-Olins (WO), asking for help in inventing a brand that would take command of an already crowded marketplace. WO agreed to position the new brand, create an identity for it, and develop its communication style.

The WO consultant team assigned to Hutchison analyzed the mobile telephony market identifying a unique position that the new cell phone could occupy. They defined their recommended position along two dimensions. One of these was transparency with regard to what customers paid for when they signed up to receive cell phone service. In the U.K. market at that time, all companies charged by the full minute, regardless of the amount of time customers spent on the phone (so the sixty-first second meant buying another minute). Along with complex and confusing contracts that tied customers to their providers over long periods of time, this lack of transparency had become a sore spot that discouraged many potential customers from signing on.

WO agreed with the client that one way to differentiate the new cell phone service and capture existing market share would be to offer per-second billing. Showing customers what they were billed for would be rewarded with a reputation for honesty and openness. It would give the new brand its reputation of having improved the industry because this highly competitive move would have to be copied. However, because competitors could easily copy per-second billing, the positioning strategy needed more than that.

The second dimension of differentiation WO proposed to Hutchison involved challenging the highly technical character of the telecommunication industry. Telecoms have traditionally been the domain of engineers and their most enthusiastic customers are often people who love gadgetry. The WO team believed that the new cell phone service could differentiate itself by taking the position of "the mobile phone for the rest of us." For example, in contrast to the technical jargon that greeted customers of other companies, the new cell phone service would relate to its customers in a refreshingly friendly way. This approach would seem dynamic in comparison to the dull, dry, technical world of other cell phone providers and attract people who had never used cell phones before. In this way Hutchison's brand could grow the market for cell phone services and capture much of that growth for itself.

To represent the brand's identity of friendly, honest, straightforward and refreshing dynamism, WO chose the innovative name "Orange." The big idea behind this name was that it let the consumers know that this brand would belong to them. The idea of Orange is having the opportunity for a more individual and optimistic future where you can manage your life. The logo it created to go along with the name was novel as well. Instead of using an icon, the brand would be represented by a single square of bright orange color. In addition to the positioning, naming, and design work, WO convinced Hutchison to build dedicated retail stores to deliver its Orange products and service, and wrote scripts for its sales associates to use when they spoke with call-in customers. The scripts and the well-lit, uncluttered stores were designed to communicate an organizational identity that supported the designated brand values. They would also differentiate Orange from other cell phone operators who sold their wares through shops crowded with competitors' products all jumbled together.

Advertising agency WCRS was brought into the development of the brand at the concept stage so that it could simultaneously produce advertising for the brand launch. The resulting Orange ads featured simple stick figures that appeared as if drawn on a chalkboard, the white figures dancing merrily over the black background of the TV screen. The figures were always shown engaged in activities with other people, presumably family or friends, such as flying kites, picnicking, and riding bicycles. Though none of the ads featured anyone talking on a cell phone, they all showed positive aspects of human interaction and emphasized fun. The only mention of the brand came at the end, when the Orange logo (a square of bright orange color with the word "orange" superimposed on it) appeared as the only color in the otherwise black-and-white ad, with a warmly inflected voiceover that optimistically announced: "The future's bright. The future's Orange."

The successful launch of Orange in late April 1994 was much discussed. Within three months Orange polled at 45 percent spontaneous awareness. Ten months after launch, in spite of having spent less on advertising than its competitors, the new brand beat all U.K. mobile and fixed-line networks in TV ad awareness. In March 1996, two years after launch, the London and New York stock exchanges valued Orange at $4 billion; by 1999 its market cap reached $9 billion, with the brand alone valued at around $3 billion.

The only trouble was that Orange customer-service representatives became so enamored of the brand that they wanted to know why the company was not more like Orange. They began using the power of their financial success to pressure Hutchison for cultural change! Before anyone knew what was happening, Hutchison had sold Orange to Vodafone for a handsome sum. Because Vodafone also bought Mannesmann in Germany, regulators concerned to reduce Vodafone's potential for monopoly power mandated the sale of Orange, which went to France Telecom for $50 billion. Although Hutchison and Vodafone both made huge profits on their sales of Orange, a profitable exit was not what either had in mind at the beginning of its association with the brand. The sequence of events shows how intimately culture is linked to branding. It also suggests that branding can be a potent means of generating bottom-up organizational culture change.

In terms of the VCI Alignment model, Hutchison needed a cell phone and, with WO's help, developed its strategic vision around a brand position and an identity to suit the target market. This strategy, once executed, produced a new organizational unit within the company that developed its own culture as it delivered the Orange brand promise. Both the culture of Orange and Hutchison's vision were well aligned with customers' images, but the larger and more traditional culture of the parent company was not in alignment with the Orange brand. The mismatch between the subcultures at Orange and at Hutchison created tensions inside the company that intensified when the upstarts used their financial success to argue that the *company* should change, not them.

An entrenched and internally powerful mind-set inside Hutchison convinced decision makers to alter their strategy for Orange and implement a new plan to sell it off. This brought Hutchison's overall vision back into alignment with its now internally consistent culture. No doubt the handsome profit earned served to assuage any sense of guilt or failure on either side, but the lesson concerning vision-culture alignment is to consider who you want to be before you create a new subculture in your company the way Hutchison did with its Orange cell phone. This story might not have had such a happy ending.

When Vision Does Not Align with Images

Some years ago Denmark's Bang & Olufsen (B&O), producer of stylish, high-quality (and high-priced) audio-video systems, was facing the most dramatic losses of its long history.[3] To be fair, B&O never enjoyed long periods of high earnings because it always reinvested profits in innovation. Up to this point everyone seemed satisfied by the steady stream of outstanding products, of which the company was justifiably proud, and for which it was widely admired. Tracing its values to minimalist design traditions across Europe (most notably the Bauhaus movement), the company sought to avoid becoming just another producer of luxury products by carefully balancing its distinctive design heritage with the needs of its global and often wealthy customers. This path led the B&O brand to its iconic status, which in the 1980s became particularly attractive to high-spending yuppies, their attentions boosting the brand's visibility and enhancing its equity, at least for a time.

But the air came out of the yuppie balloon during the economic decline of the early 1990s and B&O faced financial disaster. The board's response was to name a new CEO. The man chosen, Anders Knutsen, immediately orchestrated a reorganization to gain efficiencies and flexibility in the company's cost structure. One of his first decisions was to cancel plans to produce a highly visible new product, which he explained was necessary for financial reasons. For a culture steeped in new product innovation, this unprecedented and symbolic act sent a chill through the organization. It also sent a clear message to the world about this technologically sophisticated brand: its future products would strike a better balance between the demands of competition and the company's celebrated innovations.

Knutsen labeled his program of change "Break Point" to symbolically underscore his belief that B&O's future depended upon staying competitive in a marketplace crowded with newer and better-designed products from Phillips and Sony. As part of his strategic vision, Knutsen streamlined development and manufacturing processes and forged closer ties with dealers worldwide, encouraging them to sell B&O products exclusively.

Management also attacked the company's consumer image, but because it could not afford to do this on a mass scale, it targeted specific audiences in an effort to spread insufficient resources far enough to attain global reach. As a first step, a task force studied B&O's image in two target markets. France was selected as representative of the rapidly growing market forming in Latin cultures, and Germany to represent B&O's core market. The team expected to find differences that would feed into the execution of the company's strategic vision. They were in for a surprise.

Customers across both market segments defined B&O's brand similarly—it was all about aesthetics combined with technology. They ranked the immediate perception of technological excellence as their primary brand association, followed closely by the emotional and aesthetic aspects of B&O products (for example, as reflected in movement, materials, and design). Additionally, some of B&O's design principles were found to be only marginally significant to customers. These included the ability to integrate all products into a single audiovisual system, and the advantages of having one remote control run the entire system. Following this study, the company conducted numerous focus groups that confirmed the earlier findings. As a consequence of this extensive market analysis, the task force recommended that B&O describe its corporate brand essence as: "The best of both worlds: Bang & Olufsen, the unique combination of technological excellence and emotional appeal."

Top management embraced the work of the task force and concluded that there was nothing wrong with B&O's basic products. What had been missing all along was strategy execution and communication with customers. Eventually, the "Best of Both Worlds" brand statement helped refine the company's strategic vision, focusing it on internal efficiency *and* connecting or reconnecting with customers' aspirations. Executing "Best of Both Worlds" meant establishing or reestablishing vision-image alignment.

Coherence between vision and images is generally believed to grow as customers are drawn to the products of a strategic vision. In B&O's case the opposite occurred—management changed its strategic vision to reconnect with existing customer images. Because top managers recognized that in its struggle for economic survival the company had lost sight of the emotionality of its products and retail experience, they were able to adjust their vision to embrace what was essential to customers and thereby make it central to the organization.

The B&O case demonstrates the effects of vision-image misalignment while the Orange case showed how a culture-vision gap affected a brand. But both examples will mislead you if you think that one gap can be isolated from the others for long (see Figure 4.2). Because VCI forms a dynamic system that defines the enterprise, a gap in one part of the system will often lead to a gap in another.

Figure 4.2. Three sources of VCI misalignment that can damage your corporate brand.

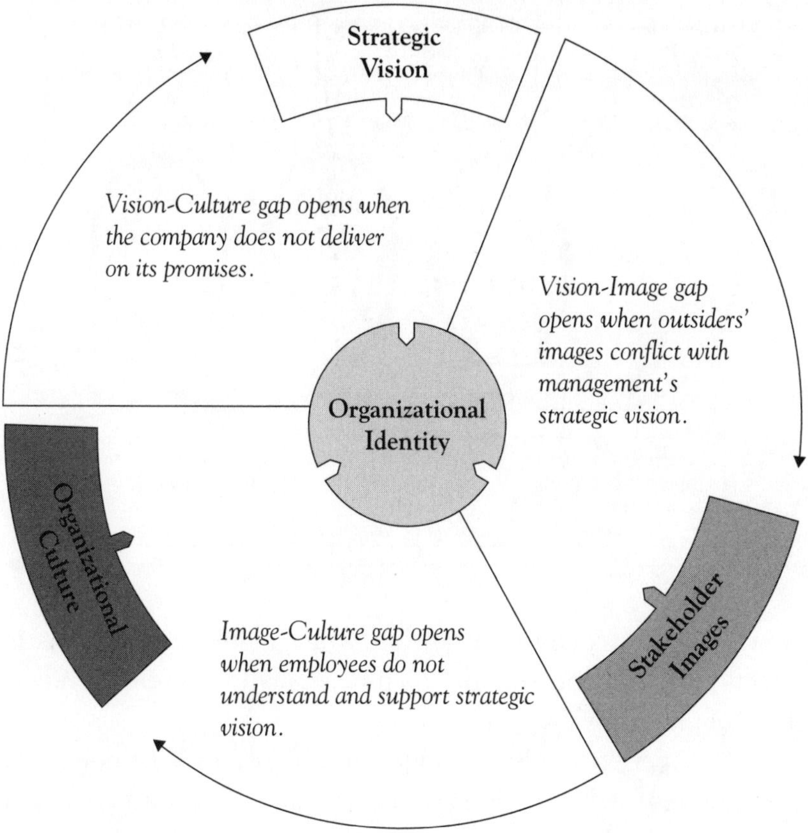

Strategic Vision

Vision-Culture gap opens when the company does not deliver on its promises.

Vision-Image gap opens when outsiders' images conflict with management's strategic vision.

Organizational Identity

Organizational Culture

Image-Culture gap opens when employees do not understand and support strategic vision.

Stakeholder Images

Source: Based on M. J. Hatch and M. Schultz, "Are the Strategic Stars Aligned for Your Corporate Brand?" *Harvard Business Review,* February 2001, pp. 128–134.

Facing Gaps Between Vision, Culture, and Images

Another look at British Airways (BA) will reveal the interrelationships between VCI gaps more clearly. The story of BA told in Chapter One showed how a company repeatedly mismanaged its brand by addressing vision, culture, and images sequentially, thereby failing to master the VCI alignment principle. Figure 4.3

**Figure 4.3. As British Airways closed one gap,
another would open.**

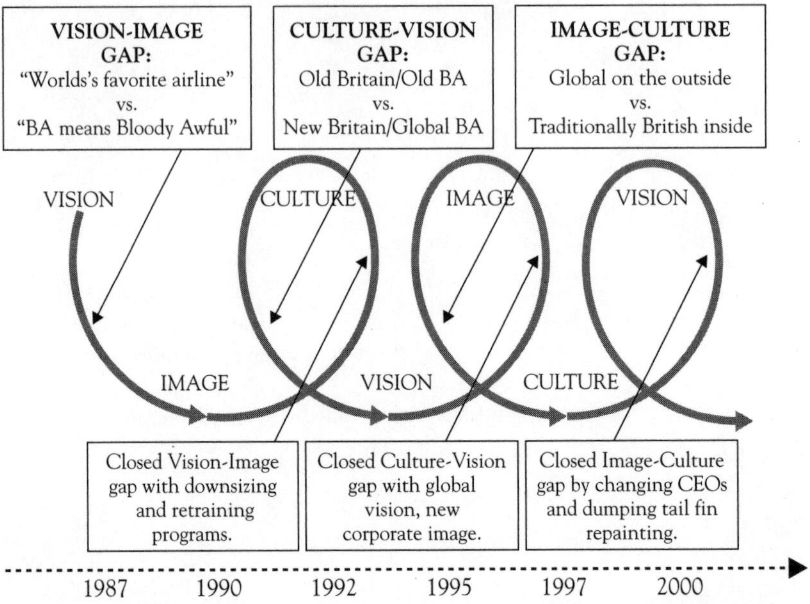

VISION-IMAGE GAP:	CULTURE-VISION GAP:	IMAGE-CULTURE GAP:
"Worlds's favorite airline" vs. "BA means Bloody Awful"	Old Britain/Old BA vs. New Britain/Global BA	Global on the outside vs. Traditionally British inside

VISION   CULTURE   IMAGE   VISION

IMAGE   VISION   CULTURE

Closed Vision-Image gap with downsizing and retraining programs.	Closed Culture-Vision gap with global vision, new corporate image.	Closed Image-Culture gap by changing CEOs and dumping tail fin repainting.

1987   1990   1992   1995   1997   2000

shows how this sequential attention, while addressing problematic aspects of BA's alignment one at a time, actually created an endless chain of recurring VCI gaps.

BA's experience raises an important question: Why does VCI misalignment reduce corporate brand value? The confusion and negative attitudes created by poor alignment of vision, culture, and images damage the value a company can expect from its corporate brand because they interfere with motivation to act on behalf of the company. BA's employees could not support the launch of their company's new image campaign (for example, the repainted tail fins and the slogan "the *world's* favorite airline") because they felt that the company was working against them. Some of them even deliberately sabotaged the new look by conducting a strike timed to coincide with the launch of the brand. Meanwhile, conservative British business class passengers, appalled by the removal of the Union Jack from BA's planes, publicly decried the new image. Thus the vision Ayling promoted for a new, global airline was left in tatters by inattention to its alignment with organizational culture and stakeholder images.

Had Ayling considered vision, culture, and images as mutually influential, he might have developed a more integrated enterprise-wide approach to BA's corporate brand and avoided the series of mistakes that still haunts the company today. While it is not always easy to get your vision, culture, and images aligned, it may not be as difficult as you think.

The Alignment Problem and Silos

Every organization needs specialists and specialized functions to do business: Strategic Planning, Human Resources, Customer Relations, Marketing, and so on. When it comes to branding, however, the need to integrate across functions is imperative. Otherwise different groups doing different things pull the brand in different directions and fail to realize synergies.

Mapping functional specialties and the programs they are responsible for onto different parts of the Organizational Identity Dynamics Model highlights the problem created when these activities are pursued independently (see Figure 4.4). It happens far too often: marketers tracking the corporate image are not in conversation with HR folks handling the culture, and internal communication specialists aren't talking to those who promote the company externally. Result: the right hand doesn't know what the left hand is doing and confusion abounds.

The failure to integrate typically means that the change programs a company has going on at any one time rarely build on the corporate brand, nor do they deliver full value to stakeholders or the bottom line. Most tragically, this lack of integration fragments the organizational identity conversation, putting all the equity invested in the corporate brand at risk.

But if this describes your company, take heart. You can pull these threads together in your corporate brand management process. In this way you can derive new value from programs already

Figure 4.4. How different corporate functions need to be integrated to achieve brand alignment.

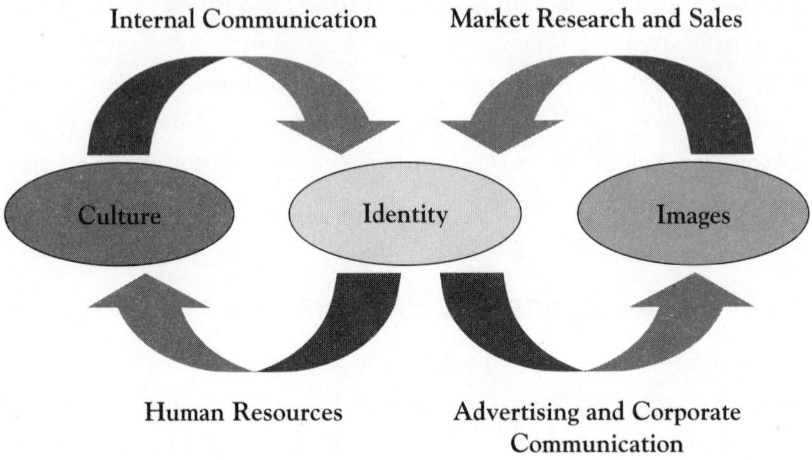

Internal Communication   Market Research and Sales

Culture   Identity   Images

Human Resources   Advertising and Corporate
Communication

A silo mind-set can disrupt the identity conversation that defines successful corporate branding.

paid for but not yet delivering their full potential. VCI alignment will help you achieve the corporate integration needed to counter the effects of fragmentation.

Imagine bringing the different people responsible for all the change programs going on in your company together in one room: the brainy business development team working on improving your vision; the passionate HR people engaging your employees in training and development activities while figuring out how to attract the right people into your talent pool; the creative marketing types working around the clock to refine the style of your next global advertising campaign; and the clever communicators who dart in and out of the room as they respond to the press or to an NGO that has taken an unexpected interest in your business. What would all these people tell you?

The branding questions you might want to address to such a group are numerous. Here are a few of our favorites:

- Is the corporate brand a valued resource in your eyes? Is it helping you realize the purposes and goals of your function?
- What do you contribute to strengthening the corporate brand? Who helps you with this the most?
- What do you do to help the stakeholders you interact with recognize that they belong to the brand or the company? Who in the company can make this easier (or more difficult) for you?

As you listen to the answers to these questions, ask yourself:

- Do the individuals and groups agree about how and when to use the brand and for what purposes?
- Are they each doing their own thing? Or do they seem to be communicating with each other and working together? Do they inspire ideas in one another?
- Are they gathering information from their stakeholders about the brand and its relevance? Do they share this information appropriately and widely enough for it to have an influence on decisions about corporate strategy and the corporate brand?

Discussion sparked by these questions and others that arise will help you find the information you need to uncover VCI gaps. If you cannot arrange to have this conversation take place in a single room, you will need to find a way to facilitate it throughout your organization. Either way, people working across your enterprise, inside the organization and out, need to share information with one another to connect the two sides of the identity conversation. This information sharing can be facilitated by someone able to gather what is learned and communicate it to those responsible for the corporate brand and to all those who are able to act on its behalf, but direct interaction between the members of different functions will produce results that are usually better and always available more quickly.

Some companies try to formalize this complex process by spec-
ifying all stakeholder touch-points and then developing systems
for monitoring and communicating with them. We have found it
more useful to keep addressing the three central questions of the
VCI model: Who are we? What do others say about us? Who do
we want to be in the future and what will our stakeholders think
about us when we get there? (see Figure 4.5). Of course, nothing prevents you from dong both. But whatever course you pursue,
addressing the proposed questions will aid you in finding any VCI
gaps that threaten your corporate brand.

**Figure 4.5. Keeping these three questions in mind will help
you close VCI gaps.**

Alignment Assessment Tools

While companies use many different techniques to obtain the knowledge needed to diagnose VCI alignment, those we have found to be most helpful are laid out in Table 4.1. Each of these tools is used by one or more of the companies we have worked with, and they can all be used in combination, provided you have the required resources and your managers are ready for this much

Table 4.1. Alignment Assessment Tools.

Technique	Activities Involved	Challenges You May Meet
Stakeholder Surveys (be sure to survey members of your organization along with your other stakeholders)	Compare market and reputation data on different stakeholder groups with data from regular surveys of employee perceptions of the company and confront any disparities. What does each group think of the company, what it stands for, what it delivers?	Make sure the way you measure performance and stakeholder perceptions matches the vision and identity for your corporate brand. All too often inside and outside data are not comparable or do not tap the uniqueness of your brand platform.
Dialogue between middle managers from key business functions	Bring together a team of middle managers from the functions most essential to your corporate brand and let them diagnose any VCI gaps your company faces. Include at a minimum representatives from Corporate Marketing, Corporate Communication, Human Resources, Business Development, and Sales.	Different functions use different concepts, often referring to the same ideas with different terms. They will need to develop a framework and a language that everyone can use when talking about the corporate brand. Make sure all managers understand that no single function controls corporate branding—it is a shared responsibility requiring shared leadership.

(Continued)

Table 4.1. (continued)

Technique	Activities Involved	Challenges You May Meet
Dialogue between brand managers and stakeholders	Look for or invent opportunities to bring the people living and experiencing your brand together in conversation about what the brand means to them and how well it fulfills their expectations and desires. Find the stakeholders who can make the biggest difference to your brand—your most enthusiastic supporters and critics.	Instead of talking about how others perceive your brand, invite them to meet your management team or take your management team to visit them. Do not avoid criticism, but be clear about how you will respond; promise no more than you can deliver. Link these conversations to internal change processes and to internal debate about strategic vision.
Events and routines that connect stakeholders to each other via your brand	Locate the most critical events and routines that deliver your brand promise. Confront top management with the day-to-day realities of how your brand is executed in "moments of truth," both inside the company and across its boundaries. Learn how your brand is experienced by stakeholders. What makes them feel like they belong? What makes them feel like they don't?	The truth about your brand is often found in everyday details. If you never experience these details yourself, how will you know your brand? How will you influence it? Managers can easily become distanced from stakeholder experiences of the brand. Counter this trend.

input. Otherwise consider working up to a combination by adding first one and than another of these tools to your brand assessment repertoire.

Many companies insist on objective measures as well as data from qualitative studies. Novo Nordisk has a long-standing tradition of measuring brand performance, collecting massive amounts of data inside the company and out using proprietary surveys and multiple brand and reputation tracking services.[4] To make better use of this data and to monitor the impact of their recently refined brand focus on "Changing Diabetes," Novo Nordisk's Marketing and Branding groups collaborated with the Reputation Institute to come up with the Corporate Brand and Reputation Tracker, a measure with forty-four attributes, including "high quality educational services for people with diabetes," "regularly introduces innovative diabetes products," and "provides access to healthcare in third world countries." The attributes factor into the five dimensions of service, products, market leadership, corporate responsibility, and innovation. The tracker is designed to measure Novo Nordisk's efforts to become "the world's leading diabetes care company" and whether the company is perceived to be "leading the fight against diabetes," the latter ambition being measured specifically in relation to both Type 1 (congenital) and Type 2 (induced by dietary and other lifestyle factors) diabetes. The Tracker can be customized to assess any of the company's programs and initiatives.

For example, Novo Nordisk used a customized version to monitor how its "Changing Diabetes" corporate brand platform affected internal and external stakeholders in four core markets around the world and to compare these stakeholders' perceptions with those of employees at corporate headquarters. Measures from the tracker helped the company assess the extent to which its culture and stakeholder images were aligned with the strategic vision of "leading the fight against diabetes." Data showed that while there seemed to be good VCI alignment with respect to leading the fight against Type 1 diabetes, there were gaps with respect to leading the fight against Type 2 diabetes.

Another application of the tracker revealed a gap between vision and the images held by primary care professionals and patients, who were relatively unaware of the company, even though secondary care professionals specializing in diabetes perceived Novo Nordisk as leading its competitors in all markets. This study also revealed that headquarters personnel were more skeptical than those working in global affiliates about the company's claim to be leading the fight against diabetes, indicating a vision-culture gap in this part of the organization.

When Are Gaps Most Likely to Emerge?

The ability to assess VCI gaps is one thing, but anticipating gaps and dealing with them in a timely fashion is another, and it is what will put your corporate brand on track for lasting success. Given enough time, every brand is going to experience occasional VCI gaps. Misalignment may happen when an organizational culture becomes self-satisfied, or when stakeholders get bored with the company. Or it can happen because strategic vision ceases to engage stakeholders, or because the brand's differentiating power is lost. The potential reasons for VCI misalignment are many. That is why well-managed brands facilitate their ongoing identity conversations and track the mutual influence of and changes in VCI elements.

Of course situations arise where gaps between vision, culture, and images can be expected and may even be a necessary part of adapting to a new marketplace or to the changing rules of competition. In general, situations of radical strategic change (for example, new market entry, merger, downsizing, CEO succession) place the greatest pressure on a corporate brand and play havoc with VCI alignment. But smaller changes can affect alignment, even changes seemingly unrelated to branding such as the introduction of a new technology, shifts in the competency profile of your employees, or new governance practices. Be aware that different strategic change ambitions have different implications for how you should manage your organizational identity conversation, VCI alignment, and your corporate brand. Many of these will be specific to your company, but some general patterns seem clear.

The most talked-about strategic change that affects corporate branding is entry into new lines of business.[5] Few companies have done this better than Virgin. This brand's friendly, funky, challenging style was translated successfully from the recording to the airline industry, from soft drinks to wine, and from financial to cell phone services. Managed well, VCI alignment and the sense of belonging it nurtures can transfer stakeholders' passion and loyalty for your brand to new ventures. But this still leaves you with the cultural challenge: How wide is the gap between the organizational culture in your new operation and the vision and images of your corporate brand? Will you align the new organizational culture with your vision and images? Or will your culture fragment, spinning off a subculture that upsets VCI alignment, as happened with the Orange brand? This challenge may make your employer brand your top managerial priority for a while, particularly if your brand extension involves the turnaround of an acquisition whose organizational subculture conflicts with that of the parent company or with your strategic or corporate brand vision. Virgin faced this problem when it incorporated British Railways' train services into its corporate brand and renamed it Virgin Trains.

When Virgin acquired British Rail's U.K. train service in 1998, success was far from guaranteed. The trains were getting more dilapidated by the day, and the new state-of-the-art trains Virgin had ordered were not expected to arrive for at least four years. Add to this the widely published opinion of industry experts that Virgin could not possibly succeed where British Rail had failed since the company had no experience running a railway. But, according to Richard Branson, Virgin's iconoclastic founder and CEO:

> Nobody else was going to invest in it. I think that sometimes in life you just have to take risks. I personally believe that if you turn the clock forward five years and . . . [ask] "what was the biggest difference that Virgin made to this country?," people will point to the trains. . . . Virgin loves to, we all love to, take industries and shake them up and make sure they're never the same again. We've done it to the airline industry, we've done it to the financial services industry, we will do it to the rail industry.[6]

Recognizing that the train service staff could easily become demoralized by continuous criticism from customers, the public, and the press, Branson sought to bolster their resolve while waiting for vindication by giving them perks such as uniforms they enjoyed wearing and spruced-up employee lounges. Branson also welcomed the new employees into Virgin's exclusive organizational culture, complete with legendary annual parties for the company's employees.

Other companies have confronted the need to reinvent, or at least rejuvenate, their corporate brands when they moved into new markets. Many of the former European public monopolies, like British Airways, faced this challenge when they were privatized to make them globally competitive. Privatizations have been numerous in telecommunication, postal services, and airlines where past monopolies such as TeleDanmark, British Telecom, and Telefónica Spain were rebranded to communicate their new private and international circumstances and ambitions.

Such massive transformations, often involving global corporate brand management, require substantial organizational change efforts that, in Telefónica's case, combined rapid expansion in Latin America with the need to orchestrate a full-scale restructuring of the headquarters operation in Madrid. According to Telefónica's CEO Julio Linares, a series of changes occurred as the company globalized its brand, beginning with needing to "embed new values and change attitudes and develop marketing capabilities."[7] Later change processes focused on quality improvement and the development of new distribution models.

In terms of VCI alignment, Telefónica's top management first had to close the gap between its global vision and the organizational culture left over from its monopolist years, and then confront its existing brand images in order to find ways to align them with the new vision. Just as in the case of Orange, creating new brand images puts pressure on distribution channels as customers learn to expect a branded service experience whose quality matches the brand promise. This expectation points to the need for culture-vision alignment, not just at headquarters but on the front lines where customer service takes place. These and other challenges are going to crop up from time to time, producing opportunities for VCI misalignment throughout the life of any organization.

Large-scale mergers of equals present some of the most challenging problems for VCI alignment. In cases such as the merger of AOL and Time Warner, everything including the merger itself was up for negotiation, making it impossible to answer any of the core VCI alignment questions (included in Figure 4.5). When facing challenges of this scope and scale, some companies choose what at first might seem like a golden compromise: create a merged corporate brand but leave local subbrands intact.

For example, the now defunct cross-Atlantic merger between Daimler and Chrysler was legendary for this sort of thinking—and even after many years most people familiar with the deal failed to grasp the business case for the DaimlerChrysler corporate brand. Most interestingly, corporate executives placed the blame for the merger's ultimate failure on the subculture of the Daimler engineers, who refused to share their famed engineering with the Chrysler side of the house. Without sharing this element of DaimlerChrysler's brand, there was little benefit and much cost associated with the merged identity. And without managing the organizational identity dynamics underpinning the corporate brand, the problems were never resolved.

Closing VCI Gaps with the Nordea Brand

A happier outcome followed the merger of four banks from Sweden, Finland, Norway, and Denmark. Their combination represents an ambitious attempt to create a completely new corporate brand in the context of this complex, multicountry, multicompany merger.[8]

Launched in 2001, the Nordea brand introduced a pan-Scandinavian institution based in Nordic ideals that was formed from the merger of several banks that had previously served the different nations of Scandinavia. Nordea entered the market with a campaign that heralded the superiority of the merged bank's products and services, implying that other available bank brands lacked the Nordic heritage of excellence. The link between pan-national pride and local identity was expressed through ads that positioned, for example, a distinctive Alvar Alto vase (Finland) beside ordinary vases, a high-design Arne Jacobsen chair (Denmark) against a backdrop of rows of ordinary chairs, and a sophisticated snow tire (Sweden) amid hundreds of ordinary ones.

As an advertising campaign, the concept might have been sound, but the audience was not buying it. A first problem concerned the link between image and identity. Although the four Scandinavian countries may seem alike to outsiders, they differ linguistically (Finnish has a completely different origin from other Scandinavian languages), politically (Denmark joined the European Union early, Sweden and Finland later, and Norway has declined membership twice), and economically (Danes favor small and midsize companies while Swedes prefer larger companies; Norway's economy is based in natural resources—shifting from fishing to oil-and-gas; and Finland is making the transition from forestry to high-tech—best represented by Nokia). Worse, the countries have been at war periodically over the past centuries and are nowadays rivals in sports, education, and certainly commerce.

A second problem concerns the gap between image and culture. Scandinavians maintain strong national stereotypes, and these were very much evident in a post-merger study of attitudes in Nordea. For example, the Swedes characterized themselves as having a "consensus" culture. But to others this culture meant that Swedish managers would just talk and talk rather than make decisions. A Finnish manager likened them to "Duracell bunnies." By contrast, the Finns saw themselves as "action-oriented," combining effectiveness with toughness and stamina while others saw them in a less favorable light, some saying they "act like an army."

The Danes were characterized as negotiators, but in less glowing terms like wheelers-and-dealers. Finally, the Norwegians were seen as "straightforward"—meaning fully predictable and homogeneous. As one Finnish manager expressed it, "The Norwegians, they are most of all—Norwegians!"

Of course nationalistic stereotypes often develop among neighboring nations, and they may or may not relate to the way people actually behave in a common environment. Still, Nordea found that these national differences had "explanatory power" during the first years of the merger, particularly in relation to decision making, leadership styles, and various initiatives launched to aid in the post-merger integration process. The Nordea managers simply could not agree on "who we are," in part because of their stereotyping and denigration of one another based on national origins. Nor could they project a common image to the employees and the public, no matter what the advertisements conveyed. The strategic vision of one united Nordic company clashed with the diversity found in the subcultures of the four merged national banks and in the stereotyped images they had of one another. These VCI gaps vexed Nordea's early efforts to achieve alignment (see Figure 4.6).[9]

The cultural complexity Nordea faced internally was complicated by diversity in its marketplace. Each of the four merged banks had a long history in its own local market with different positions and customer segments. For example, the Finnish partner, Merita, held a leading position in its local consumer market and dominated the corporate market in Finland. In contrast, the Swedish partner, Nordbanken, was a midsize and predominantly retail bank. These were the first merger partners in the formation of Nordea. Next came Danish Unibank, which itself had recently joined with a leading insurance company. Norway's Christiania Bank og Kredittkasse (Credit Union) finally joined the merger—but only after fierce negotiation with its public owners. In most markets, the merged banks suffered initially from a lack of Nordea brand recognition among customers, especially pronounced when compared to their pre-merger ratings. In some markets Nordea was

Figure 4.6. The different VCI gaps in the Nordea brand at the time of the merger.

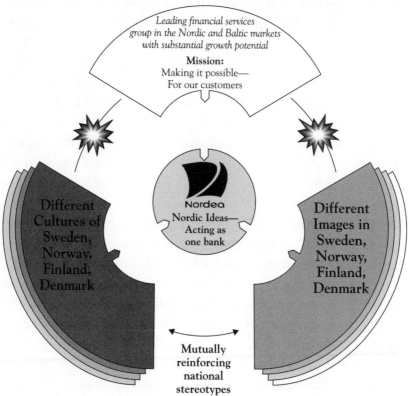

also seen as a big, undifferentiated foreign player. Poor financial performance in the first years of the merger, a growing cost/income ratio, and the dramatic replacement in 2002 of Danish top manager Torleif Krarup with Lars G. Nordström from Sweden further demonstrated the struggles the company faced in credibly launching its corporate brand.

Now, five years after the merger, the Nordea brand is doing much better and has a market position of number one or two in most Scandinavian markets, attracting 11 million customers in all, and having twenty-nine thousand employees and a market cap of €24 billion. According to Nordea's top management team, the company worked hard to integrate business processes, business functions, and employee mind-sets across markets to be able to act as one pan-Scandinavian enterprise. The cultural differences in particular were recognized early in the integration process and were met with a company-wide cultural integration campaign under the slogan "Making it possible." For example, a series of "common culture" seminars allowed managers in each business area to meet, exchange mutual stereotypes, and share ideas about how to best bring the Nordea brand to their local cultures.

In 2006, *Euromoney* gave six awards, several celebrating Nordea as the best M&A House in its local markets.[10] It is unclear whether or not Nordea could have avoided the VCI gaps that are so typical during the first years of any multicompany, multicountry merger. What is certain, however, is that no brand advertising campaign is robust enough to counter such gaps between vision and company subcultures or to overcome initial tendencies to stereotype the other parties in a merger. What is encouraging is that, unlike the failures of Time Warner/AOL or DaimlerChrysler, Nordea worked hard to establish VCI alignment and enjoys, at least for the time being, a well-integrated position in the eyes of its employees and customers.

Part Two

MANAGING CORPORATE BRANDS

5

MANAGING CORPORATE BRANDS AS ORGANIZATIONS GROW

It is common to attribute business acumen to the leader in charge during the time a company achieves success, yet most leaders recognize the debt of gratitude they owe to their company's founder. Furthermore, failing companies can sometimes right themselves by renewing the vision, values, and principles their founders bequeathed to them. This is perhaps most evident when founders themselves return to restore luster to a tarnished brand, as Steve Jobs did at Apple in the late 1990s. The VCI Alignment Model offers an intriguing explanation for these and other "founder effects."

When a company is born, it is usually because stakeholders share the entrepreneur's desire to see something accomplished. This early vision-image alignment plants the seeds for an enterprise that will develop if the many elaborations of the original idea that occur over time permit the company to thrive and grow. However, although the initial vision-image alignment gets a company through its start-up phase, without an organizational culture to give the brand life and guide employee activities, early success is unlikely to be sustainable. Thus somewhere during the transition from entrepreneurial start-up to corporate behemoth, organizational culture emerges as a force for both stability and change, and once culture is established, the branding picture is forever complicated by the need to align strategic vision with both organizational culture and stakeholder images.

But creating vision is not a one-way street; the process takes the form of an ongoing conversation between the founders and those who become their stakeholders. This is an early version of the organizational identity conversation described in Chapter Three (and illustrated in Figure 3.2): when entrepreneurs listen to stakeholders, they discover what they can achieve that is of potential value to the world; when they respond to stakeholders, they realize that potential. Thus vision rarely springs full-blown like Athena from a founder's mind. Instead it involves listening and responding to stakeholders from the get-go. It seems fair to say that vision-image alignment occurred at start-up for each and every company in existence today.

But even after the idea on which a company is founded has been established in its marketplace, the company will encounter countless challenges, some anticipated and others unforeseen. One of these is success! Growth often causes a company to drift into territory that is unfamiliar and dangerous because it means bringing people on board who have not grown up with the founder's intuitive connection to key stakeholders. What is more, the culture of the organization that carries the founder's original vision alters with the values and ideas new employees bring, causing misalignments between vision, culture, and images. The change that accompanies growth is natural and much of it will be welcomed, but providing some mechanism for relating past and future is required to protect the identity of the budding enterprise. That mechanism can and should be corporate brand management.

This chapter introduces Larry Greiner's popular theory of the stages of organizational growth, which we extend to include the effects of growth on corporate branding. First we explain the relationship between entrepreneurs and corporate brands, next how specialization and delegation create pressure to extend the brand, and finally how organizational silos can jeopardize a corporate brand while effective corporate brand management can put to rest the turf wars silos create.

Corporate Brand Management and the Stages of Organizational Growth

In the now-classic *Harvard Business Review* article "Evolution and Revolution as Organizations Grow," Larry Greiner laid out five stages of development and four accompanying crises organizations pass through as they grow from entrepreneurial start-ups, passing through stages of collectivity (culture development), delegation (professional management and control structures), and formalization (bureaucracy), to become fully mature enterprises ripe for renewal (see Figure 5.1).[1]

According to Greiner, the first crisis a successful start-up faces is a need for leadership that extends beyond what its founder can provide. Resolving the leadership crisis ends the entrepreneurial

Figure 5.1. Greiner's Growth Stages.

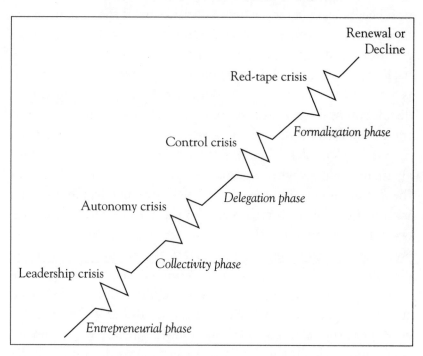

Source: Based on L. Greiner, "Evoluton and Revolution as Organizations Grow," *Harvard Business Review*, 1972, 50, 37–46.

stage by installing professional management and replacing the cult of the entrepreneur with a more complex organizational culture. These developments take the company into its collectivity stage, a predominant feature of which is centralization of control in the new management team.

Collectivity ends when the need for autonomy overwhelms the benefits of centralization, and management responds by delegating much of its responsibility. The delegation stage involves decentralization, and the company experiences growth in its middle management ranks as a means to handle the control issues that delegation leaves in its wake. But further growth leads to loss of top management control that continues until the crisis of control ends the delegation stage.

Creation of formal rules and procedures introduces new types of control that allow management to direct the activities of the now much larger and more complex organization. But formalization begets bureaucracy, which flourishes until the mounting red tape precipitates either overt rebellion or such a slowdown of all processes that the organization must choose between renewing itself or going into decline and finally dying. If the path to renewal is followed, the organization will typically regress to an earlier developmental stage and try to learn from its past mistakes as it travels once again through the stages of evolution and revolution.

Greiner's model indicates how and why corporate brand management changes with organizational growth. For example, in the entrepreneurial phase, corporate brand management occurs within the relationship the founder establishes with stakeholders, a direct connection that makes it easy to communicate vision and align it with images and expectations. Intentionally putting corporate brand thinking into decision making during this stage of organizational development gives the organization a real head start in life. This is what Richard Branson did at Virgin with his concept of the "challenger brand" and the slogan "We're on your side against the fat cats." But if entrepreneurs do not naturally think in these terms, the company's corporate brand will have to await a visionary CEO, as happened when Howard Schultz and his stakeholders developed the idea that Starbucks would be "the third place" between home and office.

In the collectivity stage of organizational development, corporate brand management is complicated by the emergence of organizational culture and the growth of a middle management group that intercedes between stakeholders and top management. The resulting distance between top managers and the everyday lives of organization members increases geometrically as the organization moves toward bureaucracy, by which point its systems and processes are likely to have fragmented and crystallized into numerous fiefdoms and subcultures. These form the infamous silos from which most large organizations suffer.

Internal fragmentation will be echoed externally in the number of markets the organization will have entered by this advanced stage of its development, globalization serving to magnify the problem. The combination of these factors results in replacement of the original intuitive connection between founder and stakeholders by a set of systems and tools for managing stakeholder relationships. Without a compelling corporate brand supported by an aligned organizational culture to recreate the founder's emotional and symbolic connection to stakeholders, only the functional side of the business remains to hold the enterprise together. Meaning is lost.

Decreeing brand programs from on high may seem like a cinch, but making them work for employees and other stakeholder groups becomes progressively harder as the organization develops through Greiner's stages. In this chapter we first focus on corporate brands created during the entrepreneurial stage, then turn to examples of what corporate branding looks like after the entrepreneurial stage but before bureaucracy has set in. These examples make it possible to explore the important topic of managing brand extensions. Finally, we explain why the organizational fragmentation caused by functional silos and turf wars is a key reason corporate brands in mature companies struggle to renew themselves.

The Entrepreneurial Corporate Brand
(VI Alignment)

The founders of a business always leave a lasting impression on the organization they establish. Edgar Schein has shown that founders shape their organization's culture, and we believe they also imprint the corporate brand with their personalities, strengths, and weaknesses. The VCI Alignment Model suggests that this founder effect emanates from vision-image alignment. Two stories of entrepreneurial start-ups illustrate founder effects on corporate brand creation.

Skype: Vision = Image

The vision was grand, the message simple. The results speak for themselves. Niklas Zennström and Janus Friis, a charismatic young Swede and a shy Dane, changed the world with Internet applications that continue to revolutionize the music and telecommunication industries. Although they did not invent peer-to-peer file-sharing technology, they adapted it to enable users to freely share music files, phone calls, and now television. And they built several global corporate brands on its foundation.

Constant family relocations had made social interactions with other kids difficult for Janus Friis, who only managed to finish tenth grade. In spite of this limited formal education, he landed a job at a small start-up company that provided Internet service to its subscribers. Here is how his career got started and how it evolved. One day, after spending hours trying to establish an Internet connection on his father's computer, Friis called customer relations at Cybercity, his father's ISP. But the customer service representative who picked up his call could not help him, so he churlishly asked for a job as, in his words, the company was "apparently lacking the competencies."[2] Much to his surprise, Friis was hired!

During his years at Cybercity, Friis developed considerable expertise on the Internet, and when the entire service staff was laid off some years later, he transferred his skills to Tele2, one of Copenhagen's local telephone companies. There he met Niklas Zennström. The two budding entrepreneurs shared an interest in embryonic file-sharing technology that connected users to each other without relying on central server capacity. They sensed opportunity in the rudimentary technology and created KaZaA, a brand under which they offered the world a free music file-sharing program. Their application was easy to use, and with its funky name and funny bubble-like logo, KaZaA attracted young people all over the world.

In no time KaZaA became the world's most downloaded Internet application and brought Friis and Zennström considerable fame. But fame turned to infamy in 2001, when the music industry accused the two of encouraging music piracy and illegal Internet file sharing. The case went before the Dutch Supreme Court, which decided that the young entrepreneurs could neither be blamed nor punished for distributing the technology, nor could they be held accountable for how it was used by others. But in spite of legal success, the notoriety left KaZaA with a lingering image of unfair play. In January 2002, following several failed attempts to partner with firms in the music industry, Friis and Zennström sold KaZaA to Sharman Networks for a modest price.

Undaunted, the two entrepreneurs moved to London, where they spent their time searching for additional uses of the peer-to-peer technology. This time they steered clear of anything musical. Their next idea came to them during the summer of 2002. Friis later recalled in a televised interview: "We wanted to provide free calling, and become one of the largest phone service operators in the world."[3]

Initially, their idea met with skepticism from potential users and investors—perhaps they thought it was too good to be true. But both Zennström and Friis believed in their budding vision. To develop it they began interacting with members of the Internet culture that was emerging throughout Europe at that time. They first teamed up with some dedicated young programmers from

Estonia and later with others from London and Paris. According to the founders, this is how they started as "a small big company." In April 2003, Friis and Zennström launched a Web site with the catchy name Skype and an easy-to-use home page.

From the beginning Friis and Zennström wanted the Skype brand to represent freedom to talk with others throughout the world at no charge. But they also wanted to make certain that *free* was associated with "freedom" rather than "discount" or "poor quality." According to Malthe Sigurdsson, Skype's brand director and the designer of its first user interface, the core principles behind the brand were "Keep it simple, be generous sharing technology, and stay humble."[4] They wanted clean and engaging designs to communicate these principles.

Skype designers found many ways to express the young company's values. For example, they created the green (place call) and red (end call) telephone receiver symbols that intuitively communicate how the system works while demonstrating simplicity. Logo designers similarly sought to express Skype's positive and friendly spirit. The cloud surrounding the Skype name, for instance, originally changed colors to symbolize the diversity of the brand, but the baby blue color won out and today presents the brand with simplicity throughout the world (see Figure 5.2).[5] Of course, for some the symbol will take on more playful associations such as "blue skying it" and "the sky's the limit," or maybe even "go fly a kite!"

The desire to be down-to-earth gave Skype part of its original identity, but the engagement between the founders and their stakeholders, and later among Skype users, complemented and completed it. Skype's managers, for example, made themselves available to their users through blogs. By listening to kudos and complaints about the service and the brand, they allowed stakeholders to guide the development of Skype while at the same time protecting its brand from complicated techno-speak, which they did by sticking to plain talk. Sigurdsson reinforced the founders' original intentions to concentrate on providing users with a free international calling service rather than focusing on the

Figure 5.2. Skype logo and user interface.

technology that makes Skype work: "We are about sharing free calls all over the world. We are not about peer-to-peer technology, telephony and VOIP."[6]

Skype's founders thought globally and built diversity into their organizational culture from the beginning by establishing multiple international locations for doing business and hiring a variety of people and personalities. Sigurdsson claimed: "It would be dangerous for a company like us to consist of white boys from business schools in Western Europe. We would not be able to reach the 'BRIC markets' in [Brazil, Russia,] China and India."

At a rate of approximately 150,000 new users per day, Skype quickly became the world's fastest-growing Internet company. According to Friis:

After one month we had at least one user in more countries than there are member nations in the UN. The vision was so clear, and

I really had a hard time understanding some people's skepticism. I think that many people have problems with the simple fact that these types of good ideas always are simple and obvious.[7]

By the end of 2004 Skype employed roughly 150 people in fifteen countries who were responsible for providing free service to more than 3 million simultaneous users. Development continued, unconstrained, until the summer of 2005 when rumor spread that Skype had turned down media-mogul Rupert Murdoch's offer to purchase the site. The company said nothing until the following September when the world press reported the flabbergasting news that Skype had been purchased by eBay for $2.6 billion in cash plus eBay stock and additional performance-based considerations.[8] By January 2007 Skype usage surpassed 9 million simultaneous users. Asked whether it is reasonable to refer to shy Janus Friis as a computer nerd, his partner Niklas Zennström answered laconically: "By no means—he doesn't know how to code. He's a visionary."[9]

Friis and Zennström are at it again. They are now busy testing their vision and branding skills on a new application of peer-to-peer technology for television. Their new undertaking promises to bring free access to TV channels via computer file sharing under the brand name Joost. Like many other entrepreneurs, Skype's founders move from start-up to start-up, preferring to let others lead the organizations they create beyond the entrepreneurial stage.

Noir: Fashion = Corporate Social Responsibility

Women's clothing designer Kathrine Hammett became one of the first to embrace socially conscious branding when her luxury label offered a popular line of T-shirts displaying political slogans such as "No Nukes." More recently, rock band U2's lead singer Bono and his wife Ali Hewson founded Edun, a socially conscious clothing company that helps the developing world create viable commercial relationships with the developed world. But in adhering to the funky aesthetic of environmentalism, none of these early efforts produced anything remotely approaching competition with trendy fashion labels such as Dolce & Gabbana or Balenciaga. That is, not until Noir came along and wedded "socially responsible" to "sexy" with its visionary luxury fashion brand.

The *Financial Times* recently proclaimed, "Green is the new black as designers embrace fair trade" and went on to describe how Noir stretches the boundaries of fashion to include social responsibility without losing any of the style associated with high fashion for women.[10] Sarah Bailey, the U.S. editor of *Harper's Bazaar*, put it this way: "I know [Noir] will capture the zeitgeist in years to come and the market is ready for a sexy brand which embodies corporate governance."[11] Noir's vision is to offer its customers the best of both worlds (see Figure 5.3).

Noir was co-founded by Danish fashion visionary Peter Ingwersen, formerly European brand manager for Levi Strauss and later CEO of Denmark's Day Birger & Mikkelsen, an international fashion brand known for its bohemian-chic style.[12] Although these experiences gave Ingwersen deep knowledge of the fashion industry, he was "getting tired of just clothing, clothing itself without any meaning—without any bigger value or symbolism associated with it. I needed to have more substance in my life."[13]

Although trained to think in terms of fashion trends, Ingwersen found himself looking outside the fashion industry for inspiration. That was when he noted what he claims is the "zeitgeist trend" of business—corporate responsibility. This observation suggested building a brand around the idea of enabling meaningful consumption. He envisioned consumers' feeling good about spending money on themselves when their purchases improved the lives of others.[14]

Ingwersen found that his vision appealed not only to potential customers but to the investors he needed to get Noir off the ground. One unforeseen benefit of this appeal was that investors from outside the fashion industry wanted to back the company. Some of them had considerable experience in the developing world

**Figure 5.3. The yin and yang of the combined
Illuminati II and Noir brands.**

Source: Noir Illuminati II.

and they helped Ingwersen create Noir's social and environmental policies. But Ingwersen found he needed more hands-on help at the helm. For this he turned to someone who knew the corporate responsibility side of fabric purchasing and manufacturing processes.

Mutual friends introduced Ingwersen to Annelise Ryberg, a Dane who had lived in New York for many years while helping Bill Clinton with his fundraising campaigns and working for the United Nations and several human rights organizations. Together

Ingweren and Ryberg created two interdependent businesses, Noir and Illuminati II. Illuminati II provides Noir and other companies with fabrics made from sustainable cotton produced in Uganda, where the company developed production methods with local farmers to meet standards set by the Global Compact and other international corporate social responsibility groups. Right now Illuminati II is a part of Noir. It will be launched as an independent brand in 2008.

Setting up sustainable harvesting of cotton and weaving processes in Uganda is no small feat for a new company in northern Europe, so these activities were outsourced to local suppliers. Ingwersen and Ryberg quickly discovered that they needed someone to oversee these activities to ensure they were aligned with strategic vision and with the standards of social and environmental responsibility that both Noir and Illuminati II claim. The two entrepreneurs teamed up with French company Axios, which was noted for its years of experience monitoring social responsibility standards in health care in developing countries. Ingwersen describes how their search for a third partner started at Google:[15]

> We actually went online. . . . That's the beauty of modern technology. And we stumbled across Axios. And by pure chance, Marlene Juel Jørgensen (who just started to work for us) had a very good friend that knew Ann, who is running Axios. So we [searched online] even more and within weeks it all came together. So this was more than a chance encounter; this was meant to be. Ann was Danish and married to an American, but living in France. She goes to these weird and wonderful places in the world where she applies the whole documentation of corporate social responsibility making sure that standards are followed. She flew up to Denmark, and we told her the whole story. Now, she's normally only involved with the medical business, but we said to her: "Listen—would you like to take on a fashion company?" and she said: "I never thought about that, it's not normally what we do" and we asked her: "Would it be interesting for you?" and she replied: "Yes," obviously.

By marrying fashion to social responsibility, Noir made its business opportunities grow, spreading quickly from investors and partners to buyers from leading department stores worldwide. According to Ingwersen, the more stakeholders became involved with the brand, the clearer the vision became. But he found that his fashion training had not prepared him to deal with the social responsibility side of Noir's brand promise. He continues:

> You need to educate—you need to educate your board, your employees, your customers the way you educate a child. So I'm here to educate with the same story. . . . Because fashion is fickle, I would love to tell a new story tomorrow, because that is the nature of fashion. Here I need to stick to the same story. That is the first challenge I had as a leader and a founder.

The Noir–Illuminati II vision thus emerged from the contradictory combination of sexy fashion and social responsibility. Here's how Ingwersen expresses the aspiration of the brand as a balance point:

> So never cut, but bring together. Then I started to understand, that maybe that is what life was about—yin and yang. It was about the juxtaposition of white up against black. It was a juxtaposition between female and male. It was a juxtaposition between rebellious-ness and consistency. It's the balance between the two of them. One in one direction is too much—and the other in the other direction is too much—you can't cope with it when you start to bring these two things together; you need to get to the balance point.

Yin-and-yang dualism shines through all the symbolism Ingwersen developed around the brands he created. The Noir name, for example, sprang from the founder's personal tastes and signature style exemplified by his fondness for Edgar Allan Poe, punk rock, and mythological rebellion emanating from the dark world. Searching for the yang to Noir's yin, Ingwersen played with concepts of "white" and "light." These associations suggested *lumin* (Latin for *light*) and enlightenment, from which the name Illuminati II was derived, contributing to the vision: "to enlighten consumers to buy in a different way" by offering a clothing brand that was committed to social responsibility. The reference to enlightenment further inspired the creation of the Noir Foundation, which is dedicated to sustaining the lives of Illuminati II farmers and their families who grow and weave the cotton for Noir's clothing. Yin and yang intermingled.

Throughout the Noir–Illuminati II story yin and yang combine the sexiness of trendy fashion with the morality of sustainability and the luxury demanded by the developed world with the subsistence the developing world seeks. Noir's organizational culture also reflects the duality of the brand. The company deliberately nurtures cultural diversity to attract talent from the fashion world while also being credible to people who are fully dedicated to social responsibility.

Post Start-Up, Pre Bureaucracy

Placing vision in the context of corporate branding makes it clear that a successful vision never stands alone; in the Skype and Noir stories strategic vision thrived on the support of stakeholders. But success and the growth it brings threaten VCI alignment, and Skype and Noir will no doubt each face misalignment challenges down the road. To anticipate what lies in their future, consider how Nike and Virgin dealt with the brand extensions that are part and parcel of organizational growth from the entrepreneurial, start-up stage into and through the collectivity, delegation, and formalization stages.

Nike: How, and How Not, to Extend a Corporate Brand (CI Alignment)

When Phil Knight and Bill Bowerman founded Nike, people inside the company knew instinctively how customers would respond to product and brand decisions. This was because they *were* Nike's customers! Knight and Bowerman had made a practice of recruiting from the athletic communities in which they were active (as runner and coach, respectively).

But the company's early success in the athletic shoe import business led to growth in its customer base and much of that growth came from people who bought Nike shoes for reasons other than to run in them. Some found Nikes more comfortable or more stable than competing brands of shoes; others wanted to share the aura surrounding athleticism or simply regarded Nike as a "cool" brand. But beneath the surface of the company's seeming good fortune lurked an unsuspected and dangerous problem—this growth damaged Nike's intuitive connection with its customers.

Market research had shown Nike that many of its customers were using its shoes for noncompetitive purposes—running errands or going to the mall. This knowledge prompted Nike to expand into casual shoes. However, the company lacked the insight into casual shoe purchasing behavior that it took for granted with athlete customers and thereby failed to see that its casual shoe customers wanted the same high performance shoe that athletes demanded. A casual shoe better suited to the purposes to which it would be put did not carry the symbolic meaning of the shoes the Nike brand had made synonymous with edgy star athletes like Michael Jordan and John McEnroe.

The consequence of this oversight was that Nike's extension into casual shoes nearly destroyed the company. Fortunately, it did not destroy the Nike brand, which carried the company through to recovery. Nike managers used this hard-won lesson well when they later acquired Cole Hahn and wisely chose to retain the Cole Hahn brand. They did, however, provide the acquisition with shoe technology that subsequently became a co-branded benefit for Cole Hahn customers. In this way Nike avoided overextending its brand while still profiting from greater use of its corporate resources, including the Nike name, to remake another shoe brand.

Today Nike connects with customers, not only with its award-winning advertising but also through its branded stores (Nike Town) and its engaging Web site and telephone sales efforts. But all this hard work does not make the company as fully involved as it was during those early years when employees spent their spare time running races and hanging out at athletic competitions. Staying in that kind of touch with the multitude of customers Nike now serves is a significant challenge. And do not overlook the company's constant struggle to converse with its other stakeholders (investors, suppliers, regulators, local communities, special interests, and the public).

The continuing risks of noncommunication were demonstrated a few years ago when Nike was implicated in a scandal over the exploitation of laborers at the overseas factories that manufacture its shoes. We return to this part of Nike's brand story when we talk about stakeholder involvement in Chapter Seven, but the point here is that being mindful of your corporate brand means unending listening and responding to keep the organizational identity conversation balanced.

Virgin: A Legacy of Brand Extensions (VC Alignment)

Virgin's founder comes as close as anyone to being the grand master of corporate brand consciousness. Richard Branson describes his company as "the premier challenger brand." His vision was forged within a conversation that initially took place in the recording industry. As one of the first independent record labels, Virgin Records sought to give struggling new bands a means to be heard when the "fat cats" at the major labels refused to deal with them. Branson's business instincts were sound, and he took the record industry by surprise with the success of the Virgin brand and the bands that recorded under its label.

Having led revolutionary change in the record industry, Branson sold Virgin Records and used the proceeds to fund other projects, the next one being a challenge to the airline industry. Virgin Atlantic is probably Virgin's best-known brand, but the conglomerate also operates music and bridal shops, sells cola and wine, and provides mobile phone, financial, and train services alongside a host of other ventures that cohere around the central idea of offering something new and different in otherwise stodgy industries. The Virgin brand promises good value for money in ways that dare its major competitors to respond, all the while exuding youthful energy and boyish charm. All this has led to widespread appreciation of Virgin as a brand with a distinctive personality, symbolically represented by the flashy red and white Virgin name that adorns all the company stands for and does.

Virgin uses its provocative corporate name, logo, and style in all its markets and across all its businesses by associating its hip, anti-establishment symbolism with generic product labels like Virgin Megastore, Virgin Money, Virgin Trains, Virgin Wine, Virgin Brides, and so on. Again and again Virgin managers have used the brand promise to provide challenge, value for money, quality, innovation, and fun to spin out new business ventures steeped in Virgin culture. As each new Virgin venture matures, others are added, keeping the distinctive spirit of the Virgin brand both current and true to its heritage. Virgin continually responds to and manages its web of relationships with stakeholders by calling on these same values and desires, albeit in ever-new ways. By embedding strategic vision, organizational culture, and a popular image in the spirit and style represented by Virgin's sexy symbol, the company continuously reinvigorates the values and desires that sustain its brand as it dares its employees and other stakeholders to join it in taking on new challenges.

Virgin's core idea has held this company together from start-up through numerous brand extensions as it grew into a mature company. In relation to Greiner's theory, Virgin is atypical in that it has used a brand extension strategy as its business model since start-up. Brand extensions more typically coincide with the delegation phase of organizational growth, when responsibility for the brand

is passed to middle managers, franchisees, and other business partners. Once the integrative mind-set of the collectivity stage has
been replaced by the move toward autonomy, brand extensions
become a natural way to carve up corporate territory.

LEGO: Managing Brand Extensions as the Company Grows

There are many lessons to be learned in regard to maintaining brand discipline in the face of the allure of corporate growth
through brand extension. In the early 1990s, executives at the
LEGO Group neglected the logic of their brand concept and began
copying their competitors. But while Disney, Mattel, and others
successfully expanded their brands into clothing and accessories,
the LEGO Group had quite a different experience. As it turned
out, its competitors made substantially different brand promises.
Whereas customers wanted Disney clothes to be entertaining and
fun, customers expected LEGO clothes to last forever, just like
LEGO bricks. They also expected the same imaginative design
elements in the clothes that they enjoyed in the construction toys,
such as extra zippers and hidden pockets, and they wanted the
clothes to sport the bold colors of LEGO bricks. Unfortunately,
the company's representatives did not think about the core brand
concept when they negotiated licensing agreements with their
clothing suppliers. As a consequence of these and other poorly
planned brand extensions, the LEGO Group's brand meaning got
stretched too far, contributing to severe financial troubles.

The difficulty that is so clear in brand overextension can be
traced to the identity conversation. What was true for the LEGO
Group seems also to apply to Nike: a strong brand produced narcissism at the top while changes in the marketplace along with
pressure to exploit the brand sent the rest of the organization into
hyper-adaptation. This fault line between the left and right sides
of the identity conversation (pictured in Figure 3.6) eventually
ruptured, creating the potential for financial ruin. But the very

thing that got these two branding powerhouses into trouble also got them back out of it. Both returned to their core brand ideas, which helped them regain competitive advantage and return to profitability by reestablishing connections between vision, culture, and images.

Intriguingly, in spite of working in so many unrelated industries, Virgin has not faced brand overextension. We put this down to Branson's vision of the company as a means to extend its challenger brand. In other words, Virgin was founded on a business model and a brand idea that have extension written all over them: go out and challenge the fat cats, industry by industry, until the "little guys" are well served. Instead of the brand serving the company, the company exists to serve its corporate brand. Branson's legacy is more than the business, it is the brand he built on stakeholder involvement.

Bureaucracy Brings Functional Silos, Subcultures, and Turf Wars

The LEGO Group and Nike cases also show how, as organizations grow and adapt to greater complexity both internally and externally, some of the difficulty of maintaining VCI alignment is due to factors other than brand overextension. Chief among the other branding challenges that mature organizations ultimately have to face is the organizational fragmentation caused by silos and turf wars.

As Greiner's stages show, an organization's inexorable march toward bureaucracy frequently means fiefdoms, turf wars, and, eventually, crystallization into permanent and uncommunicative silos. At some point in an organization's development, integration starts to break down and different functions cease to inform one another about things that should be of mutual concern. Given time, siloed communication patterns solidify into routines that can produce impenetrable jargon and competing perspectives on organizational issues, making it difficult or impossible for members of different parts of the organization to understand one another, let alone collaborate to solve problems or take advantage of corporate opportunities. Any politics between functional areas will further interrupt the flow of information and undermine joint effort, while busyness will magnify any and possibly all of these challenges. When silos become institutionalized as subcultures, they measure out the ground on which turf wars will be fought.

The beginnings of a subculture formed at the LEGO Group when the company established LEGO Media International (LEGO Media) to handle the development and worldwide marketing of interactive software and music, film, television, and magazines for children. London was chosen as the location for LEGO Media, rather than Billund (in Denmark), where the company headquarters sits, because London was believed to be the center of creative talent in the media business. Accordingly, the company staffed LEGO Media with people in their early twenties, most of whom came from the software and publishing industry, many having international backgrounds. These new employees did not want to be overly influenced by the culture at "Mount Parnassus," as one manager described LEGO Group headquarters. Believing that the LEGO brand was "fantastic" but that headquarters treated it with too much reverence, one LEGO Media manager summed up the group's feelings by stating bluntly: "The way the brand is interpreted in Billund is restrictive and keeps them from seeing opportunities. We try to follow the guidelines that make sense, but we would like the brand to be vibrant rather than boring, conservative, and not creative."[16]

LEGO Media employees believed themselves to be more in touch with the demands of contemporary young people than the rest of the company was, and that the "coolness" of media would revitalize the LEGO brand, certainly for young adults and possibly for others. They also felt that headquarters was skeptical toward new ways of seeing the brand and did not accept them as full members of the company culture. According to one employee: "I always had the feeling that we were treated like the redheaded stepchild of the company. This has something to do with the difference between producing toys and developing software in terms of the time frames involved—they haven't really understood that in Billund."[17]

In spite of not feeling they were accepted as a legitimate part of the company, members of LEGO Media described themselves as being "more LEGO than LEGO." What they meant by this was that they felt they understood the LEGO brand, its products, and its customers better than anyone else in the company. Operating at a considerable distance from headquarters, the subculture of LEGO Media developed its own unique and distinctive version of narcissism. At the same time, their new products were contributing to the company's hyper-adaptation. Of course, LEGO Media's influence also brought needed changes to the LEGO Group. One of these was the introduction of "fun" to the mission statement, which LEGO Media employees felt was missing from the brand expression. From 2001 on, the mission statement was amended to say that the LEGO Group provides quality products and experiences that "stimulate creativity, imagination, *fun*, and learning."

Telefónica: Confronting Subcultures

Another company that has faced serious internal challenges from among its many subcultures is Spain's Telefónica. This company, in the throes of privatization and internationalization, acquired a mobile telephone service, Movistar, that rapidly grew into one of the biggest profit centers in the organization. As Movistar and its profits grew, so did its people's arrogance, and before long this upstart was making demands that were wreaking havoc at corporate headquarters.

Brandishing the book *Testosterone*, Alberto Andreu Pinillos, Telefónica's managing director of corporate reputation, brand, and CSR, decried the numerous battles over who would control decision making within the firm—those who inherited control of the aging utility, or the aggressive new kids on the block who thought they were pointing the way to the future. The identity conversation they engaged in told them they needed both, one for the heritage and stability that stood behind this established brand, the other for the connection to the many users who were sick and tired of stodgy, bureaucratic telephone service. Telefónica continues to struggle with the tensions between its old and new subcultures as it acquires privatized national telephone companies across South America.

Nearly every practicing manager knows that functional silos can cause organizations to underperform by making communication and coordination between different parts of the organization difficult. Because an organization's opportunities are also available to its competitors, any underperformance can lead to a threat to survival. Furthermore, because silos provide the basis for turf wars, they often show the reprehensible face of organizational politics. Without communication and cooperation, an organization cannot implement new strategy to maintain its fit with the environment and hence its competitiveness.

Turf wars are also deadly to corporate brands, because corporate brands rely on the cross-fertilization of competencies, knowledge, and perspectives offered by a range of different professional disciplines and business functions. Silos interfere with the communication and cooperation necessary to align culture with vision and with the dissemination of information gleaned from stakeholders.

Nissan: A Cross-Functional Approach to Brand Management

The most common cure for the fragmentation problem is renewal through collaboration. Many companies, such as Nissan, are currently treating this problem with the elixir of cross-functional teams.

When Nissan's new CEO, Carlos Ghosn, set out to turn Japan's third-largest automotive company around, one of his first moves was to create cross-functional teams (CFTs) to look into pretty much every aspect of running the business. Ghosn believed solutions for Nissan's problems would be found inside the company rather than in the recommendations of high-priced consultants.

Nissan's CFTs were led by members of the senior executive team, but the working group consisted of employees from lower levels, reflecting a wide range of different functional and geographic backgrounds. Ghosn purposely selected members who might not have direct operational experience with the issue and blended these newbies with more experienced team members. CFTs worked on cost-cutting ideas, process improvements, and other projects, with a select few tasked with growing the business and finding new opportunities.

Focusing on Brand. The one that became known as the "Brand CFT" was among the first of those tasked with growing the business. Mark Perry, passionate about corporate marketing and a believer in the power of branding to "move the metal" where pure price promotion could not, lobbied to serve on this CFT. Perry, who is currently director of product planning for Nissan Sedans, told us:

> When Ghosn showed up he put together the first twelve cross-functional teams; these were put in at the turnaround stage and it was his first attempt to use CFTs here. Since that time cross-functionals—we call them "Value-Up Pilots"—became his over-arching way of working. It's our version of Six Sigma, really, and to be on a cross-functional team is a career-development move. All the high-potentials were on all the cross-functional teams together; and after a while we realized [we had to reach] into the organization and start picking other people to play on these teams, (a) because they need to get the visibility, and (b), how many of these teams can you be on and still get your work done? Ghosn ended up creating an entire department around Value-Up practices where there are lots of Value-Up Pilots that are black-belt Six Sigma guys who are all skilled in facilitating and how to help the cross-functional teams operate.[18]

Back when he took the helm, one of the first questions Ghosn asked was: "What about the brand?" Having shelved a corporate-brand-building plan some years earlier in the absence of support or interest from headquarters in Tokyo, Perry's group of Nissan's North American managers let this query spur them into action. After the first global CFT team meeting in Tokyo, Perry's group realized some of the non-marketers on the team needed to be convinced branding was important and could be a powerful catalyst for future growth.

Intuitively, the Japanese culture reveres heritage, story, and tradition, but the connection to corporate branding was not well understood. In some minds, Nissan was not a brand but rather a company that just made "stuff." Although the vehicle models—240Z, Maxima, Pathfinder, Xterra, Skyline, and GTR—were recognized as strong product brands, they had no mutual cohesion. The corporate culture was proud and engineering-driven—but, after years of sales declines, losses, and shrinking R&D budgets, its strength waned and Nissan lost its direction. The Brand CFT needed to find the path that would align the organization, but its members were not engaged in corporate vision and mission work so much as they were searching for the brand's DNA.

One World One Brand.   Once all the Brand CFT team members agreed that the idea of developing a corporate brand was needed to support Ghosn's strategy of enduring profitable growth, they had to clear two hurdles. As Perry explains:

> Nissan was a loose association of regions that happened to sell similar products. Each region had been allowed to drift apart driven by local sales objectives and short-term pressures. We began to gain traction when the non-marketing types on the team were able to see the common themes that emerged when we did it right. And by *right* I mean when we had successful product concepts, well executed, well received by the markets and with lasting sales.

We realized that when we were at our best was when we stepped out from under the shadow of Toyota and produced unique concepts with bolder styling, better performance, and technical innovations. Nissan struggles every time we develop a me-too concept because we are actually "me three" in the marketplace behind Toyota and Honda.

Based on this insight, the CFT spent eight months crafting our brand position. We argued and debated every word. Each word's meaning was checked in thirteen languages to make sure we were clear—it was both a stimulating and frustrating experience. In hindsight the journey and debate honed our thinking and the direction became very clear.

Finally, when we were ready, Mr. Ghosn and the executive committee listened to our CFT team's proposal. He asked each executive around the table whether they understood, agreed, and could support the direction. We couldn't move forward until there was 100 percent acceptance. I would be lying if I said we got approval after the first presentation, we didn't. It was like passing the bar, on our third try we successfully addressed all concerns and we were approved to move forward toward implementation. My work was just beginning.

To communicate the positioning, Perry's team realized, they would need to inspire people both inside and outside Nissan. At the head of their plan stood the "Shift_" campaign. "Shift_" presented a stream of TV and magazine ads that encouraged consumers to reassess their attitudes, stereotypes, affections, and, of course, their images of Nissan. One ad, under the tagline "Shift_perspective," featured two burly motorcyclists in an art museum intently peering at a famous landscape painting, their arms gesticulating broadly as they discussed their impressions and interpretations. Another ad from the Shift_campaign is shown in Figure 5.4.

Nissan had experienced several U.S. brand re-launches in the past. Typically these started and ended with an advertising

Figure 5.4. Still from Nissan's Shift_campaign.

Source: Nissan.

campaign having immediate but no lasting impact. Insiders described these efforts as everyone coming out to watch the rocket go up, but turning their attention to other interests before the thing came crashing to the ground, which it did more often than not from lack of follow-through. With Ghosn's arrival, the team vowed they would drive *this* brand turnaround into every nook and cranny of the enterprise.

In pursuit of their objectives, Perry led a separate team tasked with bringing the brand direction to life at retail. Nissan's customer face and key touch-point is, of course, its products, but the retail experience happens at eleven hundred dealerships across the United States. Perry knew that, in order to engage the dealer body in the new brand direction and provide another strong visual signal to the market that change was under way at Nissan, a key would be bringing a common look and feel to the retail brand experience. Working with a global team of branding and architectural experts from Lippincott & Marguiles (now Lippincott Mercer), Perry's team developed a retail design for Nissan dealerships across the globe.

The exterior design (illustrated in Figure 2.1) was developed to present the modern, innovative, and technically advanced characteristics of the brand. The interiors were warm and inviting with easy "way finding" and nonconfrontational "sales free" zones for consumers who just wanted to take a look at the new cars and trucks. The new brand symbol was prominently displayed, almost like a precious jewel as a center point on the showroom floor. Even the Auto Show display properties were revised to pick up key branding elements. This branding project sparked a billion-dollar improvement in dealership facilities in the United States alone. Globally the design spread to all markets and became a strong signal of Nissan's corporate brand. As Perry is fond of pointing out: "Nothing happens until it happens at retail."

Meanwhile Jane Nakagawa's team of advanced planners continued to carry out extensive psychographic and ethnographic market research, providing a richly detailed profile of the ideal and unique Nissan driver that would be used to redefine the Nissan brand promise in a highly differentiating way. They created cross-functional product development teams to help engineers design cars that would align with the now distinctive brand promise and appeal to the ideal Nissan driver. And they planned how they would tackle rebranding Infiniti, Nissan's line of luxury cars, once the Nissan brand turnaround was under way.

The brand CFT's efforts to improve sales dovetailed nicely with Ghosn's many cost-cutting initiatives to give Nissan, for the first time, the best profit margins in the industry. But without the corporate brand-building effort that renewed the enthusiasm and dedication of employees and got the attention of stakeholders, the much-heralded turnaround of Nissan would probably have been considerably more difficult to realize. Investing in corporate branding to define "authentic Nissan stuff" provided an integrating focus to the many change efforts, and it seems likely the massive improvement would have been impossible to achieve otherwise.

A Role for Culture

The value of the brand for the enterprise emerges from its integrative force—aligning different stakeholders and the business functions that serve their interests. The competitive strength of corporate branding depends on top management's ability to overcome the silos that business functions ultimately create. The cross-functional synergies that can be realized at the advanced stages of organizational growth are the very connections that were natural and unproblematic when the organization was a start-up. Recovering the spirit of those early times and translating it into the present and future is much of what corporate branding can do for the mature organization. But if you are managing a young organization, you can build corporate branding into the web of relationships that will sustain your company in the future, making the difficulties of growth easier to manage along the way.

6

THE INFLUENCE OF EMPLOYEES AND THEIR CULTURES

Frederick Crawford, former CEO of TRW, the automotive systems supplier, liked to tell these stories:

> There was a machine in the plant that was water-cooled. The water was discharged through a hole in the floor, and it splashed everything, the floor was a hell of a mess. A week or two after my meeting with the employees, the operator of that machine asked me to take a look at his invention. He had rigged an awning over the machine from canvas and wire that he had bent himself. The awning channeled the water so that it dropped down neatly into a pan. He had solved the problem. For the first time, that fellow had begun to think about the efficient operation of the business. I asked him why he didn't think of this before. He said, "I didn't know I was supposed to think."
>
> About a month later, another worker came to see me with a tie-rod end (a steering part made by Steel products) and a blueprint. This fellow couldn't speak good English, and he had never had much schooling. But he had spotted something in the way two pieces of the part were joined that seemed awfully complicated. He then showed me a much simpler way to put the parts together. Nothing fancy, just pure common sense. That single idea saved us 40 cents per part. And we were making a lot of parts. I asked him why he didn't bring the idea up before. He said he did, but he was told to shut up and do his job.[1]

How many times have you had what you considered a great idea—and nobody wanted to listen? Or maybe you never bothered to share your idea because you just knew it would be a non-starter. If you multiplied the number of times this has happened to you by even half the number of employees in your company, you would realize what a goldmine you are sitting on.

Sir Richard Branson, Virgin's founder and chairman, maintains that people don't leave their jobs because of not feeling they're paid well enough, but because of "not being proud of the company they're working for and not being listened to."[2]

Branson practices his philosophy of listening every chance he gets: "I always have a notebook on me, I don't just talk to my staff about ideas for service but also ideas for improvements for them personally. I come back with 20 to 25 little suggestions: whether it's 'the blouse is too thin', 'the shoes are uncomfortable', 'I'd love to have some unpaid leave'; just lots and lots of things that will make their jobs more pleasant." Branson doesn't just listen, he acts on many of the ideas he collects. In contrast to managers who perceive such requests as self-serving and thus improper behavior, Virgin's leader knows that satisfying jobs build enduring employee loyalty. His managers know it too.

Branson and his management team have also learned that when they listen to their employees, their employees are more responsive to customers, and this builds Virgin's brand. Under the leadership of CEO Chris Green, Virgin has institutionalized listening. Green initiated Virgin's customer-service council to deal with customer complaints. The council, made up of customer-serving employees, looks into what Virgin is doing wrong and figures out how to change the company to solve the problem. At Virgin Express, says Green, "People who thought they never had any kind of input and even if they did nobody would pay any attention to them, are now making the decisions."

Most employees jump at the chance to use their ideas, and if they have any insight into their corporate brand, they will find ways no one else could have imagined to make brand thinking

> Our final responsibility is to our stockholders.
> Business must make a sound profit.
> We must experiment with new ideas.
> Research must be carried on, innovative programs developed
> and mistakes paid for.
> New equipment must be purchased, new facilities provided
> and new products launched.
> Reserves must be created to provide for adverse times.
> When we operate according to these principles, the
> stockholders should realize a fair return.

Source: Johnson & Johnson.

feel as though they are truly living the Credo as well as serving an active role in the company.

The idea of letting employees question management decisions may sound strange at first. But consider how having so many eyes focused on corporate behavior helps J&J ensure that its Credo values are upheld. What is more, for J&J employees, watching out for the corporate brand is a matter of integrity—a privilege as well as an expectation and a big part of the organizational culture.

Like Virgin, Johnson & Johnson manages its organizational identity by listening and responding—and by doing so it helps build an organizational culture that supports its corporate brand. Just as listening and responding to external stakeholders aligns vision with images, listening and responding to employees aligns culture with vision. When culture aligns with vision, employees personalize top management's aspirations for the organization. They then have motivation to pursue strategic vision that goes well beyond following the boss's orders; they bring creativity to their work and to corporate branding efforts.

If, at the same time, culture aligns with images, employees will receive positive feedback from customers and other stakeholders. This, too, has motivational consequences, since praise is a reward that enhances self-esteem and contributes to feelings of self-efficacy. This link between VCI alignment and employee motivation connects directly to corporate branding (as well as to the bottom line!).

But it is not as simple as it looks. It is not the mere existence of the Credo that makes it work so well for J&J. It is the way in which employees show continued faith and loyalty to the Credo that ensures the company's brand equity and reputation. Describing J&J as "a family of companies," the Credo provides just the right amount of cultural guidance within the distributed power structure to allow wide latitude to divisions without jeopardizing corporate brand equity. The Credo does not always prevent mistakes, but in those cases, it can help correct them. The Credo has helped J&J through many harrowing moments in its long history.

One test the Johnson & Johnson Credo faced was the company's widely acclaimed decision to pull its products from store shelves nationwide following a Tylenol tampering incident. This decision was immortalized in a famous Harvard Business School case.[3] According to those involved, even though the financial ramifications were enormous, the question of what to do after the poisonings were discovered evoked little debate. The top line of the Credo states that J&J's first responsibility is "to the doctors, nurses and patients, to mothers and fathers and all others who use our products and services." With that commitment in mind, the decision was easily made.

While the use of the Credo shows that J&J truly lives its brand, the dictum "live the brand" has become a watered-down commonplace in too many companies. In some it smacks of manipulation or hypocrisy. But even when the sentiment is genuine, if top management does not set a high standard to which they hold themselves accountable in the way J&J managers strive to do, it will be hard for employees to know what to expect when they act to support the brand. While on its surface "live the brand" may seem like a reasonable request, in most cases it means changing the way the organization functions, all the way to the top.

Organizational Culture and Change

In many ways organizational culture is your silent partner in corporate branding. The silence comes from the fact that so much of what can be known about culture is implicit, or tacit. One implication of culture's implicitness is that most new hires require about a year to learn the ropes. Trying to tell them what the culture is like rarely gives much insight. To be of any use, cultural knowledge must be absorbed into one's innermost being, and thus culture cannot be taught like an academic subject.

Organizational scholars who study culture often use the metaphor of an iceberg to explain the difficulties managers face when they try to control or change their organization's culture—chipping away at the surface does little to alter the overall mass (see Figure 6.1). The visible part of the iceberg represents what you can easily see, hear, and touch—the artifacts of the culture (these include objects, words, and deeds). The far larger portion hidden beneath the water represents the tacit layers of values, beliefs, and assumptions that guide life inside the organization. The deeper layers of organizational culture shape the behavior of employees, so it is typically these that managers want to change even though their change efforts always begin with, or as, artifacts.

Edgar Schein, an organizational culture scholar so famous he appears in Philip Kerr's novel *Gridiron*, developed this layered model of culture and a theory of culture change based upon it. According to Schein's model, the artifacts, values, and basic assumptions of a culture are interrelated. Deep meanings held within members' assumptions and beliefs are expressed as norms and values that then shape behavior. It is culturally influenced behaviors that produce the artifacts you see above culture's water line.

There is more to culture than this, however, because cultural artifacts are symbolic as well as tangible—they carry meaning. Taking a symbolic view shows that culture arises from the numerous ways its members use artifacts to create meaning and communicate it.

**Figure 6.1. Edgar Schein's model of organizational culture
overlaid on an iceberg represents culture's many layers.**

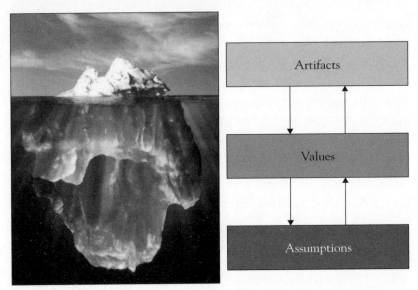

Notice that values lie just under the waterline so that any changes on the artifact level
will most likely produce a reaction here before being transferred to basic assumptions.

Source: Based on E. Schein, *Organizational Culture and Leadership* (3rd. ed.).
San Francisco: Jossey-Bass, 2004.

This meaning-making activity links artifacts back to culture's
deeper layers. Meaning making, and the interpretive process that
produces it, introduces the possibility of change since even when
artifacts remain the same, their meanings can shift when members
interpret them differently.[4] The meaning held in cultural values
and assumptions is attached to objects, words, and deeds through
association, thereby turning the artifacts into symbols. Members of
the culture share and then use symbols to communicate with one
another, which is how an artifact like a national flag comes to be so
laden with meanings.

According to Schein, change is introduced into a culture when new values carried by objects, ideas, or behaviors (artifacts) demonstrate their worth to members of the culture who then absorb them into the tacit layers (values and assumptions) represented by the lower regions of the iceberg. These deep layers contain the knowledge that has worked well enough and long enough to be taken for granted within the culture. Members will only start to change when new values prove their worth by improving organizational life. When management can persuade members that new cultural material is useful, something best done by management's own behavior, the values that the new artifacts carry with them will work their way deeper into the culture. Negotiation over meaning is required for this to happen, and that negotiation occurs chiefly in the symbolic realm.

Embedding new meaning in the value layer of culture is what constitutes culture change. Bear in mind, however, that the cultural change that occurs rarely ends up looking like what managers planned. This is because any change initiative starts at the level of artifacts, and new artifacts will be understood in the context of existing values and assumptions. There will always be give-and-take between old ways of thinking and new cultural material, because it is the meanings in play within a culture that determine what changes and what stays the same.

This uncertainty is what makes controlling culture so difficult—managers are far from alone in determining which meanings are in play within a culture. What is more, the process of absorbing new meaning into tacit knowledge takes time during which competing meanings can send intended change in unintended directions. The amount of interpretation involved makes it difficult to trace cultural change using quantitative measures. However, ethnographic research can provide insight that will help you learn how best to manage your brand in relation to your employees and their cultures.

How ING Group Embedded Its Corporate Brand in Culture Change

When ING Group sought to renew its corporate brand, management began by asking employees to regard customers not as economic resources with a purely financial relationship to this banking institution but as whole persons with multiple needs. In service to this broader definition of the customer they decided to "refresh" their brand through new artifacts and activities designed to better align their organizational culture with vision and stakeholder images. Among the most impressive of these was a new headquarters building located near Schiphol Airport, just outside Amsterdam in the Netherlands. Through design features such as a glass and steel structure built according to sustainable building principles, an interior full of open spaces that bring in light, and walls painted in bright colors, the architects sought to express the brand values of freshness, transparency, and openness that management wanted to nurture within the culture.

But symbols only express the values given them by their users. Since a symbol is an object, word, or action that is rich with meaning invested by one or more interpreters, in order for culture change to take hold, stakeholders must attach suitable meanings to any new artifacts introduced or replace old meanings with new ones. Accordingly, ING employees and community members invested the new headquarters building with their own meanings. For example, responding to its unique shape, people took to calling ING's new building "the shoe," adopting a sense of playfulness when they did so. ING managers listened and responded to this playfulness by incorporating it into another piece of their corporate brand initiative: the Globerunner program.

Globerunner involved ING Group in the sponsorship of international marathons including those run annually in New York and Amsterdam. Through Globerunner, top marathoners are ranked and rewarded with public recognition and prize money. Inside ING Group, the sponsorship program was designed to encourage employees to get involved in activities that connect them with other stakeholders and with a lifestyle focused on health and fitness. ING's managers developed Globerunner with the intention to refresh the company's cultural norms of being challenging, approachable, proactive, and sincere.

As often happens with cultural artifacts, Globerunner became intertwined with the new headquarters building. At the Globerunner launch, which coincided with the first ING-sponsored Amsterdam Marathon, the new headquarters building was decorated with a gigantic crisscrossing red lace tied with a bow. The lace transformed "the shoe" into a running shoe (see Figure 6.2). Management's willingness to respond in kind to the playfulness of the shoe association created a conversation not just between the two artifacts, but also between stakeholders and ING's culture, thus promoting image-culture alignment.

In terms of cultural change, ING's two new artifacts and the meanings employees associated with them may or may not contribute to deep cultural change; the new artifacts might only end up expressing old meaning. If it is to work its way into the deep layers of ING culture, then the new meaning needs to be valued by employees and carried forward into future organizational activities.

Leadership in Culture Change

Even though managers cannot change organizational culture on their own, they are not helpless. According to Schein, members of a culture are more likely to embrace new values that management has introduced if it is clear to them what practical contribution the new values make to their lives. For example, if the people of ING interact in more open and sincere ways during marathon events and then carry this way of relating to each other and to customers into other aspects of their work, then they will begin to embed the values of openness and transparency along with the corporate brand symbolism into their culture and thereby align it with top management's strategic vision for the brand. This change

Figure 6.2. The Dutch ING Headquarters building dressed up to reflect its informal nickname "the shoe."

Source: ING Group.

will affect both vision-image and image-culture alignment when stakeholders respond to the refreshed ING brand.

Many managers mistakenly believe that the deep layers of culture are amenable to the techniques by which tangible corporate assets are managed. The nature of culture shows why this type of thinking is misguided. Culture requires new management techniques that recognize and use its tacit and symbolic nature. Much brand management has been overly concerned with the tangible properties of brands—logo, name, colors, typography, and other stylistic elements. Instead, Schein's theory makes clear that top management's actions are the most direct way to influence the deep levels of culture.

Schein describes two types of mechanisms by which leaders embed new values in the organizational cultures of their employees (see Table 6.1). Primary embedding mechanisms involve leaders' direct attempts to mold the meanings employees use at work

Table 6.1. How Leaders Embed New Values in Organizational Culture.

Primary Embedding Mechanisms	Secondary Embedding Mechanisms
What leaders pay attention to, measure, and control on a regular basis	Organizational design and structure
Reaction to critical incidents and organizational crises	Organizational systems and procedures (for example, control systems, corporate branding processes)
Allocation of resources, rewards, and status	Rites and rituals of the organization
Role modeling, teaching, and coaching	Design of physical space, facades, and buildings
How leaders recruit, select, promote, and excommunicate	Stories told about important events and people

Source: E. Schein, Organizational Culture and Leadership, 3rd. ed., San Francisco: Jossey-Bass, 2004, p. 246.

(through personal example and speeches). Secondary embedding mechanisms operate through organizational structures and cultural artifacts other than the leader's own words and deeds. While the secondary mechanisms may escape interpretation (perhaps for lack of interest), primary embedding mechanisms are more difficult for employees to ignore due to the power of top management to attract and direct their attention.[5] This explains why role modeling by managers is such an influential cultural change practice. However, while managers may direct attention to themselves or other artifacts, it is the stakeholders who ultimately determine the meanings these artifacts carry.

The values for transparency and openness ING's top managers proclaimed when they declared their intention to refresh the corporate brand worked their way into the organizational culture through both primary and secondary mechanisms. To the extent that constructing a new building and investing in Globerunner redistributed resources, rewards, and status, top management exercised primary embedding mechanisms. But these changes also involved the secondary mechanisms of altering the physical and social structures of the organization to support the brand's values, and of influencing formal policy and philosophy statements. Thus the design of the new headquarters building and the Globerunner program communicated top management's intentions both directly and indirectly. Still, if these artifacts are to change ING, members must weave them into the larger organizational culture by incorporating their meanings into the deep layers of values and assumptions.

While it is true that installing one or two new artifacts will not change much about the overall patterns of a culture and its core meanings, over time the thousands of new interpretations made of a constantly changing mix of artifacts within an organization will do so. The introduction of new artifacts and cultural values will typically invoke new meaning-making activity, and often brand artifacts are designed with rich symbolic meanings in mind. These are supposed to be communicated to stakeholders through advertising and other kinds of marketing, but if current brand meanings and stakeholder images are not taken into account along with the dynamics of organizational identity, expectations can lead actual meanings in unintended directions. It is difficult to manage the direction meaning will take as multiple stakeholders weigh in with their interpretations.

Remember when BA intended to symbolize its new global strategic vision with multicultural artwork boldly displayed on the tail fins of its fleet of airplanes? BA's intended symbolism did not resonate with business class passengers who clung tenaciously to their image of BA as a national, not a global icon, nor did it resonate with employees who were out of step with top management's strategic vision for different reasons. In the end the meaning of the tail fins became linked, on both the culture and the image sides of the VCI model, to strategic failure instead of to global vision. Likewise the Orange brand, through clever advertising and an innovative service concept intended to symbolize a free lifestyle, aligned employees with consumers but was out of kilter with the organizational culture of Hutchison, the Orange brand's corporate parent, and ultimately with top management's strategic vision for the company's future.

Both examples show how failure to align the meanings made by employees with vision and images leads to trouble. Only through deep listening and engaged response can you create the balanced identity conversation among managers, employees, and stakeholders that makes VCI alignment possible.

Aligning the Walk with the Talk at Novo Nordisk

Novo Nordisk's cultural facilitation program was designed to embed top management's philosophy, known as the Novo Nordisk Way of Management (NNWoM) in its organizational culture. Launched in 1997, the program was initiated in part to address issues arising from the company's global expansion, which was bringing in many new managers and employees.

Since the new managers and employees were not used to practicing the NNWoM, company executives felt they needed to go beyond measuring employee awareness of company values to align its culture with its strategic vision. Facilitations are conducted throughout the company to assess the status of implementation of NNWoM and to create consensus on "actions for improvement." The consensual aspects of the plan for future improvement are worth underscoring. Within the highly collegial culture of Novo Nordisk, what might look like the mind-set police calling at your door is instead perceived as a way to facilitate the sharing of best practices and channel the wisdom of a group of "guardians of the NNWoM culture" to align company units with the company's distinctive management principles and create a better and more dynamic place to work.

The team of "facilitators" consists of senior people with deep insight into the business. They come from different functional units and have a variety of national backgrounds. In smaller teams they intend to visit each unit in the company at least once every three to four years to evaluate the unit's current alignment with the NNWoM and to brainstorm and analyze ideas about how to improve.

The standard facilitation process includes three phases: pre-facilitation, facilitation, and post-facilitation, each step of which involves two facilitators meeting with the units' managers to help them define and carry out the process, create a report on how the unit is doing in respect to living the NNWoM, and develop an action plan for improvement (see Figure 6.3).[6] The process only works when managers and their units learn for themselves that facilitation improves their work lives. Taking ownership of the process is a good example of the NNWoM.

Before a facilitation begins, the unit will be asked to provide documentation regarding the unit's mission, business plans, and organization, including results and action plans from climate surveys and examples of individual goals and development plans. The facilitation itself starts with an opening meeting during which the process and scope of the facilitation are reviewed with the unit's employees. Subsequently, anywhere from 25 percent to

Figure 6.3. The three phases of the facilitation process at Novo Nordisk.

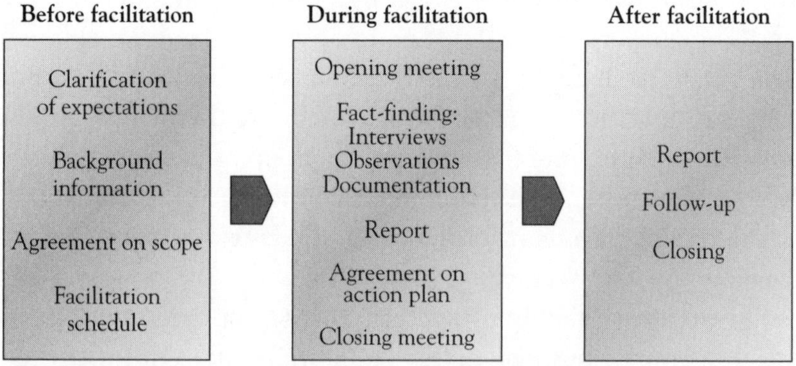

Before facilitation	During facilitation	After facilitation
Clarification of expectations	Opening meeting	
	Fact-finding: Interviews Observations Documentation	Report
Background information		Follow-up
Agreement on scope	Report	Closing
Facilitation schedule	Agreement on action plan	
	Closing meeting	

Source: Novo Nordisk.

100 percent of the employees in the unit will be interviewed as part of the fact-finding, which also involves reading additional pertinent documentation, examining the unit's record of business results, observing the work unit in action, and verifying the information provided by unit managers.

Facilitators use the information collected to find opportunities for improving alignment of the unit's way of working with NNWoM and for sharing best practices. Following data analysis, the facilitators present a draft report on the unit. Managers and the facilitators assigned to the unit discuss the report, agree on any changes, and sign off on the final version to verify its accuracy and confirm agreement on the action plan. The facilitation report and action plan are shared with the executive vice president of the specific department. According to Lone Hass, SVP of the Novo Nordisk Facilitation Team, what emerges from most facilitations is a high level of compliance with the NNWoM with only minor issues of misalignment between local practices and the NNWoM.

Six months after the facilitation, the facilitators follow up on how the action points have been addressed. Follow-ups have so far shown more than 90 percent fulfillment of agreed-upon action points. Conclusions from all facilitations are gathered together in one report for the Executive Management Team and Board of Directors twice a year. The recurring nature of facilitation provides an ongoing reality check on how the company's cultural behavior aligns with its stated vision and values.

Some Ideas for Branding HR Practices

Many companies make the mistake of creating an employer brand that is largely independent of the corporate branding process—a sure sign that the organization has fallen prey to the ill effects of silos. The urge to create an employer brand is not a bad one per se—it stems from the desire to carry on a conversation between HR and its key stakeholders (for example, employees, potential employees, colleges, and others who are involved in the recruiting process). But separating this part of the organizational identity conversation from the rest endangers the corporate brand.

Instead of thinking about employment relationships as a standalone brand, HR should focus on customizing its practices to align them with the corporate brand. This makes the employer brand seamless with the corporate brand so that there is no need to make a distinction. It also integrates the HR function into the entire process of corporate branding so that all branding efforts can do double duty (that is, serving employees and building a strong brand). It's better to get the brand behind your employees than to try to get your employees behind the brand, which is what most branding specialists mean when they talk about "living the brand."[7]

Getting your brand behind your employees involves making sure your HR policies and practices express the brand meaningfully. Everything you do with respect to employees, and everything you expect of them, should be infused with the spirit of your brand. One by one, consider every HR policy and practice and ask yourself: How can we better express our identity as a company (who we are, what we represent, our heritage, values, purpose, and ambition) in the way we go about doing this? Only then should you expect employees to be supportive of the brand. If the brand does nothing for them, why should they serve the brand?

Once the culture has been aligned with vision and images, employees will carry the branding mission onward by adjusting the ways they do their jobs to bring the brand to the company's other stakeholders, as the example of Virgin at the beginning of the chapter illustrated. HR can role model this desirable behavior by listening and responding to employees, helping to make this a key characteristic of your organization's culture. If you honor your employees by putting the full weight of the corporate brand behind them, they will be more likely to bring honor to your corporate brand. The following sections describe some examples of how some well-branded companies have put their corporate brands behind their employees by customizing their human resource practices.

Brand-Based Recruiting

Southwest Airlines, whose brand exudes playfulness, often improvises during interviews to see how potential employees will react. One story about such practices tells how, on a hot August day, several pilots came in for interviews. They arrived wearing typical pilot attire: black suits, white shirts, and ties. Seated in a hanger at the start of their day, a manager gave his introductory pitch. Seeing them suffering from the heat in their business suits, the manager offered each recruit a pair of Southwest-issue Bermuda shorts from a pile on a nearby table. A few of them made the change in spite of the fact they looked a little silly in the combination of shorts, black socks, and dress shoes! But at the end of the long day, it was the pilots who changed their clothes that were asked to work for Southwest. Their willingness to look silly showed they were the kind of people Southwest wants flying its planes. If you are someone who cares more about comfort than appearance, this company is willing to bet you will pitch in when bags need to be unloaded in a hurry, or when a customer has a problem. While many pilots have become used to standing on ceremony and asserting their status, Southwest's brand-relevant recruiting improvisations serve to identify those who are most likely to fit into the company's "we're all in this together" culture.

Brand-Based Performance Assessment

Southwest Airlines assesses its corporate performance in part by counting how many bags of peanuts its people serve. This rather odd measure is an example of a brand-expressive assessment tool. It is highly correlated with more generic performance measures, like passenger miles flown, but speaks symbolically to the value of playful customer service that this culture worships. Normally you target investors and the financial community with performance measures and hope that employees will be engaged by this technical discussion. By using the peanut measure, Southwest acknowledges an artifact of its organizational culture (the ritual of serving bags of Southwest peanuts to customers) and reinforces its brand.

Brand-Based Training

The LEGO Group adapted its Brand School training process to provide leadership development for the company's Top 100 Coaching Circle, Top 300+ (managers), and its Brand Ambassadors (brand fans who volunteer their time to work within the company). Communication tools were created to help these leaders link the brand to the business and its people and to embed it in daily work practices throughout the LEGO Group. For example, in accordance with the statement "Children are our role models," the Brand School team developed dilemma games to help the Coaching Circle learn to balance LEGO brand aspirations (being open-minded, playful, and curious like children) with business realities (being consistent, responsible, and profit-focused as adults). The Top 300+ LEGO managers similarly used the Brand School format to learn to collaborate on brand-relevant managerial tasks and to share ideas for assessing employees on their willingness and ability to act according to brand values.

A version of the Brand Schools was also created to train Brand Ambassadors for roles in support of LEGO in-house training programs, including the role of Brand School trainer. The company selects a hundred LEGO Ambassadors every year based on thousands of applications from its brand communities. These individuals visit the LEGO Group's headquarters to immerse themselves in company knowledge and participate in corporate programs on product innovation and knowledge sharing with LEGO employees. The use of brand fans as company trainers shows employees how serious management is about listening, inspiring them to begin practicing this important behavior.

Brand-Based Volunteering

Novo Nordisk, one of the world's leading producers of diabetes therapies, designed its TakeAction! program to engage employees directly in expressing the values of their brand and to link brand-expressive activity to the company's triple bottom line, meaning that the company "conducts its activities in a financially, environmentally and socially responsible way."[8]

TakeAction! encourages employees to act on the triple bottom line in their work life by giving them opportunities to engage in voluntary activities in their local community or to do volunteer work in developing countries. The program has prompted many employees to form volunteer teams to do bigger projects. For example, some teams spent time working in diabetes centers in Tanzania, while others built summer camps for young diabetics in Zambia. Some employees created a "Dream Catcher Project" to work on U.S. diabetes care and prevention with native Americans, while others talked with sixth grade schoolchildren about what it means to have a diabetic friend, or a healthy diet. According to the project managers responsible for the program, TakeAction! has many corporate benefits: "It promotes leadership capacities, builds employee skills and generally enhances employee satisfaction. It is a great teambuilding exercise and a very constructive way of bringing the corporate values to life."[9]

Brand-Based Team Building

The Helios Awards Program at British Petroleum (BP) pits teams of employees from all over the world against each other to translate their company's values into new activities and innovations. The values guide the company's employees "to be performance driven, innovative, progressive and green." The program, which was designed "to unite over 100,000 people under a single brand with a unified sense of purpose," allows BP to recognize employees "who put our brand attributes into action."[10] Not only does the program stimulate innovation, it gives employees all over the world brand stories to tell for years to come, thus helping develop culture as well as rewarding teamwork. The company Web site includes descriptions of the winning teams for each brand value, as well as video showing how their ideas came about.

Brand-Based Organizational Learning

LEGO Spirit, a program that encouraged managers and employees to tell stories about how they executed LEGO values, used the brand in a variety of creative ways. For example, stories told by employees were made available online to provide vivid vicarious experiences of brand-relevant behavior that often led to discussions among other employees and inspired further brand-building activities. The stories were organized according to different themes, such as living LEGO values, consumer and brand focus, leadership, developing professional skills, and business drive.

One LEGO Spirit brand story recalled how a Danish LEGO team traveled to Greece with two trucks of LEGO bricks that they used to build a copy of the Parthenon in a public square in Athens. Hundreds of children showed up in larger numbers than expected and local Greek people spontaneously jumped in to help the LEGO team succeed. In another story a U.S. employee realized that she had left a cutting knife in one of the DUPLO boxes she was assembling and notified her manager immediately. They located the truck carrying the box before it could reach the toy store in Washington, D.C., where the box was to be delivered, and employees opened 250 boxes before they found the knife. After this close call the employee who had lost her knife was instrumental in inventing a new safety procedure for tracking knives to reduce the chance that this would happen again. LEGO Spirit encouraged employees to tell these and their own stories by giving them opportunities for storytelling. This built LEGO culture as well as disseminating best practices throughout the company.

From Employees to Stakeholders

The status of employees as organizational stakeholders who are expected to deliver the brand promise gives them a special role in corporate branding, and the organizational culture that helps them make sense of and enact this role makes a major contribution to brand value. Herein lies the problem most brand managers eventually face: to manage a brand effectively, you must either adapt the organizational culture to the brand or adapt the brand to the culture. Either way, getting the brand behind your employees is an important first step.

The examples in this chapter are meant only to whet your appetite. They illustrate brand relevancy confined to the HR function within each firm. Yet these function-focused activities illustrate the potential for more widely shared brand-based efforts capable of affecting the whole company and reaching all the way to the deepest layers of its culture.

The possibility of bringing external stakeholders into the branding process as you develop your brand-based thinking and techniques for applying it is the subject of our next chapter. If you regard the corporate brand as an integral part of the solution to every problem your company faces and every action it takes, eventually the entire company will be touched by the brand and stakeholders will be drawn into the brand experience.

7

THROUGH STAKEHOLDERS' EYES

In 2007, Aspen Ski Company, owner of several large resorts in the Rocky Mountains, learned from Greenpeace that Kimberly-Clark (K-C), maker of Kleenex brand tissues and other paper products, was not keeping pace with industry standards for recycled paper usage. Worse still, it was sourcing some of its wood pulp from the endangered boreal forest in Canada. While skiing in Aspen, a member of Greenpeace noticed Kleenex at one of its lodges and complained to Richard Brooks, forest campaigner for Greenpeace Canada, who contacted Aspen Ski Company and alerted them to the issue.

Although at the time some considered K-C an environmental leader (for example, it held the No. 1 rank among personal care companies in Dow Jones Sustainability World Indexes), the information Brooks provided and its own research into the matter convinced Aspen to pull K-C's products from its establishments. According to *Fortune*'s Marc Gunther, Auden Schendler, who heads up Aspen's community and environmental responsibility efforts, wrote: "We are taking these actions because Kimberly-Clark's use of pulp from endangered forests and lack of recycled fiber in consumer tissue paper products is contradictory to our guiding principles."[1] Gunther also recorded that Aspen removed a sign marking a spot on one of the mountains as "Kleenex Corner."

Aspen Ski Company is justifiably concerned that global warming could destroy its business, but it also wants to be a good corporate citizen by catering to the principles it shares with its key stakeholders—people who want to keep skiing and others who want to reverse the effects of global warming for different reasons.

For K-C, on the other hand, Aspen and Greenpeace are becoming hard to ignore, particularly when they are joined by one of the company's largest customers. Wal-Mart recently added its powerful voice to those who hope to change K-C's behavior.

This complicated story reflects the even more complex world companies enter when they listen and respond to stakeholder concerns. There are competing interests to serve and conflicting information to sort through, and any of these could at any time combine in unforeseen ways to create a scandal that does irreparable harm to a corporate brand. But the world of stakeholders is not only a landscape dotted with time bombs and booby traps, it is filled with opportunities to engage with people who are as concerned about and willing to serve your enterprise as you are. Stakeholders have their particular, often idiosyncratic, reasons to engage with your organization and, like Aspen Ski Company, Greenpeace, and Wal-Mart in the K-C story, increasingly demand to do so. How will you respond to their overtures, what will you gain, and what do you risk?

Companies have long understood their dependence on the societies in which they operate—for market access, labor, raw materials, capital, and technical knowledge—but only recently have they started recognizing that stakeholders' concerns are their concerns, and that actively listening and responding to stakeholders produces fresh ideas for product innovation, enthusiasm for the enterprise, and enhancement of organizational reputation. Our description of the organizational identity conversation in Chapter Three explained why listening and responding to stakeholders improves a corporate brand and builds lasting corporate reputation.

In this chapter we explore what the companies we have studied do to engage in conversations with their stakeholders and why they make stakeholder engagement a routine part of their corporate brand management process. Our aim is to explain in detail how brand-relevant stakeholder engagement practices produce both symbolic and economic value when stakeholders invest their emotion, energy, and money in supporting the corporate brands they favor. We also explain how these same practices feed into vision and culture-building activities inside the firm to align stakeholder images behind the corporate brand.

We can't cover every aspect of corporate branding that involves stakeholder engagement, so we concentrate on four important themes: stakeholder maps and dialogues, brand communities, corporate social responsibility (CSR), and stakeholder partnerships. These themes should stimulate your thinking about what you might do in concert with your stakeholders to make better use of your corporate brand. We begin with the basics of stakeholder theory and some key findings from research on brand communities.

Stakeholders and How Companies Know Them

According to Edward Freeman, the father of stakeholder theory, corporations operate via social contracts that guarantee certain rights to those who have an interest (a stake) in their activities or outcomes.[2] Every company has a variety of stakeholders. On the inside are the company's own managers and employees. Outside are members of the firm's supply chain: customers, suppliers, and joint venture or alliance partners. Less direct relationships to the company make stakeholders of the communities in which a company operates and those who serve them, including politicians, regulators, NGOs, and the media. If employees are unionized, then their unions should be considered part of the stakeholder mix as well.

In its simplest form, Freeman's theory states that organizations that attend to the demands of all their stakeholders will outperform organizations that privilege some stakeholder groups over others (for instance, giving shareholders more weight than customers or employees). While this may seem sensible, most organizations are only beginning to consider this broad picture of their responsibilities, and few have yet to fully grasp its implications for managing their corporate brands.

Many companies get to know their stakeholders by mapping their influence on the organization. For example, Figure 7.1 shows

Figure 7.1. How the LEGO Group balances all stakeholder interests.

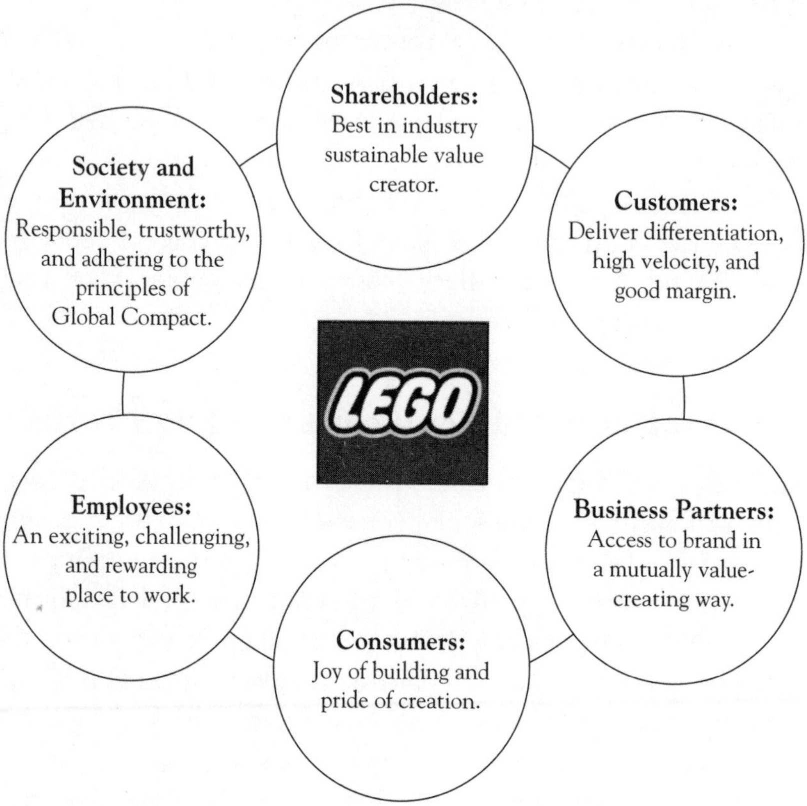

Shareholders: Best in industry sustainable value creator.

Society and Environment: Responsible, trustworthy, and adhering to the principles of Global Compact.

Customers: Deliver differentiation, high velocity, and good margin.

Employees: An exciting, challenging, and rewarding place to work.

Business Partners: Access to brand in a mutually value-creating way.

Consumers: Joy of building and pride of creation.

Source: Adapted from the LEGO Group, Shared Vision 2007.

everyone who has a stake in building a sustainable business for the LEGO Group. Stakeholder mapping formed a big part of the LEGO Group's "Shared Vision," which top management is currently using to guide the company toward excellence. The figure shows how the founder's vision of being the best is interpreted differently by each of the six core stakeholder groups. During the mapping process top management used the slogan "only the best is good enough" to remind everyone inside the firm that they faced endless opportunities (a play on the core brand idea "endless play") to improve the company.

Maps like the one the LEGO Group developed help companies define stakeholder touch-points they can then monitor and manage, typically by defining the experience the company expects its employees to deliver to various stakeholders and assessing their performance against this ideal. Stakeholder dialogues, another popular activity at many companies, provide input from selected individuals on everything from product ideas to image and reputation.

Early efforts to converse directly with stakeholders focused almost exclusively on customers. During the 1990s, Dell Computer Company started using customer intranet sites and Platinum councils to tap its largest global customers for product ideas and other forms of feedback. At the time, founder and CEO Michael Dell explained:[3]

> Our Platinum Councils are regional meetings—in Asia-Pacific, Japan, the United States, and Europe—of our largest customers. . . . In these meetings, our senior technologists share their views on where the technology is heading and lay out road maps of product plans over the next two years. There are also breakout sessions and working groups in which our engineering teams focus on specific product areas and talk about how to solve problems that may not necessarily have anything to do with the commercial relationship with Dell. . . . And we send, not only our top technologists and engineers, but also the real engineers, the people who usually don't get out to talk to customers because they're too busy developing products. All of our senior executives from around the company participate, spending time with the customer, listening to how we're doing.

Dell pointed out what the company learned as a result of listening to its customers:

> A few years ago, the engineers responsible for our desktops were operating on the theory that customers really wanted performance from these products—the faster the better. But what I really want is

a stable product that doesn't change. . . . So our engineers thought one thing, the customers thought another thing. It took the direct feedback from the Platinum Councils to spotlight this failure to communicate. . . . As I think back to some of those council meetings, things that would seem fairly small at the time have often turned out three or four years later to become the basis for billions of dollars of revenue—notebooks with longer-life batteries, for example, or loading customers' software for them in our plants.

Somewhere along the line, most companies learn not to ignore their customers. But where building a strong corporate brand is concerned, stakeholder involvement means more than delivering good customer service or creating focus groups to gather feedback. The companies whose branding practices we most admire constantly look for ways to involve their brands in the lives of their customers and other key stakeholders and sometimes bring stakeholders directly into their management and branding processes.

Discovering what conversation your stakeholders would like to have with you is key to making stakeholder dialogue effective. What is it about your corporate brand or your practice of brand management that offers valuable resources stakeholders can use to achieve their objectives? It is important to see the brand through your stakeholders' eyes, and the only way to do that is to listen to them and respond to their ideas and concerns, as Pfizer did with the issue of HIV-AIDS.[4]

Through debate with its many stakeholders—patients, physicians, pharmacists, regulators, business partners, NGOs, health care opinion leaders, and its own employees—Pfizer saw an opportunity to do "something worthwhile" by investing resources to fight AIDS in Africa. Although the company does not offer drugs to combat this horrible disease, activist pressure and employee opinion combined to make the company feel responsible. After all, shouldn't the world's largest pharmaceutical company take on the world's biggest health problem?

In response to its stakeholders, Pfizer sent eighteen of its medical and managerial professionals to seven NGOs operating in nine countries. As members of the pilot group for the Pfizer Global Health Fellows that launched in 2003, part of the group began training African health care providers in the effective treatment of AIDS victims. Though a seeming drop in the bucket, Pfizer claims a tremendous multiplier effect from the efforts of its Pfizer Fellows. For example, the company calculated that by 2007 the first hundred Pfizer Fellows had graduated their thousandth AIDS health care provider in partnership with the Infectious Diseases Institute at Makerere University in Uganda.

Although fighting AIDS is not a significant strategic issue for Pfizer, responding to the concerns of its stakeholders is. One immediate benefit of programs like the Pfizer Fellows has been feeding the passions of its employees. Another is that, by addressing health care on a global scale, Pfizer is positioning itself to lead the entire enterprise of which it is a part, with long-term benefits to both its brand and reputation as a citizen of the world. However, by not focusing its energies on activities more central to its business, it runs the risk of losing the support of management or investors along the way.

Later in the chapter we describe how Johnson & Johnson and Novo Nordisk similarly mold their identities around enterprise level action. However, because their business concerns are central to their corporate social responsibility (CSR) efforts, their branded programs more directly link stakeholder engagement practices to their organizational visions and cultures. But before we get to these examples, the story of stakeholder responsiveness has a further wrinkle that connects stakeholders to corporate brands even more directly: brand communities.

Brand Communities

Lugnet, a community of LEGO fans, uses the Internet to connect users from all over the world with sub-communities organized by country, city, or particular interest (for example, robotics, trains, or space). These groups continuously create interconnected Web sites and blogs and have joined forces to celebrate the LEGO brand with competitions and other events. Other brand communities are similarly organized. For example, Bimmerfest and the United Bimmer Community provide digital meeting places for BMW enthusiasts to link to numerous smaller and often specialized groups that serve a variety of interests and needs.[5]

Brand researchers Albert Muniz and Thomas O'Guinn coined the term "brand community" to describe the specialized and non-geographically bounded set of relationships that develop among admirers of a brand.[6] Their study of the communities that formed around the Saab, Ford Bronco, Harley-Davidson, and Apple Mac brands showed that brand communities share the characteristics social theorists use to define human communities in general.[7]

First, people who joined the brand communities Muniz and O'Guinn studied shared a strong feeling of "we-ness," that is, consciousness of being different from "others." For example, Mac users have long believed that they are part of a crusade against PCs, which they consider inferior to Apple's computer products. Their sense of being different from PC users fuels the experience of shared identity on which the Mac brand community is based.

Social theorists tend to qualify groups like brand communities with the term *imagined* because their members are willing to share their strong sense of belonging with people whom they have never met.[8] However, it is not uncommon for members of imagined communities to find reasons for meeting face-to-face. Many brand communities create occasions for this purpose, and companies sometimes sponsor or host their events. The activities offered through MacPulse, Harley Community Rides, and the annual Bimmerfest are all examples of company sponsored events that cater to brand fan interaction and give company employees a chance to converse with members of their brand communities.

Second, like human communities in general, the brand communities Muniz and O'Guinn studied created rituals and traditions that they celebrated in stories. For example, Saab community members celebrated the heritage of the company via ritualized storytelling about how the company originally built airplanes and fighter jets, a history that emphasizes the innovative spirit of the brand. As a member of the Milwaukee Saab club remarked, "They were engineers. They didn't change anything unless there was a good reason. They were building PLANES."[9] It is not uncommon to find brand fans constructing Web sites that, like user-built museums, provide elaborate details of a company's past. On Saab's community Web sites these histories always go back to the company's 1937 founding and, of course, the planes. The stories protect and preserve the relished traditions of the brand community and become sacrosanct through the reverence members bestow upon them.

A third feature of all communities, including those devoted to brands, is their members' propensity to protect what they consider sacred heritage. Everyone knows the story of Coca-Cola's botched attempt to change the original formula of Coke. Outraged Coke fans forced the company to return the original product to the marketplace, which the company did under the revised name "Classic Coke," selling it alongside the newly differentiated "New Coke." Although this fiasco later pointed the way to numerous lucrative brand extensions, for a time the confrontation with loyal customers left many stakeholders feeling that Coke was out of touch.[10] Something similar happened to the LEGO Group when it tried to change the colors of LEGO bricks. Word of the change leaked out, prompting an outcry among furious LEGO fans. They quickly organized a protest via the Internet and convinced the company to reverse its decision.[11] Consider how engaging in conversations with these fans prior to taking action would have built goodwill for both these companies. Instead, making the decisions in isolation led to confrontations that left a bad taste in everyone's mouth.

Members of the LEGO Group and Coke brand communities developed a shared moral responsibility or sense of duty to safeguard the brand that united them against what they perceived as brand misbehavior on the part of the company. A code of ethics is the fourth characteristic that brand communities share with other human communities. For example, an Apple Mac user expressed clear moral outrage when he said: "Skip used to be a Mac person, but switched. I found this morally reprehensible. . . . He's kind of a Mac turncoat."[12] Understanding the morality that develops within brand communities can give a company important insights that help brand managers guide decision making and avoid ugly stakeholder confrontations, such as those institutionalized at walmart-blows. com and other anti-corporate Web sites.

The moral dimensions of brand community can also produce motivation to act in positive ways. Think about it like this: if feeling offended on behalf of a brand can mobilize resistance to a company or its brand, what other behaviors can community culture produce? One possible answer comes from Wikipedia, a free online user-written encyclopedia. Unforeseen by Wikipedia's creators, contributors engage in an amazing amount of self-monitoring. In fact, this aspect of Wikipedia may be the key to its success. Not only does self-monitoring improve Wikipedia's content and protect it from abuse and error, it gives a central role to those who voluntarily contribute their knowledge, time, and energy, thus building a Wikipedia culture along with a global corporate brand.

Another example of community morality in action comes from a joint effort by Nike and Google to form JOGA—a community of soccer players "dedicated to keeping the game beautiful and . . . reminding the world how the game was meant to be played." The co-sponsored joga.com Web site provides Internet space for exchanging pictures, videos, and experiences of soccer games, but its members also use JOGA, which is shorthand for the Portuguese phrase *joga bonita* meaning "beautiful play," as a platform for combating the phenomenon of aggressive fans' turning soccer games into violent and sometimes life-threatening experiences. Known as *hooliganism*, this phenomenon has traveled the world—painting the sport in a negative light and uniting the JOGA community around a shared desire to revitalize the beauty of the game. By focusing on positive game experiences,

members remind each other what they believe playing soccer is all about and create a powerful set of interests to combat
hooliganism.

By co-sponsoring JOGA, Nike extends the boundaries of its
corporate brand to include the entire enterprise of soccer. By associating the Nike brand with the cause of promoting the ideals of
the game, Nike becomes part of a global movement to uphold soccer. Of course the community's dedication to soccer will benefit
the Nike brand and support sales of Nike's products, but by standing up for athletic ideals and the morality of soccer as a game for
everyone to enjoy, Nike strengthens its brand image in much more
subtle and indirect ways than by making self-serving brand claims
through advertising. It also ups its quotient of "cool."

The Quest for "Cool" and Control Issues

It would be a mistake to expect members of brand communities
to embrace your corporate brand in the same way that you do.
Often special product features or idiosyncratic experiences serve to
attract brand fans and fuel their imagination. Because you do not
experience your brand in the same ways your stakeholders do, listening in on brand community debates or interacting directly with
community members can give you important insights into your
organization's identity as well as ideas for product innovation and
brand improvement. No detail is too small to escape the attention of brand fans, so brand community members often possess
knowledge that is otherwise unavailable to the company behind
the brand. Many companies find brand communities irresistible
even though they don't welcome the way community members
sometimes try to police their behavior. This is because these communities also provide a means of disseminating brand messages
that is faster, cheaper, and often more effective than what traditional marketing techniques can provide.

In the quest for "cool," consumer-generated viral marketing
plays an increasingly important role, particularly for brands that

target young people. For example, when Nike posted a video clip showing FC Barcelona's superstar Ronaldinho on youtube.com, the company benefited from practically immediate worldwide dissemination and the debate that followed in its wake. In the clip, Ronaldinho was shown kicking the crossbar of a soccer goal four times in a row, his foot clad in a new golden Nike boot. The clip was passed from Web site to Web site and was seen by millions of people who began blogging about whether Ronaldinho's football magic was fake or real.[13] Either way, a closer look at Ronaldinho and his amazing shot made a lot of football fans feel that the new boot from Nike represented the ultimate in "cool."

On the other hand, it can be awfully "cool" to use brand symbolism against a company. *Adbusters*, a Canadian magazine known for taking a critical stand on capitalism and for its enthusiastic support of culture jamming (using corporate symbolism against itself, for example, to undermine a brand or raise questions about its morality) published a photo of Tiger Woods, his famous grin bent into the shape of the Nike Swoosh. While some firms might be inclined to sue, this humorous reminder to Nike that everyone knows Tiger is paid to use Nike gear helps keep the firm honest with itself. The identity conversation, of which this gesture is a part, is ongoing and this is but one opportunity for Nike to reflect on its practice of using paid testimonials and what they mean to stakeholders. Alongside anti-company Web sites, such perversions of brand symbolism offer counter-associations to those produced by company-controlled messages about a brand.

How the LEGO Group Learned to Listen and Respond to Its Stakeholders

For far too long, LEGO managers underestimated the importance of listening to vocal brand fans who tried to tell the company what they saw as missed opportunities and bad decisions. Even when these individuals developed their own communities to converse about the LEGO brand, its products, and the brand they loved,

LEGO managers considered this "shadow market" too small to be worth their attention. But once LEGO managers started interacting with these brand communities their resistance faded, and now brand fans are routinely invited into the company to improve decision making.

The way that the LEGO Group carves out space to interact with its stakeholders is illustrated by the company's intensive interaction with four Mindstorms enthusiasts from the United States. Figure 7.2 shows how their involvement in the company extended the LEGO Group's organizational identity conversation in ways that added value to the LEGO brand. Although it had long conducted market research, the LEGO Group discovered that the direct listening and responding that occurred through conversation lent weight to what these stakeholders had to say to the company. The importance given to this stakeholder input ultimately

Figure 7.2. How listening and responding to brand communities improved the LEGO corporate brand.

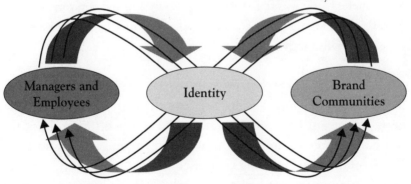

Invite four brand fans to help redesign Mindstorms; give users a "license to hack."

Challenge the company and initiate own improvements on Mindstorms available for community.

LEGO feels need to address problems with Mindstorms.

Mindstorms could work better and the company doesn't seem to move fast enough.

led the LEGO Group to make significant product improvements based on fan ideas.

What is more, now that the boundary between the LEGO Group and its brand communities has been crossed, other brand fans have participated in key product and branding decisions, such as the LEGO Hobby Train. Brand fans designed this product using the LEGO Factory and it was marketed under their names. Incorporating brand community input reinvigorated both the brand and the company, and it also sensitized management to the fine distinctions between engaging active and independent fans and attempting to influence the brand community by imposing corporate structures such as the Ambassador Program and LEGO Club for younger children. Involvement stimulates fans to act as guardians of the brand but also exposes the company to ongoing stakeholder surveillance in regard to brand credibility. As CEO Jørgen Vig Knudstorp explains:

> There is an explosion in communities with Flickr and YouTube and what have you. And it turns out that our fans are frontrunners at LUGNET. This makes us more exposed than ever before. For example, this guy I know and have met several times at BrickFest told me: "I have just received a personal letter from the CEO of the LEGO Group that I want to share with all of you where he is admitting that there is a mistake in one of the boxes recently launched!" So we are living in a pretty interesting environment all of a sudden. And to the old inside-out thinking you can just say—totally forget it.[14]

Along with Knudstorp, the managers at the LEGO Group have learned that the more closely users interact with the company, the more important it becomes to stay on their own turf and not try to manage the community the way they manage the company. Based on his considerable experience interacting with the LEGO brand community, the LEGO Group's senior director of business development, Tormod Askildsen, offered the following advice for building relationships with brand community members:[15]

- *Be clear about what you stand for.*
- *Understand your users' perceptions of value.*
- *Encourage user-to-user conversations.*
- *Trust and build trust.*
- *Don't sell.*
- *Don't try to "manage" your community.*
- *Be smart in the way you control your intellectual property.*
- *And often, don't do anything.*

How Johnson & Johnson Links Social Responsibility to Its Corporate Brand

The role of business in society, along with the related issues of sustainability and social responsibility, has moved to center stage for many companies precisely because stakeholders consider it important. Furthermore, Greens, NGOs, environmentalists, anti-capitalists, and like-minded others are pushing these issues onto the agendas of governments around the world that have changed or are considering changing laws to force compliance. Whether it is in anticipation of regulation or because business leaders see opportunities to build their businesses with, rather than for, their stakeholders, organizations are voluntarily becoming more responsive.

Like Pfizer taking on AIDS in Africa or BP looking for solutions to global warming, it seems that companies everywhere try to associate themselves with good causes. The question is, can this be done in a way that maintains a brand's integrity rather than putting it at risk of earning a reputation for hypocrisy? By recognizing that a brand is, at least in part, what its stakeholders make of it, companies learn that putting stakeholders front and center in their brand-based decision making saves them anguish down the road. The best brands are built by helping stakeholders find ways to use them in their own lives and examples of this provide models for integrating corporate social responsibility with corporate branding.

Take Johnson & Johnson. The top line of this company's Credo states: "We believe our first responsibility is to the doctors, nurses and patients, to mothers and fathers and all others who use our products and services." In a review of its service to these "top line" stakeholders, Johnson & Johnson asked doctors and nurses about their most vexing problems. When they repeatedly responded "the shortage of nurses," the company decided to get involved. Growing demands for health care services due to shifting demographics, combined with lower enrollment and retention rates and lack of educational opportunities, had created a critical shortage of nurses. In February 2002, working in cooperation with professional nursing organizations, schools, hospitals, and other health care groups, the company launched the Johnson & Johnson Campaign for Nursing's Future, a "multi-year, $50-million national campaign designed to enhance the image of the nursing profession, recruit new nurses and nurse faculty, and help retain nurses currently in the profession."[16]

Johnson & Johnson decided that its people would use their skills and resources to create public awareness—not of the shortage but of the value of nursing to society and of the profession to its members. Since J&J is a branding powerhouse, one of its first activities involved treating the nursing profession as a brand that it then promoted with a series of ads featuring real nurses in action, telling the country about what it means to be a nurse. Johnson & Johnson is only referenced at the end of each commercial with a voiceover saying simply: "This has been a message of caring from Johnson & Johnson," more to add weight to the message than to claim credit.

In addition to advertising, J&J's cooperation with other organizations involved a range of different activities including recruiting efforts, scholarships, nursing ambassador programs, leadership and communication training for newly promoted nurse managers, mentoring programs for new nurses, fundraising galas, and media events. Services provided can be accessed through two Web sites: discovernursing.com and the new campaignfornursing.com. Discovernursing.com contains searchable links to hundreds of nursing scholarships and more than two thousand accredited nursing educational programs, funding resources including tips on finding loans and scholarships, and information on more than a hundred specialties and career paths for those with nursing degrees. As of 2007, J&J claims to have hosted more than 4 million unique visitors at the Web site—visitors who spent an average of ten to twelve minutes exploring it with more than 12 million page views.

In addition to its other activities, J&J uses its brand tracking and reputation measurement tools to assess the campaign's impact. At the launch in 2002, J&J defined three success criteria: to enhance the image of the nursing profession, to recruit more nurses and nurse educators, and to retain them. At the end of 2005 the company gathered relevant data from its multiple partners to create an overall assessment of the campaign's impact. Table 7.1 summarizes how much the campaign has changed attitudes toward nursing among those already in the profession and potential recruits.

Table 7.1. Assessment of the Johnson & Johnson Campaign for Nursing's Future.

Impact	2002	2005
Image: 18–24 year olds thinking of nursing as a career choice	<10 percent	> 30 percent
Image: Ranking as possible career choice among general public	#9	#3
Recruitment: Enrollment in nursing schools	Down 30 percent	Up 13 percent cumulative: 2002 (8 percent), 2003 (17 percent), and 2004 (14 percent)
Recruitment: Vacancies at nursing schools	100,000+ vacancies	42,000 qualified applicants turned away
Retention: Planning to leave within next three years	43 percent	22 percent

Source: J&J. From talk in New York City, May 2006, by Andrea Higham, Director, The Johnson & Johnson Campaign for Nursing's Future.

In addition to the measured aspects of the Johnson & Johnson Campaign for Nursing's Future, many members of the nursing profession reported feeling a surge of pride every time they viewed one of the commercials. And although the company did not engage in the campaign to promote itself, it believes that it has contributed to the enhanced affection nurses feel for Johnson & Johnson. Another unanticipated outcome of the campaign is the current shortage of space in nursing programs, which now cannot accommodate all the applicants who want to become nurses.

In relation to corporate branding, the Johnson & Johnson Campaign for Nursing's Future has drawn upon the company's Credo to help solve a health care crisis in the United States. Having met with so much success, J&J now plans to expand the campaign to other countries that face nursing shortages. There is little doubt the success of the campaign is one reason the company continues to enjoy its award-winning reputation. According to the Reputation Institute, from 1999 when it first made its annual reputation assessment and through 2007, the general public has regarded J&J as one of the top two most admired companies in the United States (J&J topped the rankings from 1999 through 2006).[17]

Stakeholder Contributions to Strategic Vision and Organizational Culture

When companies embark on stakeholder involvement programs, they often begin a process that ultimately changes not just their approach to corporate branding but other aspects of their business as well. In particular, stakeholder interaction will force people in the company to reassess how they view their future (vision) and will reorient them to their past (culture), thus influencing VCI alignment. An example comes from Novo Nordisk.

Diabetes is a disease that can either be inherited (Type 1 diabetes) or induced through obesity and other lifestyle factors (Type 2 diabetes), and it poses major health risks for a growing percentage of the world's population, particularly in its Type 2 preventable form. Studies of the projected growth of this disease led Novo Nordisk's top managers to renew the company's original vision statement: "We will be the world's leading diabetes care company. Our aspiration is to defeat diabetes." Novo Nordisk subsequently went through a period of substantial organizational change to refocus its brand around its renewed vision.[18]

First, in 2000 Novo Nordisk spun off the company's enzymes business to make diabetes once again its central concern (following the de-merger, products related to diabetes contributed about 75 percent of the company's revenues). Next Novo Nordisk's top managers called for revising the corporate vision. They formed a task force to conduct a self-study of their corporate heritage and to analyze their image both internally and around the world. Ultimately the process led top management to create a new Corporate Branding Unit. Corporate vice president Charlotte Ersbøll was put in charge and made responsible for developing and executing the corporate brand throughout the enterprise. One of her first assignments was to turn the revised strategic vision for Novo Nordisk's corporate brand into a clear and evocative brand platform that led to the 2005 launch of the "Changing Diabetes" program.

"Changing Diabetes" enabled the company to partner with others pledged to fight this horrible disease. The company was already closely aligned with the World Diabetes Foundation (WDF), which it had started in 2001.[19] "Dedicated to create awareness, care and relief to people with diabetes in the developing world," WDF was similar to the International Diabetes Foundation (IDF) except that it focused specifically on helping impoverished diabetics in the developing world. Although funded by Novo Nordisk, the WDF developed its own role and identity in the global diabetes community and acted as an independent force for change.

At roughly the time Ersbøll started leading the partnership venture, a young diabetic from the United States became active in the WDF and the IDF. Clare Rosenfeld caught Ersbøll's attention when she began to advocate putting diabetes on the UN's agenda.[20]

Novo Nordisk had recently launched its "Young Voices" initiative to bring attention to the problems faced by young diabetics and found Rosenfeld to be a striking example of a young person with diabetes making an effort to lead the world to greater awareness of diabetes' devastating effects on health and with a compelling vision of getting diabetes on the agenda of the United Nations.

Also smitten by Rosenfeld's vision, professor Martin Silink, IDF's incoming president, saw it as a platform for uniting the global diabetes community behind a worthwhile effort. Clare and her mother Kari Rosenfeld, together with Silink, shared the idea with potential partners to see if it had the power to take form. Very early in this process, the WDF and Novo Nordisk were contacted and were quick to pledge their joint support.[21]

Novo Nordisk and the WDF decided that they wanted to take a leading role in bringing the needed global alliance about, developing a global campaign in collaboration with IDF to "Unite for Diabetes." The IDF quickly brought other companies on board as well as other diabetes associations. But in those critical first phases the involvement of Novo Nordisk and the WDF helped provide the manpower and marketing resources essential to its success. Novo Nordisk contributed ten full-time staff members and the WDF produced a campaign movie.

As part of the alliance strategy, Rosenfeld, with encouragement from WDF, became active in IDF's Young Leadership Program and her mother Kari Rosenfeld was named project manager for the effort to get diabetes on the UN agenda. All the effort paid off. Only six months after Rosenfeld's team petitioned the UN, its General Assembly adopted a resolution making November 14 an official UN day to be observed annually starting in 2007. Diabetes is only the second health issue, after HIV-AIDS, that the UN has acknowledged in this way.

As another part of its contribution to pledging a UN Resolution on Diabetes, Novo Nordisk developed its Changing Diabetes World Tour (see Figure 7.3), which launched in September 2006. Over an eighteen-month period, the Changing Diabetes "Bus"

Figure 7.3. The Changing Diabetes World Tour in front of the Danish Parliament, Copenhagen, Fall 2006.

Source: Novo Nordisk.

toured five continents disseminating information on the prevention and treatment of diabetes, engaging those who approached
in conversation about the disease and their experiences with it.[22]
When the vehicle left Japan, after having toured Europe, South
Africa, and Australia, it had been visited by more than fifty-eight
thousand people and had generated media coverage reaching nearly
460 million people worldwide with messages about diabetes.

The youth of Young Voices were part of the tour at every stage,
engaging in dialogue with politicians, media, other people with
diabetes, and the general public. Their personal diaries and a diary
of the tour were featured on Novo Nordisk's Web site to allow the
public, politicians, and prominent stakeholders from the diabetes
community to follow it as it made its way to Manhattan. As we
write, the "Bus" is scheduled to end its journey on November 14,
2007, parking in front of the UN to join the celebration of the first
UN-sponsored World Diabetes Day.

Novo Nordisk's "Changing Diabetes" program continues to generate awareness of the company's focused commitment to take global responsibility for diabetes and it continues to benefit from many partnerships. Among these is the William J. Clinton Foundation, which has joined the WDF to fight obesity and diabetes on a global scale. At its launch in New York City in 2007, former U.S. president Bill Clinton endorsed the "Global Changing Diabetes Leadership Forum" that paved the way for this collaboration.

By founding the WDF, providing leadership for the "Unite for Diabetes" campaign, sending the "Changing Diabetes" tour around the world, and participating in the "Leadership Forum," Novo Nordisk has shown the diabetes community that it is willing to use its brand to persuade the world to address the growing threat of diabetes. It has also proven to its own employees, some of whom were highly skeptical, that even though Novo Nordisk is a relatively small player in the pharmaceutical industry and even smaller on the global stage, it can exercise leadership in the fight against this devastating disease. Novo Nordisk's managers believe that leadership on this issue contributed to strengthening the company's market position. In 2007, the company took a 40 percent share of the diabetes treatment market in the United States for the first time, placing Novo Nordisk ahead of Eli Lilly and Sanofi-Aventis (and its share of European markets remained greater than 50 percent throughout this period).

Novo Nordisk's stakeholder involvement efforts have created a mechanism for top managers to show the company that it is serious about its vision. Following their example, many employees have jumped on the bandwagon, volunteering time and other personal resources to "Changing Diabetes." This new behavior has created some significant changes inside the organization's culture, one of which was to rediscover the company's founder story. Out of deep love for his diabetic wife, Novo Nordisk's founder, the University of Copenhagen's professor and Nobel Prize–winner August Krogh, developed an early version of the insulin that saved her life. Many Novo Nordisk employees now regard this pioneer of diabetes

Figure 7.4. Novo Nordisk's partnership map.

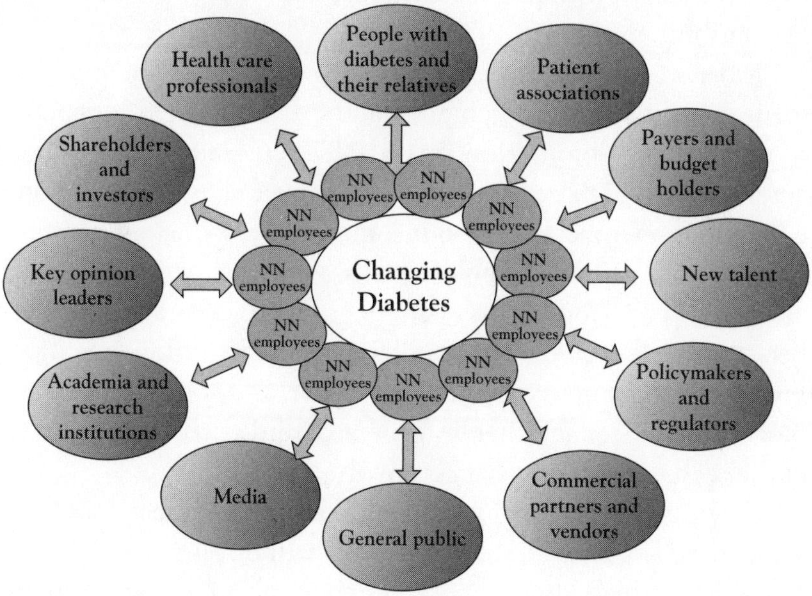

Source: Novo Nordisk.

treatment as the progenitor of "Changing Diabetes," tour and all. The years of corporate brand refinement that led to this moment have shown employees that Novo Nordisk's leadership in the fight to prevent diabetes comes from the work they do each and every day (see Figure 7.4).

Some Caveats Regarding Stakeholder Involvement

Some managers worry that involvement in stakeholder issues will not produce recognition of the company involved. Or conversely, they fear they will be suspected of getting involved only for crassly commercial purposes and thus will damage the firm's reputation. Increasingly, however, stakeholders recognize the many benefits of corporate involvement and interpret a company's support as evidence that it is taking its corporate social and environmental responsibilities seriously.

More worrisome is the issue of how to manage the involvement to make sure the corporate brand speaks for itself, as opposed to requiring self-promotion. Stakeholder communities are characterized by a high degree of transparency and exchange among community members both offline and online. Constant communication increases the likelihood that companies will be credited with their contributions to issues central to community members, but it does not mean that all will see them in the same light. Furthermore, community members serve as opinion leaders for broader audiences and thereby generate third-party endorsements of the corporate brands that get involved.[23]

Playing on the global stage with your stakeholders does have some notable drawbacks. Stakeholders will not limit their ambitions for your brand to your purposes; they have their own agendas, as Nike found out when it initially ignored stakeholder concerns over conditions in the factories that make Nike shoes. As news spread about the low pay and miserable lives of those employed by Nike suppliers in Indonesia and Vietnam, Nike faced growing pressure to change its ways. At first the company attempted to sidestep the issue by claiming it would be at a competitive disadvantage if it took action alone and that it had no grounds for interfering in the politics of foreign nations. But as pressure mounted Nike learned that it needed to step up to its leadership role as the world's biggest maker of sporting goods. Implementing policies for monitoring conditions in the factories that supply its products, eliminating child labor, and improving the pay levels and benefits provided to factory workers, Nike not only improved its reputation, it salvaged its brand.

Nike's experience shows how tight internal control over some branding activities is impossible. Stakeholders will always create meanings for your brand that will demand your response. For example, at the height of the controversy over Nike's dealings with its suppliers, one young man tried to buy a pair of customized shoes from the company's Web site. He wanted the word "sweatshop" printed under the Swoosh, and when Nike repeatedly declined to fill his order, he posted the increasingly unsympathetic corporate correspondence on the Internet for all to see. As the postings made the rounds of viral distribution, Nike realized just how little it could do to contain this issue. Having Michael Moore show up on its doorstep offering Phil Knight a plane ticket to accompany him on a footwear factory tour to be documented for his movie *The Big One* was another indicator that stakeholders were gaining the upper hand.

Once Nike took initiative in solving the problems in its supply chain, it learned another important lesson in stakeholder engagement: companies cannot prevent their competitors from taking advantage of initiatives that serve the entire enterprise of which they are a part. Novo Nordisk competes head-to-head with Eli Lilly, Sanofi-Aventis, and GlaxoSmithKline for its share of the world diabetes market, and these companies directly benefited from Novo Nordisk's "Unite for Diabetes" campaign. Yet by becoming an industry spokesperson, Novo Nordisk changed its role within the economy and society, creating new costs but also offering many new opportunities to lead positive change throughout the world. Though much of this leadership will involve partnerships that can diminish the amount of credit that Novo Nordisk can claim for itself, the key is to maintain an enterprise-level point of view, sharing in the glory of improving the world for everyone, as opposed to only lining stockholders' pockets.

This brings us to one final caveat. Corporate brands can provide stakeholders a ready-made platform from which to address the world's ills. But too many companies try to take the stage themselves, causing harm to their corporate brands. Like BP, which gained public support for a time with its brand promise to save the world from greenhouse gases, companies soon learn that stakeholders will hold them to their promises. While for a time BP enjoyed price premiums from customers who supported the brand's ambitions, the company's poor management of the Alaskan pipeline shocked and disappointed many stakeholders. In effect BP was hoist by its own petard when the public judged it by the higher standards of environmental sustainability it set for itself with its numerous green brand campaigns.

When it comes to stakeholder engagement, the range of possibilities is huge. Most companies have to learn for themselves what works and what doesn't, what stockholders will tolerate and what other interests require. Although there is no recipe for guaranteed success, keeping the conversation alive, listening and responding to those who matter from all spheres of the enterprise, will give your brand what it needs to find its particular path to maintaining success.

Part Three

PULLING IT ALL TOGETHER

8

ALIGNING VISION, CULTURE, AND IMAGES

Decades of enthusiasm for its multicolored plastic bricks and the construction activities they inspire have made the LEGO brand iconic. According to advertising and branding firm Young & Rubicam, parents with children consider it one of the most admired brands in the world, a status the company proudly shares with Disney, Kellogg, and Coca-Cola.[1] The LEGO Group has legions of brand fans and worldwide fan clubs that work nearly as tirelessly as the deeply committed LEGO employees do to ensure the brand's longevity.

Accordingly, you might assume that the LEGO Group operates in a timeless, mythic Never Never Land, where passionate customers of all ages reward the company's central idea of endless play with multiple product purchases and sustained loyalty. But changing child-development and play patterns, computerized gizmos, and multimedia technologies, as well as robust low-cost competition, have all intruded on this fairy-tale image of the business and its brand. Our longitudinal study of the company found that the LEGO brand's success story has not been one of continuous alignment between strategic vision and committed stakeholders. On the contrary, this is a story of ongoing and sometimes wrenching adaptations to a shifting marketplace that required numerous organizational changes and concerted effort to continually realign vision, culture, and images.

The dawn of the twenty-first century, when we began our investigations, found the LEGO Group savoring the fruits of its glorious past as it received not one but two Toy of the Century

Awards, beating out Barbie and GI Joe among others. These awards, along with years of solid financial performance, reinforced an air of complacency in the company. This confidence, however, would prove illusory. Rapid changes in the market

Figure 8.1 The cycles of corporate brand development at the LEGO group.

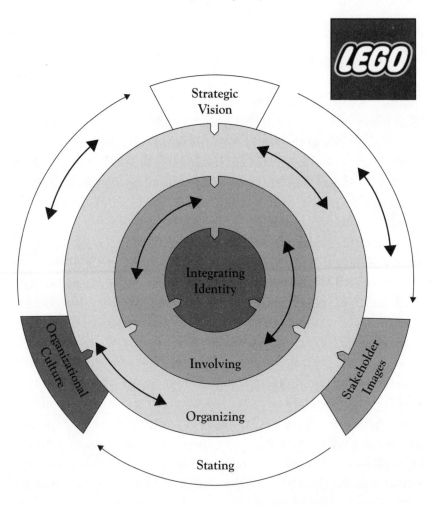

The company began by restating its values to improve alignment of vision, culture, and images, and then moved through reorganizing and involving employees and other stakeholders to integrating organizational identity with the brand and the business. Successive approximations to VCI alignment continue throughout the life of a brand but good brand management practices tighten alignment over time.

coupled with product management missteps soon placed the firm in the precarious state of experiencing both narcissism and hyper-adaptation. These maladies, in turn, helped to magnify significant fluctuations in revenues and profit.

The LEGO Group's top management team struggled to recon-figure the company without losing the organization's identity or base of customer support. The VCI Alignment Model provides a way to describe how the terrain kept shifting under the feet of top management and the brand managers as the company's corporate brand management process evolved over the next several years. In this chapter, we describe four cycles of the LEGO Group's brand-ing process as the company brought its managers and employees together with consumers and other stakeholders to realign its strategic agenda and brand identity: *stating, organizing, involving stakeholders*, and *integrating*. Each cycle is related to the company's vision, culture, and image as shown in Figure 8.1.[2]

The LEGO Group's brand story reveals the ins and outs of cor-porate brand management under the most trying of conditions. It shows not only how a corporate brand can save a company from ruin but also how, when done well, reinventing a corporate brand can lead to the renewal of the company it represents. An organi-zational change of this magnitude does not occur overnight, so the case shows what crafting a new strategy, culture, and brand image looks like close up. We describe the four branding cycles sequentially, though of course in practice they overlapped a good deal (see Table 8.1).

LEGO Brand Challenges

Ole Kirk Christiansen, a carpenter from rural Denmark, founded the LEGO Group in 1932 to manufacture his popular wooden toy designs. From the beginning he wanted his company to be the best run, not necessarily the biggest, in its industry, as expressed by the company's founding slogan, "only the best is good enough." The creative value of play was surely on his mind when he named

Table 8.1. Four Cycles of Corporate Branding at the LEGO Group.

VCI Cycle	Restating Core Values	Building a New Brand Organization	Bringing the Brand to Life for Employees and Consumers	Integrating for the Future
Key Decisions	What is the company's reason for being? What is to be its aspiration for the future?	How to reorganize structures and processes for future brand performance?	How to involve employees in brand execution that is meaningful to core customers?	How to integrate all stakeholders behind the corporate brand?
Key Concerns	Too many brand extensions indicate fragmentation and hyper-adaptation. Brand perceived as "un-cool" among customers.	Develop coherent brand organization and execution. Overcome turf-based brand ownership.	Embed brand values in company-wide behavior and reenergize stakeholder relationships.	Learn to balance focus on core brand idea with increased stakeholder participation in brand development.
Key Activities	Restate core values and define brand identity. Revisit brand heritage and confront current stakeholder brand perceptions.	Reorganize and strengthen cross-functional collaboration. Simplify global partnership structure.	Listen and learn from internal and external stakeholders.	Nurture integration between internal and external stakeholders across markets and business areas.

Source: The LEGO Group.

the company LEGO, a contraction of the Danish *leg godt*, ("play well"). Interestingly, only later did the company learn that *lego* has a Latin root meaning "to construct." Thus the fortuitous name Christiansen chose foreshadowed the toy that would one day make the LEGO brand famous throughout the world.

The first LEGO studded plastic brick appeared in 1948. It was improved over the decade that followed but has remained essentially unchanged since 1958. And even though the LEGO Group has introduced many different innovative play experiences over the course of its history, the bricks, and the endless possibilities for combining them, remain the core of its identity. To illustrate the core brand idea of "endless play," the company reports that there are 915 million ways of combining six eight-stud bricks—and that even that remarkable number is limited by the bricks' being all one color; many more possibilities emerge if different colors of bricks are combined.[3] What is more, if ownership were distributed equally around the globe, every human being in the world today would own sixty-two LEGO bricks. In 2006 the company production rate hit 19 billion bricks per year.

The LEGO Group's master brand guided the company through decades of international growth, inspiring numerous product innovations along the way. Most famous among them is the play system that combines bricks of various sizes, shapes, and colors with a cast of mini-figures that inspire users to create their own wide-ranging theatrical play scenarios. Over the years this play system expanded into a range of endorsed brands targeting different age groups, such as LEGO DUPLO for younger children and LEGO TECNIC for older boys. It also expanded through its development of themed play kits including those featuring Harry Potter, Star Wars, and its own in-house story cycle, Bionicle.

By the mid-1990s, however, the toy industry was facing shorter product life cycles, the result of shifting play patterns among children. The most notable trend, known as KGOY or "kids getting older younger," marked a lessening of the amount of time children spent in play as well as their declining appreciation for traditional activities. As children's tastes shifted to computer-aided activities, the company's competitive landscape expanded to include electronics and entertainment firms offering new kinds of games and software. Competition increased within the construction toy market too. Canadian MEGA Bloks, for example, imitated the LEGO

Group's offerings at a lower price point, and their lesser quality did not dissuade mass-market retailers who were on the prowl for brands they could offer at a discount.

Meanwhile, back at the LEGO Group, decades of continued success and growth had fostered a sense of hubris within the organization. Self-assured managers were so imbued with their own ideas about play and ambitions for growth that they underestimated the power of market signals and overestimated their company's capacities to grow. In the late 1990s, as the company set its most ambitious growth targets ever, the shift in toy consumer demand accelerated, new entrants vied for precious shelf space, big-box retailers continued to put the squeeze on costs, and traditional toy competitors moved aggressively into low-cost offshore production.

On the strategic front, the push for growth had thrown the LEGO Group into hyper-adaptation as middle managers pursued brand extensions at a frenetic pace. Middle managers extended the brand into software games, children's clothing and accessories; co-branded LEGO kits created in alliance with Hollywood producers; LEGOLAND theme parks for the United States, United Kingdom, and Germany; and television shows. Figure 8.2 shows the LEGO brand architecture fragmenting through the proliferation of brand extensions as hyper-adaptation set in.

All this, in turn, had an impact on the LEGO Group's culture. Moving into computer games, virtual reality, and Internet applications meant hiring employees with new competencies, interests, and lifestyles. Hiring from outside the industry introduced countercultural ideas and changed the LEGO Group's organizational culture in ways that sparked internal conflicts and ultimately produced a significant vision-culture gap. Internal subcultures sprang up around teams assembled to produce new products and execute new projects. Meanwhile, consumers expressed confusion over what the LEGO Group was all about as it strayed from its traditional offerings and core brand identity. Although some products had great success during this period, the gaps between vision, culture, and images grew—and profits plummeted.

Figure 8.2. The history of LEGO brand extensions, 1932-2003.

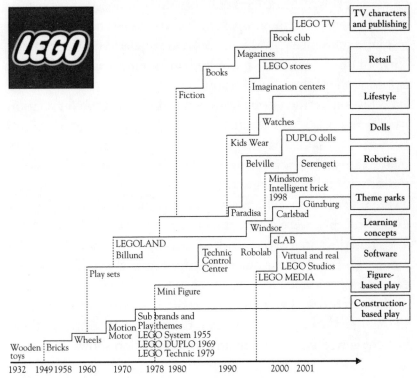

Source: The LEGO Group.

The LEGO managers were not blind to developments in their markets; they simply failed to manage the implications for the company effectively. Top management realized it needed to address the company's financial performance issues without losing its widely admired heritage or its valuable global brand in the process. Founder Ole Kirk's grandson, Kjeld Kirk Kristiansen, now the owner of the company, insisted that the construction idea remain at the heart of the LEGO brand and urged his managers to use the company's heritage to come to terms with the new play patterns among children. He had already rewritten the LEGO mission statement in 1998 to read: "It is our mission to stimulate children's imagination and creativity and to encourage children to explore, experience and express their own world, a world without limits." Guided by this mission, marketers began to emphasize the creativity of construction, moving the LEGO brand essence beyond toys to play experiences. In the process they focused on the concept "Stimulates Creativity" promoted with a marketing campaign featuring the tagline "Just Imagine . . ."

This marketing effort, however, did not end the fluctuation in revenue or address conflicts within the firm. When problems became acute, CEO Kristiansen installed a new top management team and appointed as COO an outsider with a reputation for turnaround management. The new top team was abundantly aware that children no longer perceived the LEGO brand as relevant and they were determined to reinvigorate its image. They also shared Kristiansen's desire to reconnect the brand with the company's heritage. As one of their first acts, they set the goal of creating a corporate branding process that would touch every part of the enterprise. The new team would not only re-reinvent the LEGO brand, they would redesign the company behind it. Their first challenge: Reconsidering the question "Who are we?"

Cycle One: Stating Who We Are

To create a corporation-wide branding process, top management appointed eight people representing different functional specialties or markets to serve as a brand task force.[4] The task force brief was to come up with an action plan whereby the LEGO brand would become "the world's strongest brand for families with children."[5] The task force started by diagnosing the current reality in the company and considering carefully what was happening to the identity of the LEGO brand.

Diagnosing "Values Confusion." Many legitimate business and brand-relevant questions were being debated around the company at this time: What kinds of play count as construction? How far can we stretch the construction concept? Can we ignore pressure for lower prices coming from retailers like Wal-Mart? Are we going to stick to our high-minded principles, or do whatever it takes to compete on a global scale? Uncertainty and indecision over these and other such matters seemed to trace to what the task force termed "values confusion," an indicator of a vision-culture-image gap.

For instance, the task force determined that even though the LEGO Group had long practiced values-based management, the clarity and constancy of company values had been upset through the slew of poorly conceived and executed brand extensions. Some employees were upset by products such as LEGO clothing and accessories that lacked connection to traditional LEGO values and had little to do with the core concept of construction. Others were distressed that large business investments in computer gaming, action-type figures such as Galidor, and television programs were depriving core units of the resources needed to innovate and deliver the quality that they and their customers had come to expect.

Within the company, the task force found sharp differences in values and mind-set between old-guard employees and newcomers and between Danes and those employed in the growing U.S. operation. Meanwhile, market research documented that children in seven key markets around the world perceived the LEGO brand as "dusty" and that even some new offerings lacked "street cred." And the LEGO tagline, "Just Imagine . . . " was quickly countered by SONY's competing motto, "Go Create." This was all diagnosed as symptomatic of vision-culture and vision-image gaps.

Restating Core Values. As important as this repositioning would be, the brand task force felt that the LEGO Group needed to turn its attention to full-scale corporate branding based in VCI alignment. One point employees repeatedly stressed was that it was difficult for them to translate the LEGO brand values into their day-to-day work activities because the brand was not well integrated into the company's business functions and many subcultures. Based on this feedback, and on other insights gained from the study of LEGO's culture and stakeholder images, top management green-lighted the task force's plan to focus on and update the LEGO values.

As the task force worked through internal and external data, it held six workshops, running two or three days apiece, to clarify its own thinking and sharpen its recommendation for addressing VCI gaps. Brand consulting house Red Spider facilitated these meetings and stimulated the members' creativity through brainstorming, projective techniques, and semiotic exercises. These sessions had task force members make associations between existing core values and future aspirations for the LEGO brand. Based firmly on the company's new mission statement, this process helped the task force translate the LEGO Group's original brand values into images of construction as creativity and self-expression.

Following the workshops, and after much discussion of company history and many comparisons with competitors' value statements, the task force restated the values as shown in Figure 8.3. In the following period, top management tried out a new slogan aimed at consumers: "Play on." They also launched a road show for employees to introduce the updated values and invite them to infuse their own activities with brand-relevant meaning. This demonstrated top management's seriousness about corporate branding. But branding on a company-wide scale was turning out to be more demanding and complex than top management had expected. Accordingly, the managers signed off and approved the brand task force's proposed next move: to organize for more effective brand management.

Cycle Two: Organizing for Brand Management

Top management's next step was to examine the LEGO Group's organizational structure to see if changes there might better support the new brand strategy and communicate its meaning to all parts of the organization.

Figure 8.3. LEGO values and their restatement as part of the new brand strategy.

It is the combination of our values that determines what is special about us.

A deeper interpretation of our values helps express the unique way the LEGO Group delivers them.

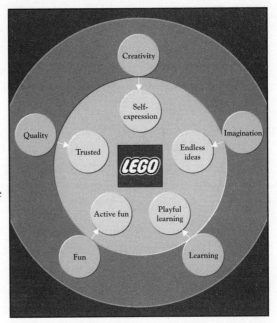

The original brand values appear in the center ring of the figure and the updated values in the outer ring.

Source: The LEGO Group.

A New Brand Architecture. Based on the rewritten mission of 1998, CEO Kristiansen emphasized the guiding value of "Nurturing the child in each of us." Internally this mission reclaimed the construction idea embedded in the LEGO Group's cultural origins while externally it committed the company to making construction play experiences more attractive to the mass market. Management believed this positioning would allow the LEGO Group to uphold its heritage, satisfy its largest retail customers today, and become more relevant to the consumers of tomorrow.

In turn, the task force began to reorganize the LEGO Group's brand portfolio. Previously the brand architecture was structured by categories of user age and type of building materials. Now it would be organized around users' play experiences. The new architecture would strengthen the company's position in construction toys by refocusing all product development and marketing on the brand's core construction concept. Of course this meant the company would need to close down non-construction-based product lines, which it promptly began to do. The streamlining and simplifying of the building platforms and product lines continued for several years.

A New Brand Organization. By now the task force had performed an organizational culture analysis and one problem stood out from the rest—the unclear definition of roles and responsibilities for managing the brand, particularly in regard to communication and to bridging the problematic relationship between marketing and product innovation.

Prior experience had taught LEGO top managers of the need for more professional brand management. To achieve it they created a new Global Branding unit and developed organizational infrastructure to support it. The head of the new unit, a senior vice president, reported to the executive office (comprising the CEO and COO) and was given responsibility both for the internal execution of the new brand values (brand integration) and for the involvement of external stakeholders (brand relations). Placing the new unit at the intersection of internal alignment and external relations called for collaboration among the functions of Corporate Communication, Marketing, Innovation, and Global Business Support.

To stimulate the desired collaboration, the head of the new Global Branding unit hired ten campaign and event management experts and placed each of them in a different new product development team to carry marketing insight into the heart of the LEGO Group's innovation processes. The new hires not only provided new product teams with better knowledge of their customers' needs, they gave their products compelling storylines. In the process of bringing communication and marketing expertise more directly into the product innovation process, the LEGO Group reduced the number of outside agencies involved in communicating the LEGO brand from forty down to one global agency and a few local ones, thus immediately realizing savings in time, effort, and money.

As you can imagine from such significant changes to organizational structure, power and status were massively redistributed. This caused a number of clashes between old and new, local and global subcultures. In the midst of the turmoil top management stressed the need for organization-wide corporate brand execution and stayed publicly committed to the branding process. Once everyone got used to the idea of rebranding and the reorganization was well under way, the brand task force was disbanded to underscore the point that successful brand execution was now everyone's responsibility.

Cycle Three: Involving Employees and Other Stakeholders

If the corporate brand was to be successfully launched, employees would have to involve themselves in building and serving stakeholder relationships much more than they had in the past. To press this point, top management, Human Resources, and the new Corporate Branding unit put on a global road show designed to encourage comprehensive internal dialogue among and between employees and managers. Although this dialogue increased awareness of the need for change, it was insufficient to make change happen. Accordingly, the company came up with a significant innovation to its management process—the LEGO Brand Schools.

Sending Employees to Brand School. The Brand Schools were devoted to helping employees develop a shared understanding of the LEGO brand's essence. In their first incarnation, the classes involved workshops that ran for one to three days and were designed to promote greater awareness of and internal debate about company values and brand strategy. The dialogue that emerged confirmed that employees were still confused about the future direction of the company and continued to have difficulty connecting LEGO values to their everyday work activities. The Brand Schools instructional team (part of the new Global Branding unit) addressed these issues by role-modeling playfulness and by incorporating the company's research on the importance of self-expression in creative play into their redesign of the workshops.

The second generation of Brand Schools invited groups of employees, led by their managers, to express how they felt about their jobs, the LEGO Group, and the challenges facing it by building symbolic images or models of their feelings and perceptions—in LEGO bricks![6] Using LEGO bricks and play figures they constructed stories about their work and organizational life. These metaphoric constructions and commentary were then shared with fellow Brand School participants. Figure 8.4 shows

Figure 8.4. Examples of how LEGO employees interpreted their company's challenges during LEGO Brand Schools.

We have some unpredictable trade partners.

The competition killed our Cash cow.

We got hung up by the safety net.

Misunderstanding the customers' needs.

Too much income from one source?

There are too many skeletons in the closet.

Source: The LEGO Group.

examples of the sort of symbolic images the employees produced in Brand Schools.

The rich symbolism of the presentations Brand Schoolers made with their LEGO constructions evoked many animated discussions. As the experience was repeated, it became clear employee involvement in branding had at last been "LEGO-ized." With the help of these programs, and through their own participation in them, top and middle managers had licensed employees to express their views and reinvent their jobs in brand-appropriate ways. This licensing of expression gave many employees a sense of autonomy and empowerment. It also offered the company a dose of the self-reflection that a healthy organizational identity conversation brings when it is balanced by stakeholder involvement, to which the LEGO Group turned next.

Listening to the Marketplace. While the LEGO Brand Schools were under way, the LEGO Group's new Global Branding unit developed and tested a revised brand architecture designed to improve the focus on connecting with consumers. Off-the-shelf brand-monitoring systems, including some provided by Millward Brown and Young & Rubicam, were used to track the emotional attachment consumers felt to the LEGO brand. Research showed that consumers' images of the LEGO brand differed by market segment. Consumers in Europe and North America, for example, had higher trust in the reliable creativity of the brand than did Asian and Latin consumers. By contrast, Asians and Latinos perceived the LEGO brand as more innovative and fun than did their European and North American counterparts.

To explore these differing opinions and develop a more refined understanding of how children and their parents engage with the brand, the Global Branding unit initiated ethnographic studies of families with children in many locations around the world. These first ethnographic studies showed that the need for play crosses national cultures; it also showed that parents and kids universally associate the LEGO brand with bricks, construction, creativity, imagination, and the experiences of authenticity and autonomy.[7] These results confirmed the distinctiveness of the LEGO brand. Encouraged by the value of these rich findings to inform product development and corporate branding processes, the Global Branding unit expanded its ethnographic research methods, combining participant observation, shadowing, and in-depth interviewing with consumer diaries and videos and photographs of children and families playing with LEGO bricks.

Brand Communities. Meanwhile the company was learning about its brand from another source—brand fans who belonged to various LEGO clubs and user groups. The biggest of these, a free online brand community started in 1998 by Americans Todd Lehman and Suzanne Rich Green, is called Lugnet (LEGO Users' Group Network).[8] Lugnet boasts international membership and is dedicated to the development and exchange of LEGO brick building concepts. Among its many activities Lugnet facilitates the formation of special interest user groups, such as those devoted to space and train travel and to robotics. Members of the Lugnet community also create and organize offline celebrations of the LEGO brand such as the annual BrickFests that take place in the United States. At BrickFests, LEGO fans have the chance to meet face-to-face to share their special creations and construction techniques.

Lugnet also serves as the biggest international network for many thousands of AFOLs (Adult Fans of LEGO). As the LEGO Group's GlobalBranding unit got up to speed, it discovered that AFOLs were joining Lugnet at a rapid and accelerating rate. Through monitoring various Web sites, LEGO managers learned that many AFOLs were eager to interact with the company. As the new brand architecture took shape, many inside the LEGO Group engaged with AFOLs in heated debates on product offerings and the new brand strategy.

To gain another kind of access to its brand communities, the company hired global community relations specialist Jake McKee to create a blog—Jake McKee's LEGO Blog—that allows the company to interact daily with AFOLs and benefit from their insights about the brand and their experiences using LEGO products.[9] Interestingly, the LEGO Group's open attitude toward consumers has its roots in the 1998–99 launch of the first Mindstorms robotics products when, a few days after the launch, some highly skilled AFOLs cracked into the Mindstorms software code. Wisely, instead of suing them, the LEGO Group invited the hackers to participate in the further development of Mindstorms products. Building on this experience, the company now invites some of its users into its product development efforts and has given customers "the right to hack" into the software for the next generation of LEGO robotics products.

As the LEGO Group became aware of the new forms of LEGO play and building processes being invented by its thousands of highly dedicated consumers, it grew increasingly comfortable interacting with these key stakeholders. Some user-generated ideas have proven to be attractive to other users, and the company noticed that these innovations were nearly always based on the brick and the core construction concept (showing that consumers understand the brand). What is more, because many users were sharing their innovations over the Web, they often took better advantage of digital technology than LEGO designers had thus far managed to do. Through interaction with users and exposure to their innovations, the company gained important new product ideas as well as knowledge about how the LEGO brand works.

Business Restructuring Amid Brand Building. In spite of steady progress in brand building, the company's legacy costs continued to be a drag on performance, and in 2003 the LEGO Group faced the worst financial results of its long history. In 2004 a new top management team was appointed and the founder's grandson and current owner of the company replaced himself with a young CEO, Jørgen Vig Knudstorp. Even before they took over the management of the LEGO Group, the new management team took advantage of the Brand Schools.

Through a special round of Brand Schools in 2002–2003, dubbed "Making It Happen," experienced employees shared their candid perceptions of the company's problems. The incoming top managers took the employees' ideas into consideration as they planned the financial turnaround of the LEGO Group. Then, as soon as they were in charge, Knudstorp and his top management team crafted a new strategy called "Shared Vision" to stem losses and move the company forward. Targeted for completion in 2010, the strategy had three phases, each with distinct must-win battles.

Cost Reductions. The first phase focused on cost reductions and the generation of cash. During 2004–2005, the company sold assets, most notably its LEGOLAND theme parks, and restructured the production and supply chain. This included closure of dedicated production facilities in Denmark, Switzerland, and Korea and the decision to outsource approximately 70 percent of manufacturing to Flextronics. In less than three years, these actions reduced the number of the LEGO Group employees worldwide from about nine thousand to around five thousand (with the stated intention to further reduce the workforce to three thousand by 2010). On the cash side, the firm focused on retail customer profitability and portfolio development of the core products.

Although the layoffs were painful, they happened peaceably, aided by the personal involvement of the new top management team. Believing in open communication and transparency, the new top team hid none of the disturbing facts about layoffs and downsizing from LEGO employees. Moreover, CEO Knudstorp personally chaired both the global and local (Danish) Work Councils that provided forums for open dialogue and the building of management trust and credibility among employees. During this difficult period Knudstorp kept an open-door policy and, to the surprise of many LEGO managers, prioritized spontaneous interactions with concerned employees. He also took time to visit factory floors to speak with workers, many of whom had been employed by the LEGO Group all of their adult lives.

The iconic status of the LEGO brand within Danish culture played its own role in the LEGO Group's turnaround. This status has been measured and confirmed by Global RepTrak, which ranks within their local populations the reputations of corporate brands in twenty-nine countries. By RepTrak's accounting, the LEGO Group was the most admired brand in the world in 2007 (it had ranked second behind Italy's Barilla in 2006).[10] The brand's highly ranked reputation led the Danish media to focus considerable attention on the company's financial crisis and this prompted Danes everywhere to support the crusade to keep the LEGO Group alive and locally owned. It was against this public backdrop of support that the affected employee unions expressed their concern for the survival of the LEGO Group rather than pressing for industrial action to save jobs. Another factor on the company's side was the considerable strength of Denmark's economy, which gave those who were laid off opportunities to find alternative work.

Creating a Platform Company. Now in the second phase of "Shared Vision" (2006–2008), top management is transforming the LEGO Group's business model. The company has had to shift its operations and identity from being a manufacturing company to being a *platform company* (that is, one that keeps competencies and technologies critical to the brand in-house, while outsourcing other activities to provide global economies of scale, access to expertise, differentiation, and entrepreneurship). The must-win battles at this phase are to shift the supply chain, improve the profitability of the product portfolio, and prepare for future growth. In Phase Two Knudstorp often returns to the founder's original vision, "only the best is good enough." The success with the turnaround up to this point has reconfirmed his belief that the LEGO brand is and always was a niche-driven premium brand. Its focus on excellence and the desire to continuously improve has been its constant source of strength. He points out that both founder and grandson were fond of repeating: "We shall be the best, not the biggest."

Identity change continued alongside the company's global reorganization as the LEGO Group moved from its old country-based organization to organizing by key accounts, consumer relations, and product innovations. As the identity shift took hold, the company began to use its knowledge about fans to improve its service to retailers. For example, its 2006 "Store of the Community" concept garnered praise from Wal-Mart for creating "the most innovative event in Wal-Mart from any supplier." As Knudstorp explained:

> The basic idea is that instead of creating a standardized in-store offering common to all toy stores, including Wal-Mart, we customize each of our sites to reflect where our fan communities live. Instead of using demography, income, or whatever, we look at club- and fan-intensity in the data from our LEGO Club and sales tracking system. The more LEGO fans living in the area, the bigger the product selection and the more expensive products they will find in their local store. We can even customize the product selection to the local clubs' special interests, such as in trains or space. The result is that the customized stores sell more LEGO products and the consumers find what they are looking for. So it is win-win for retailers, consumers, and the LEGO Group alike.

The LEGO Group's financial performance at last took a turn for the better. In 2006 the company reported its most profitable year for a long time (profit before tax was approximately US$270 million) combined with an 11 percent increase in sales (totaling approximately US$1.344 million). The market response to the new strategy had clearly been positive, the surge in sales driven by a combination of renewal in core product lines (particularly strong were LEGO CITY, DUPLO, and TECNIC), and improved sales of robotics products (LEGO Mindstorms NXT) confirming for everyone the wisdom of refocusing the brand on the construction concept.

Cycle Four: Integrating for the Future

Since the financial turnaround, top management has not stopped focusing on the corporate brand. Recognizing the role the brand plays, LEGO leaders continue to encourage interactions between employees and dedicated fans. This encouragement is producing a more mature alignment of vision, culture, and images in the sense that the company now trusts its corporate branding capabilities to guide strategy and decision making.

As one direct consequence of the LEGO Group's newly acquired appreciation for what employees and other stakeholders contribute to the brand's vitality, Knudstorp now nurtures the entrepreneurial spirit of the LEGO culture and supports strengthening the LEGO managers' open-source approach to innovation. In a recent interview with Majken Schultz, he recalled his first personal experience with the growing LEGO fan community, which occurred when he, company owner Kjeld Kirk Kristiansen, and a handful of LEGO employees from the robotics team participated in the 2005 BrickFest in Washington, D.C.:

> I came with my family, so it was a really nice event. I gave a talk for half an hour with no slides. Afterwards I spent two hours with the fans on Q & A from the stage. It was my breakthrough because I established a personal relationship with them. During the rest of the weekend they came over and talked, took care of my kids. . . . Those people are still sending me personal e-mails asking "what about this brick or that box." So to me this is where I cracked the code. When I came to BrickFest the following year, people were all over me, as soon as I got in the door. Thirty-five LEGO employees also participated. As a top manager you have to realize that you are a symbol in everything you do, and that's how it worked. The fact that I was there and pictures of me, the fans, and the owner were sent around in the LEGO Group, and so on, and suddenly all the employees of the company realized: "Hey, this is not just for fun!" That first experience was in August 2005 and already in September Kjeld and I decided along with

the rest of the board to create a new business unit dedicated to LEGO community education and direct sales to consumers.

The new attitude at the top led LEGO middle managers to experiment with new ways of working that brought some consumers right into the company. For example, LEGO user panels were created to help the company develop new products. In one case, four American brand fans participated in developing a new generation of LEGO Mindstorms.[11] Over a period of eleven months the four collaborated closely with the R&D department, motivated only by their dedication to the brand. As one of them, John Barnes, said to *Wired Magazine:* "If it had been any other company than LEGO, I wouldn't be here."[12] The collaboration culminated in the launch of LEGO Mindstorms NXT. Mindstorms has since grown to become the world's most popular line of robotic tool kits and has inspired other product developments including books, new programming languages, online brand communities, and multiple company-sponsored events, all of which are clearly linked to the core construction idea that the brand now consistently serves.

In addition to engaging its most enthusiastic users, the company has taken an interactive approach to the mass market by developing LEGO Factory. LEGO Factory allows people equipped with a LEGO Digital Designer (3D construction software that is downloadable free of charge from LEGO.com) to design their own digital models with a large palette of different bricks. They can share their designs with other LEGO fans, and, if they choose, custom-order the bricks to physically build their creation. LEGO Factory even allows them to design their own packaging. Once again, the company received help with emerging problems and opportunities involved with LEGO Factory development by engaging its users in dialogue. For example, the company invited ten LEGO enthusiasts to participate in the development of the new LEGO Hobby Train product launched in 2007. The fans designed the train models, and their names appear on the packaging along with the inscription: "Designed by LEGO Fans."

User involvement has paved the way for an integration cycle through the VCI Alignment Model that is ongoing at the present time. It was precipitated by the strategic goal for the third phase of "Shared Vision": to further revitalize the brand with a push toward organic growth (targeted for 2009 and beyond). The 2006 annual report describes the final phase of "Shared Vision" this way (page 18): "The LEGO Group considers such very direct involvement of the users an important innovative driver in relation to the coming year's preparations for growth. By means of close contacts with the users, the company obtains unique knowledge of the wishes and needs of the users, and this will be applied in the development and marketing of LEGO products."

The enhanced focus on brand community received organizational support in August 2006 with Knudstorp's creation of a new four-person group. This group will oversee a new business unit Community, Education and Direct (CED). Knudstorp, who envisioned this business unit after participating in his first BrickFest, gave it responsibility for maintaining direct contact with consumers. This means that CED is responsible for all direct contact with the company's many fans, as well as for sales via the LEGO Group brand stores and its online and mail order services. CED sits alongside the Markets and Products (M&P) business unit that serves the LEGO Group's global retail partners. As of this writing CED contributes about 15 percent of revenues and is growing twice as fast as the LEGO Group in total.

Brand Execution as VCI Alignment

An idealized view of the cycles of brand management suggests that the brand execution process will enjoy uninterrupted progress toward VCI alignment. But the reality of the LEGO Group's corporate branding process shows how fraught with human costs and temporary setbacks the process can be. As the company circled repeatedly around the VCI Alignment Model, the LEGO Group's top management team was replaced and turnover among division heads and regional managers was at times high. As might be expected, internal confusion and numerous turf wars slowed the change process and reduced the efficiency of the new organization even as corporate branding took hold inside the company. At other times the faith consumers held in the LEGO brand was shaken, and in 2000, 2003, and again in 2004 the company endured sizable financial losses due to escalating costs, to which the corporate branding process contributed.

Of course, these experiences created periods of deep concern and even some despair among LEGO managers. But top management's enduring focus on the brand and hope for its future guided the company through these difficult times and helped the LEGO Group get back on track. In a 2006 press release CEO Knudstorp explained how the strong brand carried the company through the turnaround and remained the foundation for the Shared Vision strategy: "Strategy based in core values kept the LEGO Group on the right track. The LEGO Group's core proposition continues to be at the heart of the strategy."[13] Because their efforts to renew the LEGO brand were grounded in a supportive organizational culture and in the emotional attachment its core customers felt for the company, whenever the LEGO Group strayed during these years, involved stakeholders helped the company recognize what was wrong and correct it. This recognition, we believe, was the direct result of an increasingly healthy respect for the organization's identity conversation.

The LEGO Group's branding process also shows that, because corporate branding demands continuous realignment of vision, culture, and images, taking corporate brand initiative may require extensive organizational change and most certainly demands constant attention. In contrast to British Airways' rebranding effort, which suffered from sequential and fragmented attention to vision, culture, and images (see Figures 1.3 and 4.3), the LEGO brand managers learned over time to simultaneously adjust the three VCI elements to each other.

For example, when the LEGO Group brand team moved to bring the internal reorganization of the company on board, they constantly referred to the reworked strategic vision and its implications for customers as reasons and guidelines for necessary changes. And when LEGO managers realized the huge potential to be gained by involving brand fans in new product innovation, they worked hard to prepare employees and the organizational culture to interact directly with these enthusiastic customers and to adapt their own strategy execution processes accordingly. As these organizational changes took hold, the LEGO Group identity shifted in dramatic ways, abandoning its self-image as a manufacturing organization and beginning to regard itself as a leader in the global enterprise of play. Changes like these demonstrate the intimate relationship between a corporate brand, VCI alignment, and organizational identity, and show how changes in one affect all the others.

The result of the LEGO Group's efforts was the gradual reduction of once-damaging gaps between its strategic vision of global competitiveness, its cultural heritage rooted in the construction concept, and its lost image of "cool" among stakeholders. The VCI cycles through which the LEGO Group passed from 2000 to 2007 are summarized in Figure 8.5. Compare this figure to Figure 4.3 to see how the LEGO Group's brand management experiences differed over time from those of BA. Notice particularly that, contrary to BA's experience, the LEGO Group significantly decreased the extent of misalignments between vision, culture, and images with each successive cycle of its brand management activity. This is shown in the figure by the diminishing size of the VCI spiral that depicts the LEGO Group's movement toward the tantalizing ideal of VCI alignment. The contrast between Figures 4.3 and 8.5 shows that, whereas the LEGO Group reduced the gaps between vision, culture, and images more or less continuously, BA continued to loop endlessly around and around without making headway, the result of treating its brand management process in a highly fragmented way.

The descriptions of the four VCI cycles provided in this chapter and summarized in Table 8.1 indicate the complexity of

Figure 8.5. The LEGO Group's successive approximations to the goal of VCI alignment.

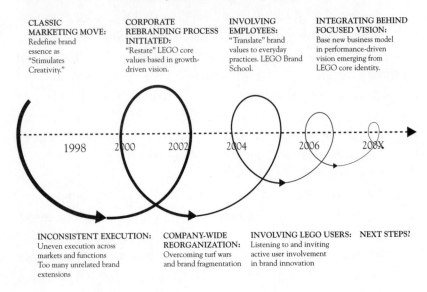

CLASSIC
MARKETING MOVE:
Redefine brand
essence as
"Stimulates
Creativity."

CORPORATE
REBRANDING PROCESS
INITIATED:
"Restate" LEGO core
values based in growth-
driven vision.

INVOLVING
EMPLOYEES:
"Translate" brand
values to everyday
practices. LEGO Brand
School.

INTEGRATING BEHIND
FOCUSED VISION:
Base new business model
in performance-driven
vision emerging from
LEGO core identity.

1998   2000   2002   2004   2006   200X

INCONSISTENT EXECUTION:
Uneven execution across
markets and functions
Too many unrelated brand
extensions

COMPANY-WIDE
REORGANIZATION:
Overcoming turf wars
and brand fragmentation

INVOLVING LEGO USERS:
Listening to and inviting
active user involvement
in brand innovation

NEXT STEPS?

corporate brand management and the shifting demands it makes on managers as they progress toward alignment. Although the overall direction of the branding cycles the LEGO Group underwent followed the sequence shown, there is no reason that the cycles of corporate branding need to proceed in any particular order. As shown in Figure 8.5, VCI alignment is a constantly moving target that involves mutual responsiveness among employees, stakeholders, and company managers.

9

GETTING INTO ENTERPRISE BRANDING

Catching the Third Wave

Branding continues to evolve from its roots in product marketing and its further development as a corporate-wide endeavor. Today branding is entering a new period where it engages not just customers and employees but all members of the enterprise of which it is a part. We believe that the managers who participated in the Corporate Branding Initiative (CBI) were among the first to experiment with enterprise-level branding. Our work with these managers and study of their firms has been instrumental to understanding the most recent evolution of this complex field (see Figure 9.1).

In this concluding chapter, we pull together the threads of corporate brand management that are woven through the book and translate them into action items. We explain the three waves of branding more fully, specify the interdisciplinary nature of third-wave brand thinking, and point out what you need to do to develop this capacity in yourself and your organization. We then describe how two CBI companies reorganized to institutionalize an interdisciplinary approach to corporate branding within their firms' multifunctional activities. Finally we discuss several dilemmas that our CBI managers confronted as they caught the third wave of corporate branding, and end with some advice about achieving VCI alignment and balancing the organizational identity conversation that underpins it.

Figure 9.1. The three waves of corporate branding.

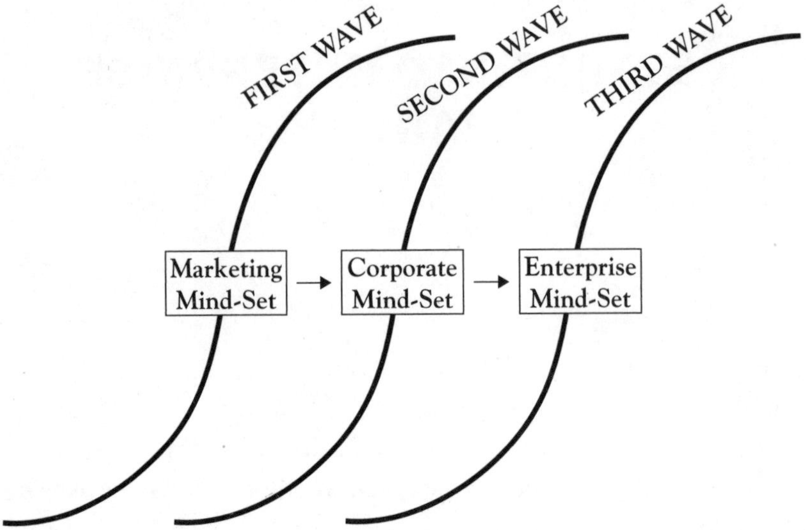

Third-Wave Corporate Branding

Branding began as a marketing endeavor to create and manage the relationship between products and consumers (see Figure 9.2). The rise of the product brand, particularly as promoted by fast-moving consumer goods companies like Procter & Gamble and Unilever, and by consultants such as Wally Olins and Walter Margulies, inspired the academic discipline of marketing to create programs to train students for brand management positions. The branding subdiscipline of marketing grew over the years but never lost its focus on the consumer, which meant that, in the main, first-wave marketers treated corporate brands as if they were giant economy-sized product brands that could be created and refreshed with advertising campaigns. This approach, however, failed to recognize the relevance of branding for nonmarketing functions within the company, and it neglected a firm's many other stakeholders.

The second wave sought to put the *corporate* into corporate branding and thereby made branding a multifunctional activity.

Figure 9.2. A structural view of the three waves of corporate branding.

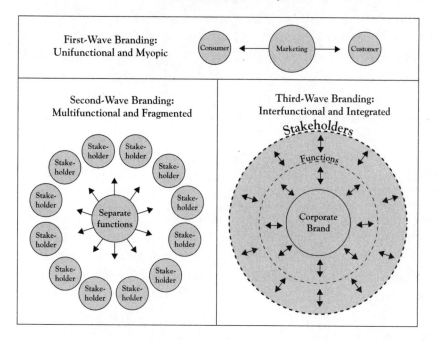

This meant that HR, PR, Investor Relations, and all the other communication functions joined with Marketing to manage the corporate brand. In turn, scholars from the myriad management school disciplines, from finance and strategy to organizational behavior, all weighed in with new ideas, models, and measurement methods for studying the corporate brand and enhancing its value.

Second-wave corporate branding led to such innovations as employer brands and a plethora of brand activation and renewal programs—each designed, orchestrated, and led by a different group within the corporation. Over time, this activity contributed to brand confusion as different groups claimed their pieces of the branding puzzle and the resources that came along with them. Because organizational identities were becoming muddled from within, second-wave branding ultimately spawned cross-functional task forces and teams whose job was to coordinate all the corporate brand efforts around the company and to bring corporate brand thinking to the firm.

Cross-functional task forces and teams can certainly help a firm integrate corporate branding activities. As diverse groups of specialists get to know and understand one another's perspectives, their ideas about what they can collectively accomplish bring clarity and focus to heretofore disjointed branding initiatives. These teams come to recognize, however, that not only do they need to tame the internal chaos of uncoordinated projects, they also need to position and manage the corporate brand amid diverse and sometimes competing stakeholder relationships.

Companies today are entering an era of stakeholder capitalism that is changing the balance of power within firms. New rules for doing business are being written as suppliers, investors, employees, communities, and a growing number of global NGOs are organizing to offset the influence global business represents. Stakeholders make stronger claims on companies than ever before, and their influence affects the identities of the firms that they relate to and target.

In the context of stakeholder capitalism, a third wave of branding is evolving to respond to these gathering forces. This shifts the identity conversation by positioning the corporate brand to be the voice, not just of the company but of the entire *enterprise* (see Figure 9.3). The third wave encompasses the interests and expectations of the full range of a company's stakeholders and makes corporate branding a strategic asset of increasing importance to corporate boards, CEOs, and top management. More time and attention at the highest levels of an organization will be given to listening and talking to stakeholders and engaging the full range of them through the corporate brand. To do this kind of complex, interactive, and inclusive communicative work requires that managers become more conversant with the symbolic aspects of corporate branding, which is key to catching the third wave.

The main implication of the symbolic view of corporate branding is that many voices will shape and inform the corporate brand

Figure 9.3. Most successful companies are now poised to take on enterprise branding.

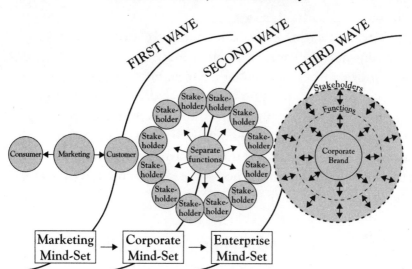

though myriad forms of communication—direct and indirect, face-to-face, and virtual—and through traditional channels as well as new media such as text messaging and Web sites like MySpace and YouTube. As a result the next generation of brand managers will spend increasing amounts of time looking at the brand through the eyes of their multiple stakeholders. Participation in brand community events will feature prominently on their schedules, and every interaction inside the firm and out will become much more of a two-way communication process. Brand managers will bring some of these stakeholders into the management process, making use of their ideas and skills in internal company activities. They will design new activities that get employees to work alongside even more stakeholders doing things that give all of their lives greater meaning.

Before long, corporate brand managers will become masters of helping their companies create what they see through stakeholders' eyes. So, for example, Novo Nordisk's brand comes to mean much more than serving diabetic customers, it is about joining forces with others to change the effects of diabetes around the world. And Johnson & Johnson's brand does not simply represent its pharmaceutical, medical, personal, and baby products; it promotes caring, whether by aiding parents as they care for their children or doctors and nurses who care for the infirm. Such visions are not pretty words, they are the heart and soul of the well-branded third-wave firm. Brands that catch the third wave will not only express these enterprise-minded aspirations, they will inspire action on the part of all stakeholders to help the company create these new realities.

The Interdisciplinary Nature of Corporate Branding

During the first wave of branding, a brand manager could get by with an understanding of marketing and consumer psychology. The second wave saw the disciplines of organizational behavior and the cross-functional business perspective of the MBA added to the knowledge corporate brand managers were expected to master. The third wave places even greater demands on managers to gain the perspective of the whole enterprise and develop their awareness of the symbolism involved.

To gain this perspective for yourself, look for resources and information outside the basic business disciplines of strategy, finance, marketing, HR, and communication. This means gaining familiarity with sociology, to understand multiple stakeholders in society; anthropology, for insight into symbolism and culture; and specialized knowledge in areas as diverse as corporate social responsibility and global economic development. It also means you will need to be open to those trained in the liberal arts and humanities. As employees, advisers, or other stakeholders, they will make valuable contributions to your corporate brand and you will want to do your best to understand them. They are steeped in the symbolic perspective that helps to differentiate third-wave brand thinking from earlier approaches.

Being conversant with disciplines that extend beyond traditional business studies will help you in several other ways. For example, it will probably stimulate your curiosity about and deepen your appreciation for the many ways people relate to brands. It will also help you understand diverse cultures and societies and get into the heads of multiple stakeholders. On a practical note, this background can help you select among consulting firms who increasingly hire experts from the social sciences, humanities, and liberal arts. And it will alert you to the value of hiring people to help you manage your corporate brand who have educational backgrounds that extend beyond business studies. Your expanded knowledge base will aid you in making use of what they offer.

You might worry that including people with even more diverse backgrounds than those represented within business disciplines will pull you and your company toward further fragmentation. This is a risk—but remember that those trained in the liberal arts and humanities also bring integrative skills. They have been trained to think across boundaries and familiarize themselves with multifaceted phenomena. Many have become comfortable with pluralistic frameworks and multiple points of view. Thus, when it comes to understanding and reconciling the contributions of different specialists, the interdisciplinary-minded have much to offer.

Still, do not ignore the functional specialties of business studies that contribute to corporate branding. They have as much to offer as they ever did—if not more; you just need to make better use of what functional specialists can do by managing their limitations and helping them appreciate each other. Marketing specialists know what consumers and customers expect and desire, and can figure out how to deliver what they want creatively. Their affinity for customers and consumers, however, often leaves them at a loss when it comes to serving other stakeholder groups. You will have to help them see why anybody else matters.

The various specialists of corporate communication, from media relations to corporate social responsibility experts, provide skills essential to effective communication of the brand to others, internally and externally. Their propensity to value consistency and clarity of message is invaluable, though you will have to temper it by encouraging stakeholders to play with brand meaning in their own ways. Although many communication specialists value two-way communication, you may have to lean on them to practice what they preach.

Human resource practitioners understand cultural matters within your firm and can help when culture change is needed. These are the people who can put training and development programs together that will encourage employees to express cultural values through their behavior, and adjust it to benefit the corporate brand. They can also ensure that the brand draws people into the firm who fit the culture well and look forward to working on its behalf with your stakeholders. Sadly, many companies have outsourced critical HR and training functions that are key to translating the corporate brand into organizational behavior. If this describes your company, you should help HR reassume its larger role and rededicate itself to ensuring that people in the company recognize that they truly matter. Putting the brand behind your employees is a good place to start.

But HR departments cannot do it alone. Their advocacy for people and training efforts will have limited influence until brand-affirming behaviors are supported by management practices throughout the company. For example, R&D, Engineering, and Operations cannot translate the brand's central idea into products until employees have a deep emotional and aesthetic feeling for the corporate brand and understand its role in the company and the enterprise. And unless culture backs employees up when they creatively use brand-based thinking to do their jobs, they will quickly learn that branding does not really matter. The same point applies to other departments. If management does not make brand thinking a requirement and brand delivery the norm, then nothing anyone can say on behalf of the brand is going to help realize its potential symbolic or economic value.

There is more at stake than corporate brand value. Once top managers begin using corporate branding to express strategic vision and align it with culture and images, VCI alignment starts to take over. Brand-mindedness reveals the big picture of what the company is about to everyone who is interested. Organizational identity, once it is fully functioning as a dynamic connecting point between stakeholders, reveals to all what the business model is and how everyone's activities contribute to its success (or failure).

This transparency makes it easier for stakeholders to engage in the strategy-making process as well as other organizing activities, and to bring recommendations and ideas to conversations about who "we" are and what "we" should become. In the end, strategy formulation gets absorbed into the identity conversation, bringing a level of integration that will aid all organizational endeavors. Keep in mind, however, that this level of integration between vision, culture, and images will eventually lead to adjustments in corporate structures.

Organization Matters

To put corporate branding front and center in all the organization is and does, brand managers find themselves either starting up branding programs and leading cross-functional branding teams or serving as the focus of even bigger reorganizations. We have already described Nissan's cross-functional team approach to branding (Chapter Five) and the LEGO Group's Brand Schools program (Chapter Six).[1] Now we describe two other CBI companies that reorganized to give branding a permanent home in their corporate structures: Novo Nordisk and Johnson & Johnson.

Creating a Corporate Branding Function at Novo Nordisk

With their company top-ranked in Europe and China and growing globally, both organically and through acquisitions, senior managers at Novo Nordisk realized that its far-flung units needed to show one face to the world.[2] The corporate brand was ideal for this purpose and could also be used to help develop a more distinctive and aggressive strategy, as well as making sure the Novo Nordisk Way of Managing was consistently applied throughout the company. To do all this work, and after much consultation internally, the executive management team decided to focus Novo Nordisk's brand on its largest and oldest business—the treatment of diabetes—and to create a permanent function to oversee the brand.

The new unit, called Corporate Branding, was created as a spin-off of the much larger Corporate Communication function, both of which report to Lise Kingo, executive vice president and chief of staff, who in turn sits on the company's executive management team. Corporate Branding's main responsibilities are:

- *Internal branding:* To be a catalyst for Novo Nordisk's strong brand culture, including internal global rollout, establishment of the Brand Academy, and building the employer brand
- *External branding:* To enhance brand involvement through partnerships, sponsorships, publications, advertising, events, and so on
- *Brand design:* To drive corporate brand visibility internally and externally
- *Brand tracking:* To ensure ongoing tracking of brand relevance and reputational impact for key stakeholders globally

Corporate Branding began with the idea of using the corporate brand as an umbrella for Novo Nordisk's many product brands (for example, NovoRapid and NovoMix). With this in mind, the new unit, under the leadership of its new VP, Charlotte Ersbøll, conceptualized the Novo Nordisk brand as a sort of house. This "Brand House" is supported symbolically by four "pillars" that Ersbøll and her team derived from the Novo Nordisk Way of Management (see Figure 9.4).[3]

Ersbøll recalls that, all the while they were creating the "Brand House," her team used the mantra: "Do few things very well and keep it simple." Apparently all the chanting worked, because the simplicity of the "Brand House" as a frame of reference has been much appreciated by those charged with executing the brand throughout the company. It also proved significant when some months later Corporate Branding based the brand platform "Changing Diabetes" on the pillars of the "Brand House." "Changing Diabetes" is rooted in the company's heritage of "Leading the fight against diabetes" but introduced substantial changes throughout the company as well.

Figure 9.4. The Brand House of Novo Nordisk.

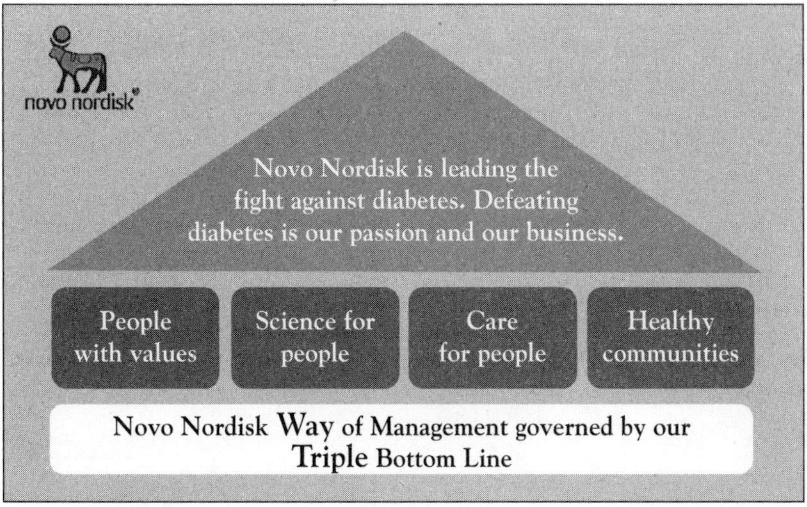

The roof states the brand vision to lead the fight against diabetes, and the four pillars align the multiple activities behind the brand.

Source: Novo Nordisk.

Motivating other business functions to start using the "Brand House" and to engage with the vision of "Changing Diabetes" was an enormous challenge for Ersbøll. To accomplish this she appointed a global cross-functional team (CFT) for corporate branding (see Figure 9.5). To ensure top management support of the collaborative effort, Ersbøll made sure the CFT reported to Novo Nordisk's steering committee, led by CEO Lars Rebien Soerensen and on which Kingo (her boss) and Jacob Riis, the vice president of international marketing, also sit. Riis's support of the new branding CFT's activities is particularly important because, according to Ersbøll, his department is the "closest partner to Corporate Branding." The two units have many overlapping responsibilities and potential conflicts and mutual opportunities need to be managed carefully.

When designing a CFT to work on corporate branding, you should include every unit of the organization that has an interest or stake in the brand or that can help you to execute its strategy. In this way the CFT will begin establishing the relationships that will make the corporate brand work for the entire organization.

Figure 9.5. Novo Nordisk's dedicated global cross-functional corporate branding team.

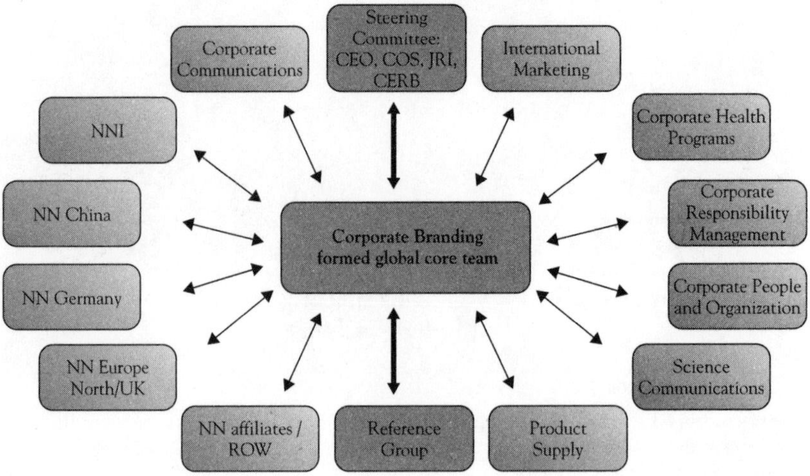

Source: Novo Nordisk.

At Novo Nordisk, in addition to collaborating with International Marketing, Corporate Branding benefited from relationships to Corporate Communication and to Corporate People and Organization, two functions that are essential to understanding and working within Novo Nordisk's organizational culture. Functions such as Science Communication and Product Supply were key to tapping the images held by stakeholders within the pharmaceutical industry. The Corporate Responsibility Management function was a natural part of the CFT on branding because Novo Nordisk has long practiced corporate social responsibility (in addition to its role leading the fight against diabetes, the company is world-renowned as one of the early adopters of triple-bottom-line reporting). The units selling to the four markets in which "Brand House" activities were first rolled out were also part of the CFT. The sales units help the Corporate Branding unit understand and manage the effects of corporate brand related change on salespeople and their customers.

As you can imagine, the CFT on corporate branding engages in a complex set of activities and meets regularly to maintain its focus on all of them. According to Ersbøll:

> We meet every second week and follow a shared milestone plan together. So we are making decisions in terms of the progress we are making with International Marketing in relation to the corporate branding effort. Then we also have a steering committee for the entire corporate branding effort. Here, we meet every time we reach a juncture in the program and need to get agreement that this is the mandate we have from top management for moving forward. We have identified a number of programs that are of strategic relevance to corporate branding and here we also have a shared branding team. We are sitting in each others' teams, so to speak. Together we identified some of the critical activities that we have and that we feel are good at exemplifying the brand promise in action.[4]

A strong indicator that including corporate branding in the strategic vision was a success came in 2006 when, for the first time,

Novo Nordisk became the diabetes market leader in the United States, beating out its archrivals Eli Lilly and Sanofi-Aventis. Revenues in North America had grown a respectable 30 percent from 2002 to 2006, but in 2006, the year that "Changing Diabetes" took hold, they jumped a further 26 percent, nearly the same increase as in the past four years put together. Market share improvements were another indicator that the brand was working well for Novo Nordisk. In 2006 the company held about 41 percent of the North American market, while Lilly served nearly 38 percent, and Sanofi-Aventis around 20 percent. This is a huge increase over the same figures for 2002 when Lilly held about 68 percent of the market with Novo Nordisk at approximately 28 percent and Sanofi-Aventis around 5 percent.

Not only did these improvements justify investments in corporate branding and in the larger North American sales force that came along with it, but—because the small company from Denmark had been chasing these giants for most of its life—they indicated that Novo Nordisk had achieved its BHAG of beating Lilly on its own turf. While Lilly and other competitors in the diabetes treatment field surely will not let Novo Nordisk rest on its laurels, with a newly strengthened corporate brand and a brand-inspired sales force to connect it with customers, the company is in a better position than ever before to meet its challengers.

In April 2007, Novo Nordisk top management decided to build on its core capabilities in the area of corporate responsibility, stakeholder relations, public affairs, public relations, and corporate branding by establishing the Corporate Branding and Responsibility function (CBR). CBR is geared to ensure Novo Nordisk's present and future global leadership as a sustainable and responsible business that is changing diabetes.

Building Corporate Equity at Johnson & Johnson

Johnson & Johnson represents another variation on the problem of how to create a permanent place for corporate branding in the organizational structure. Over the years J&J had expanded like mad into a variety of pharmaceutical and consumer businesses, becoming the world's most diversified health care company. However, the core identity of the company was captured by the idea of *care*, epitomized by the warmth and affection of the baby imagery that had represented the company for as long as most could remember.

To preserve this heritage and adapt it to the changing business portfolio, the company created a centralized corporate branding function—named Corporate Equity—to oversee the Trustmark, which is how J&J refers to its corporate brand. The Corporate Equity unit was established to integrate the many separate projects and programs the company used to support the Trustmark. The company used the term *equity*, rather than *branding* or *reputation*, to emphasize the fact that the Trustmark's value has to be earned. Additionally, *equity* bears the connotation of financial value—and everyone wanted to monitor investments made in the new activity to be certain they paid off.

Owen Rankin, VP of the new unit, described his main task as being "to invest in and nurture the equity of the company both inside and out."[5] In his opinion, the Trustmark's job is to strengthen the company's attractiveness to consumers, customers, governments, regulators, business partners, and innovators, and it is particularly important in attracting new talent to the company. Previously the numerous programs aimed at stakeholders had been distributed more or less randomly around the organization. Now the Corporate Equity unit would ensure that the same implementation approach was used everywhere and was assessed using standardized methodologies.

To give an example of how the Corporate Equity unit contributes to the company via the J&J brand, not long after the group was launched, one of the Johnson & Johnson baby product advertising teams had developed some potent ads—only to discover in testing that they did not work to sell the targeted products. The ads were too generic to suit the purpose for which they had been designed, yet they were scoring high response rates—everybody seemed to like them. They were clearly very special, and the group had the data to prove how emotionally compelling they were.

The group that created the ads contacted the Corporate Equity unit and told them how well they were testing. Since they could not justify using the ads themselves, they offered to let Corporate Equity have them. Further market research confirmed the enormous resonance between the corporate brand and the theme of the ads expressed by the tagline: "Having a baby changes everything." If you have never seen one of these ads, just take a peek at Figure 9.6 and imagine this as a thirty-second spot complete with heartwarming video and sentimental music. Now try to hear the voiceover contrasting the many things a new parent sacrifices with the warm images of what is gained, which are celebrated in the visuals. Many people get tears in their eyes when viewing one of these ads for the first time. They can really touch the soul.

Figure 9.6. One of the ads from Johnson & Johnson's "Having a baby changes everything" campaign.

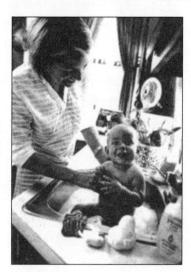

Whod have ever thought
the love of your life would be
short and bald?

You always went for the tall, dark, mysterious types. You fell in love with one, married him, and started a family. Then when the baby was born, an amazing new feeling hit you. And now, as much as you'll always love your husband, this new little man just takes your breath away. **Having a baby changes everything.**

Johnson&Johnson

Source: Johnson & Johnson.

Of course, when the new ads were aired on television and appeared in magazines, the tracking numbers soared. More interesting still from the perspective of corporate branding, J&J's medical products and pharmaceutical customers—those doctors and nurses from the top line of the Credo—were as enamored of the ads as anyone else. That the baby imagery touches all J&J's stakeholders in similarly compelling ways confirms the distinctiveness of this brand and its reputation. Having a baby truly does change everything.

Coping with the Dilemmas of Corporate Brand Management

Brand managers aspire to confirming experiences like the one J&J's Corporate Equity unit enjoyed with its "Having a baby changes everything" campaign. But the truth is that the multiple interests, issues, and concerns stakeholders bring to an enterprise will more often generate dilemmas in which two (or more!) sides to corporate brand management each make essential contributions to the organization's success yet are, in important respects, incompatible. Further tips on managing with and through dilemmas using a paradoxical approach to management follow the list of dilemmas, but as we work our way through them, notice that they are not independent of one another. This point is key to understanding not just the dilemmas but why managing VCI alignment is an ongoing and dynamic proposition.

The Dilemmas

To help you handle your dilemmas, here are some brief descriptions of how the corporate brand managers we know faced theirs.

Centralize and Decentralize. Most companies swing between the poles of centralizing and decentralizing, regularly moving from one to the other and back again. Depending on where your company sits on this trajectory, you will confront different issues in regard to managing your corporate brand. Too much centralization means too few of your stakeholders will be heard; employees give relatively more of their attention to top managers when centralization is in force. Too much decentralization means pretty much everyone is responding to stakeholders, but the company will struggle to give a coherent response, something that centralized authority makes it much easier to do. Taken to their extremes either of these outcomes will undermine your corporate brand, so you must watch as the pendulum swings and adjust the emphasis of your brand management practices to anticipate and counteract the unwanted effects of centralization and decentralization. Both J&J and Novo Nordisk handled this dilemma by establishing formal business units to oversee their corporate branding activities. These units simultaneously offer their respective organizations centralization, in that they sit at the corporate staff level, and decentralization, in that they create dialogue between functions.

Global and Local. This dilemma represents the quandary created by responding to the variety of different stakeholder images your brand invites while trying to present a recognizable face around the world. Recall British Airways (BA) and its dilemma of serving traditionally conservative British business class customers at the same time that it needed to represent itself less nationalistically to the rest of the world, which is where it expected the greatest future growth. A global BA seemed to be in direct conflict with the local BA that British passengers continued to expect when they interacted with the company. But corporate brands cannot afford to lose either their local support or their global reach. A balance between these competing interests must be managed if the brand is to avoid troubles like those that continue to plague BA. Take a lesson from Novo Nordisk's Brand House and provide a platform of basic but open-ended principles, like the four pillars of the Novo Nordisk brand. Then encourage stakeholders in local markets to bring these principles to life in their own ways and for their own purposes. In this way you can focus the local conversations on themes that are shared around the world without imposing one perspective on the meaning of your brand.

Stability and Change. Most managers today are accustomed to leading change and even more are familiar with resistance to their change efforts. Programs piled upon more programs—all designed to change daily work routines—confuse employees and make them cynical about the management process. What their managers fail to grasp is what every minister and psychologist knows only too well: to support people who want to change their lives, you must respect what they cannot change. The same holds true for organizations: if you want to change your organization, begin by reassuring those who will execute the change that the values they hold most dear will not be lost.

On the other hand, change can bring energy and, as Greiner points out, for many older organizations it is the only path to renewal. Emphasize the renewing forces of change as well as the ways in which it preserves the organization's way of life to achieve the balance you need to confront this dilemma. The consistency of Southwest Airlines' relationship to its employees has been a mainstay of this company's management practice and gives a foundation for asking employees to give their full support during times of change. The ability to face change with the confidence that some things will remain the same keeps this corporate brand on the list of perennial favorites among stakeholders.

Old and New. Related to the stability-change dilemma is the dilemma of balancing old against new. The LEGO Group, Novo Nordisk, and Johnson & Johnson all found it valuable to revisit the past, taking note of the cultural values and assumptions in which the culture first took root. This effort helped them introduce corporate branding initiatives that brought company-wide renewal, including structural changes that made corporate branding relevant for their organizations, businesses, and the wider enterprises of which they are a part. But be sure not to get so enamored of your past that you cannot try new things. In particular, do not overlook the perspectives your newest recruits offer; as members of your enterprise as well as your organization, they bring with them the capacity to recognize things that more senior employees may never see.

Strive to discover how new employees want to express your old cultural values as they acclimate to your firm and its culture, as the LEGO Group did with its young and fresh LEGO Media employees who felt that they were "more LEGO than LEGO." Often the newest employees will be able to bring about change at the deep levels of culture that others cannot reach. On the other hand, recall how Steve Jobs, the oldest and arguably the most symbolically significant employee of his firm, was able to reinvigorate Apple all the way to its core. There is simply no way around bringing old and new together in your corporate branding efforts.

Maintaining Control and Sharing Leadership. It is common to feel an urge to control your corporate brand and its meanings by dictating the images you want to embed in the minds of your stakeholders, particularly your employees. This attitude denies the enormous value employees and other stakeholders contribute to the brand, and it is simply wrong to assume that what managers say something means is in fact what it means. On the contrary, knowing the meanings stakeholders make with your brand is key to a balanced organizational identity conversation, without which you risk falling into narcissism.

However, while it is true that leaders who share their power with stakeholders give away some control, to deny that leaders have influence over the corporate brand is also wrong. Their influence derives from the fact that they themselves are symbols and their behavior and attitudes are interpreted as being part of the brand. To exercise the control they have effectively, leaders must be in tune with the symbolism of the brand and their roles within it, one of which is to share their leadership with others who are passionate about the brand, as the LEGO group does through its

Brand Ambassadors program and other stakeholder involvement initiatives. As the new CEO of LEGO Group has recently learned, dedicated brand fans will bring new energy to your organization as well as providing innovative ideas for new business ventures. They will even offer you ideas to improve your brand management practices if you are prepared to listen and respond to them.

Handling Dilemmas with Paradoxical Management

Though it may at times seem impossible to manage all the dilemmas that confront you, manage them you must. Fortunately those who research the management of paradox provide some wisdom for doing so. According to these experts, managing paradox means practicing paradoxical management. This basically involves avoiding two traps: compromise and one-sided resolutions.

The Trap of Compromise. When a young Nike corporation tried to expand its brand by offering sports shoes for the casual market, it offered neither top-quality athletic shoes nor well-designed casual shoes. The resulting compromise ended up as a semi-athletic casual shoe that nobody wanted—a tough lesson that nearly doomed the company. In contrast to Nike, an older but wiser Bang & Olufsen (B&O) seeks synthesis rather than compromise in the design of loudspeakers and audio systems. When disagreements occur, as they inevitably do, B&O's top management resists any form of compromise that leads the brand away from its heritage in the poetry of design *and* technological excellence. By not falling into the trap of compromising either of these competing values, this company differentiates itself from the mainstream.

The Trap of Resolution. The other common mistake people make when handling paradox is to try to resolve it by choosing between the horns of the dilemma. BA saw the need to build a global corporate brand as choosing global over local interests. Framing the decision as a choice caused its top management to

underestimate the powerful sentiments of their local British customers and to refuse the brand heritage that these mostly business
class passengers knew and loved. Had BA included local business customers (its largest source of revenue!) in a conversation
about the brand, it might have found a means of balancing the
many interests rather than favoring some over others.

By way of contrast to BA's experience, pan-Scandinavian
Nordea started by trying to preserve the local cultures, technologies, and leadership styles of each of the four merger partners,
but it quickly learned to balance valuable local connections
with neighborhood bank customers against the global vision of
expressing Nordic ideals. By not giving in to the desire to resolve
the dilemma, Nordea is now aligning its Nordic vision with its
emerging organizational culture and this is changing stakeholders'
images of the new bank.

How Symbolism Can Help. While avoiding compromise and
resolution are two strong moves in the struggle to deal with the
dilemmas of corporate branding, more help is on the way. Understanding symbolism and how its interpretation works will relieve
your desire to flee dilemmas and replace that fear with comprehen-
sion of the complexities involved.

If the CEO—the most potent human symbol an organizational
culture offers—models the importance of listening and responding to stakeholders, then a productive identity conversation will
develop within which managers and stakeholders share the responsibility of leading the brand to new destinations. If the CEO recognizes the importance of keeping that conversation balanced, not
forsaking the heritage of the firm yet reinterpreting that heritage
to serve the needs and expectations of its current mix of stakeholders, then culture and images will align.

If the CEO stays actively engaged with the identity conversation, it will be natural to use the information and impressions that
the organization's identity dynamics provide to improve strategic
vision and pull it in directions that cultural values and stakeholder

expectations already support. This will make future changes easier because once vision is aligned with culture and images, each will begin to inform the others in ways that, if attended to, will offer guidance regarding how to maintain or even improve alignment.

Symbols have an enormous capacity to carry multiple, even contradictory meanings that can be fluid in the face of change. But remember that it is *the act of making meaning together* rather than the precise meanings made that produces brand value. Positive associations that are formed in response to your brand symbols will provide the glue that holds stakeholders together in a community of belonging and support for the brand. Though at times you will have to manage conflicts between various uses of your symbol system, emphasizing the process of developing meaning together rather than the specific meanings involved will help you find the balance points that will enhance your brand's symbolic and economic value.

For some purposes it will be beneficial to create a unified message. Here you must remember to feed your "we" as well as your "us." On the "we" side, a consistently presented voice and demeanor that represents your cultural values does not violate the dictum of letting others make meaning with your symbolism and listening to what they say. Companies that desire strong corporate brands need to be able to do both.

When feeding the "us" side of the identity conversation, try to accept the meanings that stakeholders read into your corporate messages rather than pushing what you intended by them. If stakeholders feel they must resist your desire to shape their meanings, then they will not regard your brand as authentic. Manipulation of meaning is rarely pleasurable to anyone. Much better to openly share the role of shaping your brand with those whose interpretations are the final arbiters of its meaning and value. Tapping their conversations about who you are will help you know what your organization is capable of achieving.

If balancing the identity conversation in your organization becomes the basis of your strategic vision, you will go far as a leader and avoid the pitfalls of trying to control what you cannot—a brand's meaning. It will paradoxically also promote acceptance of your leadership because the involvement of stakeholders in forming the vision you offer them means they have already made an investment in you and the organization you symbolically represent.

Managing VCI Alignment and Identity Dynamics

As we emphasize throughout this book, striking a balance in the identity conversation is fundamental to effective corporate brand management. An organization's identity is formed from the conversation that occurs between those who create the organizational culture that backs their delivery of high-quality customer service and stakeholder responsiveness, and those whose images provide the organization with its reputation. The reputation then feeds back to employees and managers and, along with the company's efforts to mold external opinion, becomes part of the organizational identity and thus helps determine the level of self-esteem the organization achieves. Organizational self-esteem in turn affects the motivations of those who serve customers and respond to other stakeholders, which further influences the regard in which a company and its corporate brand is held. Once employees get the feel for the corporate brand and how it works, stakeholders will enjoy better brand delivery and their image of the organization will be enhanced as a result.

The improved image your corporate brand helps your company earn simultaneously exposes employees to positive feedback, which in turn produces greater self-esteem and leads to a spiral of mutual reinforcement between brand and stakeholders with positive benefits for your corporate reputation. Though your brand is unlikely to escape all criticism, organizational self-esteem without narcissism will allow you to listen as attentively to your critics as you do to your fans. Avoiding hyper-adaptation will, at the same time, keep you from overreacting to critics and fans alike. Making critics part of your decision-making processes will keep your brand authentic while maximizing the chances it has to gain converts. And belonging on the part of your loyal stakeholders will differentiate your company in a crowded global marketplace.

Strategic vision must play an integral role at each and every point in the process, but it must be as responsive to culture and images as these need to be to each other. Only through mutual listening and response among managers, employees, and all other stakeholders will the elements of VCI align to give your corporate brand the foundation it needs to mature into iconic status within the societies in which your enterprise operates, and it is the subtleties of meanings invested in brands that grease the wheels of this alignment. Here are five final pieces of advice we offer to send you on your way to creating and managing your corporate brand:

- Corporate branding is dynamic.
- Anticipate the future by celebrating your past.
- Listen and you will speak volumes.
- Serve your customers by delighting your employees.
- Think like an enterprise.

Corporate Branding Is Dynamic

The delicate balance that maintains VCI alignment means that the task of managing a corporate brand will never be completed. Continuous change in the economic, technological, regulatory, and other circumstances your company faces, and in the stakeholders who will forever try to negotiate new brand meanings that you never intended or imagined, will force you to alter one or another of the VCI components along with the way that you manage your corporate brand. Your need to shift gears and change the mind-sets that shape corporate branding practices throughout your organization will be an endless source of new challenges to keep you intellectually active and constantly engaged. But be sure to take a break from this incessant activity once in a while to celebrate your brand, its achievements, and those who make it possible.

Anticipate the Future by Celebrating Your Past

The past is where the founder first worked out an identity conversation that united stakeholders in pursuit of the enterprise that they shared. Return to that now-mythic time of origin—that is the best place to begin looking to the future, because it provides the sense of security that only remembering where we have come from can give us. But more than this, the past often holds untold treasures. In the time of origin, there were not one but many paths to be followed. Returning to the beginning can bring renewal when you discover paths radiating out from the origin point that lead in directions not yet explored. Anthropologists have shown that all tribes are fond of telling their origin stories; you can use this cultural trait to good advantage when you rebrand your organization to achieve renewal. And if you are a founder and living in the time of origin right now, be sure to make your company's origin story a good one.

Listen and You Will Speak Volumes

Never underestimate the power of listening to discover the actions your brand most needs. To learn to listen well you will need to practice. Music can be an excellent teacher here. We like to listen to jazz, a complex musical genre that invites you to hear melody, harmony, and rhythm intermixing in ever-changing ways. Listen first to just one instrument in a song that you like and hear how it is interacting with the others. Then relax a bit more, maybe closing your eyes, and hear all the instruments working together, sometimes stepping forward to take a solo, sometimes dropping back to complement someone else's solo, sometimes all playing at once to build intensity and complexity into the music. Imagine yourself in the middle, improvising along with the other musicians. This is the state you want to be in when managing your corporate brand. Play along with others to find the sound and style that befit your enterprise. Once you have mastered listening to all your stakeholders in an improvisational way, you will be able to make decisions that will benefit your corporate brand, and you will have already involved the people upon whom its success depends.

Serve Your Customers by Delighting Your Employees

Putting your brand behind your employees may be the single most important thing you can do. Only when your employees blend corporate brand thinking into their everyday work practices will customers experience the significance of your brand in their lives. So delight your employees with the meaning and fun that your brand can add to their work activities—and reap the benefits of their enhanced performance and greater stakeholder appreciation of your corporate brand.

Think Like an Enterprise

Keeping the full enterprise in mind in the midst of managing your brand in an ever-changing world means balancing on a web of intersecting interests and dilemmas. Seeing through the eyes of your stakeholders will develop your capacity to know your organization's identity and its role within society and the world. The knowledge this will bring will give you a greater sense of moral responsibility as well as many innovative ideas about the business you are in and how to manage it. Consciously adopting your stakeholders' points of view will also produce the plurality you need to manage your corporate brand both globally and locally.

Don't try this alone—bring others in your organization along with you. To prepare yourself, cultivate multiculturalism and interdisciplinarity throughout your organization. Doing so will produce the complex thinking you need to meet the dilemmas of corporate branding head-on and to catch the third wave of corporate branding.

Glossary of Key Terms

Corporate culture The values, beliefs, and basic assumptions espoused by an organization's top-level executives; expressed in official corporate documents, company brochures, and PR messages and advertising about the firm. (Compare *organizational culture*.)

Enterprise perspective The involvements of an organization viewed as a dynamic system of interests and activities, centered not necessarily on the organization or its business but on the context that makes the organization's activities useful and gives them meaning; places the organization within the context of its stakeholders' reasons for relating to it and to each other.

Organizational culture The internal values, beliefs, and basic assumptions that embody the heritage of the company and manifest in the ways employees think and feel about the company they are working for; expressed through the symbols and artifacts (objects, words, and deeds) of the whole organization and all of its members. (Compare *corporate culture*.)

Organizational identity Underpins the corporate brand; partly the effect of comparisons with competitors and of what others say about the organization, and partly of organizational self-insight; it is often expressed in the form of claims about organizational values, central ideas, or core beliefs that cause some confusion over the difference between organizational identity and culture.

Stakeholder images The meanings associated with an organization by its external stakeholders; the outside world's overall impression of the company at a particular time. Includes the views of customers, shareholders, the media, the general public, and so on.

Corporate reputation The overall estimation and assessment of an organization held by its multiple stakeholders; established over considerable time, corporate reputation emerges from the aggregated perceptions (corporate images) stakeholders form and use to communicate with one another about the organization's ability to fulfill their expectations.

Stakeholders The individuals and organizations that contribute (either voluntarily or involuntarily) to a corporation's wealth-creating capacity and activities, and that are therefore its potential beneficiaries and risk bearers; those who supply critical resources for the success of the enterprise or have sufficient power to affect its performance.

Strategic vision The central idea behind the company that embodies and expresses top management's aspiration for what the company will achieve in the future.

Notes

Chapter One

1. The BA case story is based on M. J. Hatch and M. Schultz, "Bringing the Corporation into Corporate Branding," *European Journal of Marketing* 37, no. 7/8 (2003): 1041–1064.
2. Quoted in Hatch and Schultz, "Bringing the Corporation into Corporate Branding," p. 1053.
3. See, for example, newspaper reports such as "BA Image Revamp Angers 'Unhappy' Staff," *Yorkshire Post/Reuters,* June 11, 1997, p. 3, and "Investors Attack British Airways Livery Revamp," *Financial Times,* July 16, 1997, p. 27.
4. J. Martinson, "Willie Walsh: The Pistol-Wielding Bambi Who Thrives in a Crisis," *Guardian,* June 30, 2006. Available online: www.guardian.co.uk/ba/story/0,,1809618,00.html. Access date: August 20, 2007.
5. Table 1.1 builds on Hatch and Schultz, "Bringing the Corporation into Corporate Branding."

Chapter Two

1. D. Atkin, *The Culting of Brands* (New York: Portfolio, 2004).
2. BMW's placement is according to the ranking agency Universum. Available online: http://universumusa.com/undergraduate.html. Access date: September 14, 2007.
3. This definition of *brand* is available online: www.marketingpower.com/mg-dictionary.php. Access date: August 25, 2007.

4. For more on Nissan brand presentation, see www.nissanusa.com. Access date: August 25, 2007.

5. S. J. Levy, "Symbols for Sale," *Harvard Business Review*, July–August 1959, pp. 117–124. See also S. J. Levy and D. W. Rook (eds.), *Brands, Consumers, Symbols and Research: Sydney J. Levy on Marketing* (Thousand Oaks, CA: Sage, 1999).

6. Wally Olins elaborated on these thoughts in *Corporate Identity: Making Business Strategy Visible Through Design* (Boston: Harvard Business School Press, 1989) and *On Brand* (London: Thames & Hudson, 2003).

7. A. Cohen, *The Symbolic Construction of Community* (London: Ellis Harwood, 1985).

8. This crisis was described widely at the time in national and international media, including CNN. A short overview is available online: http://en.wikipedia.org/wiki/Jyllands-Posten_Muhammad_cartoons_controversy. Access date: August 20, 2007.

9. The original source is D. Aaker, *Managing Brand Equity: Capitalizing on the Value of a Brand Name* (New York: Free Press, 1991).

10. See www.millwardbrown.com for more information on Millward Brown's consulting agency and its measurement system. Access date: August 20, 2007.

11. S. Gupta and D. R. Lehman, *Managing Customers as Investments: The Strategic Value of Customers in the Long Run* (Boston: Harvard Business School Press, 2005). The book promotes treating the consumer as a cash flow generator.

12. S. Fournier, "Consumers and Their Brands: Developing Relationship Theory in Consumer Research," *Journal of Consumer Research* 24 (1998): 343–373.

13. R. V. Kozinets, "Can Consumers Escape the Market? Emancipatory Illuminations from Burning Man," *Journal of Consumer Research* 29 (2002): 20–38.

14. Further information about the Reputation Institute and its RepTrak measurement system is available online: www

.reputationinstitute.com/main/home.php. Access date: August 20, 2007. The four emotions define the RepTrak pulse system. The results are published annually for twenty-nine countries in Forbes Online: www.forbes.com/leadership/2007/05/18/ reputation-lego-rankings-lead-citizen-cx_tw_0521reputation. html. Access date: September 20, 2007. For further discussion of the RepTrak, see C. van Riel and C. Fombrun, *Essentials of Corporate Communication* (London: Routledge, 2007).

15. Atkin, *The Culting of Brands*.
16. Interview with Jane Nakagawa conducted by James Rubin and Mary Jo Hatch, June 4, 2004, Los Angeles, California.

Chapter Three

1. The material for this example comes from J. Dutton and J. Dukerich, "Keeping an Eye on the Mirror: Image and Identity in Organizational Adaptation," *Academy of Management Journal* 34 (1991): 517–554.
2. For a short introduction to George Herbert Mead see M. J. Hatch and M. Schultz, *Reader on Organizational Identity* (Oxford, U.K.: Oxford University Press, 2004).
3. Y. Moon, "Inside Intel Inside," Harvard Business School Case 9-502-083, 2005.
4. According to Interbrand's Valuation Studies, Intel has been in the top five in brand equity since 2000, with the exception of 2001, when it was number six, and 2007 when it was number 7. Each year in August, *Business Week* publishes the most recent Interbrand results. Available online: www.businessweek .com. Access date: August 20, 2007.
5. G.-C. Guilbert, *Madonna as Postmodern Myth: How One Star's Self-Construction Rewrites Sex, Gender, Hollywood and the American Dream* (Jefferson, N.C.: McFarland, 2002).
6. For a further analysis of the turn-around in Shell, see C. Fombrun and V. Rindova, "The Road to Transparency: Reputation Management at Royal Dutch Shell," in *The Expressive*

Organization: Linking Identity, Reputation and the Corporate Brand, edited by M. Schultz, M. J. Hatch, and M. H. Larsen (Oxford, U.K.: Oxford University Press, 2000), pp. 77–97.

7. The oil reserve scandal was covered in all leading international business newspapers in the period from March through June 2004, when the scandal peaked.

8. A. D. Brown, "Narcissism, Identity, and Legitimacy," *Academy of Management Review* 22 (1997): 643–686.

9. A. D. Brown and K. Starkey, "Organizational Identity and Learning: A Psychodynamic Perspective," *Academy of Management Review* 25 (2000): 102–120; quote on p. 105.

Chapter Four

1. J. Collins and J. Porras, *Built to Last: Successful Habits of Visionary Companies* (New York: Harper Business Essentials, 1994). See also J. Collins and J. Porras, "Building Your Company's Vision," *Harvard Business Review*, September–October 1996, pp. 65–79.

2. D. Hamilton and K. Kirby, "A New Brand for a New Category: Paint It Orange," *Design Management Journal*, Winter 1999, pp. 41–45.

3. See also D. Ravasi and M. Schultz, "Organizational Culture and Identity at Bang & Olufsen," in *Practicing Identity*, edited by L. Lerpold et al. (London: Routledge, 2007), pp.103–120; and D. Ravasi and M. Schultz, "Responding to Organizational Identity Threats: Exploring the Role of Organizational Culture," *Academy of Management Journal* 46 (2006): 433–458.

4. See the Web site for Novo Nordisk (www.novonordisk.com; access date: August 20, 2007). You will find the various rankings of Novo Nordisk on this site. For Reputation Institute, see www.reputationinstitute.com. Access date: August 20, 2007.

5. For an overview of brand extensions and the different types of brand relations, see D. Aaker, *Brand Portfolio Strategy* (New York: Free Press, 2004).

6. Interbrand. *Uncommon Practice: People Who Deliver a Great Brand Experience* (Harlow, U.K.: Pearson Education, 2002), pp. 6–7.

7. See J. Linares, "Leading Change: An Interview with the Executive Chairman of Telefónica Espana," *McKinsey Quarterly* Web exclusively, August 2005. Available online: www .mckinseyquarterly.com/Leading_change_An_interview_ with_the_executive_chairman_of_Telefonica_de_Espana_ 1654_abstract. Access date: September 20, 2007.

8. For a brief overview of the Nordea merger, see the company's Web site, www.nordea.com (access date: August 20, 2007). For an in-depth study of the merger process and challenges, see A. M. Søderberg and E. Vaara, *Merging Across Borders: People, Cultures and Politics* (Copenhagen: Copenhagen Business School Press, 2003). The case description is based on this source, and all citations are from it: pp. 73, 75, 78, and 81.

9. These differences in national cultures between the Scandinavian countries are further described in the many works of Geert Hofstede. The classic is *Culture and Organizations: Software of the Mind* (London: McGraw-Hill, 1991).

10. This is published at the Nordea Web site (www.nordea.com), under Investor Relations. Also see www.euromoney.com. Access date: August 20, 2007.

Chapter Five

1. L. Greiner, "Evolution and Revolution as Organizations Grow," *Harvard Business Review* 50 (1972): 37–46. A version of the figure exists in a reprint of the original article May–June 1998, p. 58.

2. Interview with Janus Friis on *Danmarks Radio* concerning his life as visionary entrepreneur. He was featured in the Danish *Money* program broadcast on November 9, 2006. Available online: www.dr.dk/DR1/penge/arkiv/2006/1109153912.htm. Access date: September 15, 2007.

3. M. Sigurdsson, "The Skype Brand," talk given at the Reboot Conference, Copenhagen, June 16, 2005. Full presentation available online: http://skypejournal.com/blog/archives/2005/06/ malthe_sigurdss.php. Access date: August 20, 2007.

4. The Sigurdsson story builds on the Reboot Conference and an interview in *Designmatters* 2 (February 2007): 14. (A publication of the Danish Design Centre.) Available online (in Danish): www.ddc.dk/DESIGNVIDEN/designmatters/design matters_no2_2007#. Access date: September 28, 2007.

5. Skype's visual design was created by 2GD.

6. Sigurdsson, "The Skype Brand."

7. Janus Friis cited in the Danish magazine *Euroman*, December 2005, pp. 48–49.

8. "Skype Extends Leadership Position with New Must-Have Release," Skype press release, London, 2005. Available online: http://about.skype.com/2005/09/. Access date: September 30, 2007.

9. The interview appeared in *Euroman*, December 2005, pp. 48–49.

10. All these endorsements and many others can be found at the Noir Web site: www.noir-illuminati2.com. Access date: August 20, 2007.

11. "Fashion with a Heart," *Harpers Bazaar*, August 2005, p. 74.

12. To read more about Day Birger & Mikkelsen, see www.day.dk. Access date: August 20, 2007.

13. Interview with Peter Ingwersen, CEO and founder of Noir, conducted by Majken Schultz in Copenhagen, March 9, 2007.

14. The trend has been defined by Boston Consulting Group as the fastest-growing market segment: luxury affordable for the middle class and creating "mass-exclusivity."

15. Interview with Peter Ingwersen.

16. Quoted in: E. Karmark, *Organizational Identity in a Dualistic Subculture: A Case Study of the Organizational Identity Formation in the LEGO Media International* (Copenhagen: Copenhagen Business School Press, 2002), p. 140.

17. Karmark, *Organizational Identity in a Dualistic Subculture*, p. 144.

18. Interview with Mark Perry conducted by Mary Jo Hatch in Charlottesville, Virginia, April 17, 2007.

Chapter Six

1. Reprinted by permission of *Harvard Business Review*. Excerpt from "A Voice of Experience: An Interview with TRW's Frederick C. Crawford," by G. Dyer, November–December 1991, pp. 115–126; quote on p. 117. Copyright© by the Harvard Business School Publishing Corporation, all rights reserved.
2. Quotations from Virgin personnel are from Interbrand, *Uncommon Practice: People Who Deliver a Great Brand Experience* (Harlow, U.K.: Pearson Education, 2002), pp. 4, 5, and 8.
3. S. Greyser, "Johnson & Johnson: The Tylenol Tragedy," Harvard Business School Case #583043, 1982.
4. M. J. Hatch, "The Dynamics of Organizational Culture," *Academy of Management Review* 18 (1993): 657–693.
5. E. Schein, *Organizational Culture and Leadership*, 3rd. ed. (San Francisco: Jossey-Bass, 2004), p. 246.
6. We are indebted to research assistant Simon Boege for the analysis of the facilitation process and interviews with then SVP of the facilitators Lone Hass and two individual facilitators conducted in 2003, and to Mike Rulis, VP of Corporate Communication, Novo Nordisk, for his extensive comments on this material. The facilitators have recently been transferred from the Novo holding company to Novo Nordisk, but the facilitation process has remained intact since 1997.
7. For further discussion of how companies are invoking brand-based human resource and communication practices, see N. Ind, *Living the Brand* (London: Kogan Page, 2001).
8. For further description of the triple bottom line, see Annual Report 2006, p. 5. Available online: www.novonordisk.com. Available online: http://annualreport.novonordisk.com/images/2006/PDFs/Report%202006%20UK.pdf. Access date: September 20, 2007.
9. The quoted statement about the TakeAction! program is available online: www.novonordisk.com/annual-report-2004/case-stories/case-taking-action.asp. Access date: August 20, 2007.

10. For a description of the Helios Awards Program, see www
.bp.com/subsection.do?categoryId=9002633&contentId=
2002401. Access date: September 20, 2007.

Chapter Seven

1. Marc Gunther, "Aspen Nixes Kleenex," March 6, 2007. Available online: www.marcgunther.com/?cat=9; search on "Kleenex." Access date: August 20, 2007.

2. R. E. Freeman, *Strategic Management: A Stakeholder Approach* (Boston: Pitman, 1984). See also R. E. Freeman and J. McVea, "A Stakeholder Approach to Strategic Management," in *The Blackwell Handbook of Strategic Management*, edited by M. Hitt, R. E. Freeman, and J. Harrison (Oxford, U.K.: Blackwell, 2001), pp. 189–207.

3. Reprinted by permission of *Harvard Business Review*. Excerpt from "The Power of Virtual Integration: An Interview with Dell Computer's Michael Dell," by J. Magretta, March–April 1998, pp. 73–84; quote on p. 80. Copyright © by the Harvard Business School Publishing Corporation, all rights reserved.

4. See J. Levine, *Pfizer Global Health Fellows: Expanding Access to Healthcare Through Cross-Sector Partnerships* (Boston: Boston College Center for Corporate Citizenship, October 14, 2004).

5. The premiere Web site for BMW owners around the world, with interactive forums, photo galleries, and other resources, is www.bimmerfest.com. Another discussion forum and community for BMW enthusiasts to share their knowledge and passion for cars can be found at www.unitedbimmer.com. Access date: August 20, 2007.

6. A. Muniz and B. O'Guinn, "Brand Community," *Journal of Consumer Research* 27 (2001): 412–432.

7. The concept of community has a long history in philosophy and sociology. with contributions from thinkers such as Dewey, Durkheim, Weber, and Simmel. For elaboration of these references, see Muniz and O'Guinn, "Brand Community." Muniz

and O'Guinn describe three markers of brand communities. We divided their second point, adding protection of the brand heritage as a fourth marker.

8. For elaboration, see B. Anderson, *Imagined Community* (London: Verso, 1983).

9. Muniz and O'Guinn, "Brand Community," p. 422.

10. For more on the Coca-Cola story, see the short description and related links at http://en.wikipedia.org/wiki/New_Coke. Access date: August 20, 2007.

11. Discussion of the conflict over the LEGO brick colors is based on the Ph.D. dissertation of Yun Mi Antorini, who showed that this debate alone generated more then 900 Internet pages of reaction. Y. M. Antorini, *Brand Community Innovation: An Intrinsic Study of the Adult Fan of LEGO Community* (Copenhagen: Samfundslitteratur, 2007).

12. Antorini, *Brand Community Innovation*, p. 425.

13. See, for example, the video and other cool stuff at www.kahsoon.com/category/cool-stuff/. Access date: August 20, 2007.

14. Interview with Jørgen Vig Knudstorp, CEO of the LEGO Group, conducted by Majken Schultz in Billund, Denmark, April 11, 2007.

15. From a presentation at Copenhagen Business School, Full-Time MBA Program, April 2007. Quoted directly from handout presented in class.

16. "The Johnson & Johnson Campaign for Nursing's Future: 2007 Campaign Overview." Available online: www.campaignfornursing.com/download/press/campaign_overview_030107.pdf. Access date: August 20, 2007.

17. In global studies of reputation among the world's two hundred leading companies, Johnson & Johnson ranked #2 in the United States in 2006 and #4 in the United States in 2007. The annual reputation studies were conducted by Harris Interactive in collaboration with the Reputation Institute and published in the *Wall Street Journal*. Global RepTrak 2006 was conducted by the Reputation Institute and published

by Forbes online, November 20, 2006. Available online: www
.forbes.com; search for "Global RepTrak 2006." Access date:
August 20, 2007.

18. M. Schultz, J. Rubin, M. J. Hatch, and K. Andersen, "Novo
Nordisk: Focusing the Corporate Brand," University of
Virginia Darden School Foundation, Case #UVA-BC-0192,
2004.

19. For the World Diabetes Foundation, see www.worlddiabetes
foundation.org. Access date: August 20, 2007. Novo Nordisk
has made a commitment to donate $67 million to WDF over
a ten-year period.

20. For Clare Rosenfeld's story and role in the campaign, see www.
unitefordiabetes.org/youth/ambassadors/clarerosenfeld. Access
date: August 20, 2007.

21. For more information about IDF, see www.idf.org. Access date:
August 20, 2007. To read about World Diabetes Day, see www.
worlddiabetesday.org. Access date: August 20, 2007.

22. For further details on the Changing Diabetes World Tour,
see http://diabetesbus.novonordisk.com. Access date: August
20, 2007.

23. For elaboration of the benefits of third-party endorsement of
brand activities, see M. Morsing and M. Schultz, "Corporate
Social Responsibility Communication: Stakeholder Information, Response and Involvement Strategies," *Business Ethics:
A European Review* 15, no. 4 (2006): 323–338.

Chapter Eight

1. The Young & Rubicam brand survey is the Brandasset Valuator assessing the vitality and stature of brands. See http://www
.yandr.com/and go to Our Work and then to Our Brandasset
Valuator. Access date: September 20, 2007. The Brandasset Valuator is described in detail by David Aaker in *Building
Stronger Brands* (New York: Free Press, 1996). According to
brand researcher Douglas Holt, the LEGO brand has an iconic

status. See his *How Brands Become Icons* (Boston: Harvard Business School Press, 2004).

2. M. Schultz and M. J. Hatch, "The Cycles of Corporate Branding: The Case of LEGO Company," *California Management Review* 46, no. 1 (2003): 6–26.

3. This statement is taken from www.lego.com. Access date: August 20, 2007. See selected statistics in the Company Profile 2006. Other details about the LEGO brand, such as awards, are also given on the Web site.

4. The task force consisted of members from both Europe and the United States and a variety of people with marketing, communication, and people skills. Majken Schultz was a part-time external consultant for the LEGO Group from 2000 through 2003, working with the leader of the task force, among others. The first part of the brand story draws on earlier published sources: M. Schultz and M. J. Hatch, "The Cycles of Corporate Branding"; M. Schultz and M. J. Hatch, "A Cultural Perspective on Corporate Branding: The Case of LEGO Group," in *Brand Culture*, edited by Jonathan Schroeder and Miriam Salzer-Mörling (London: Routledge, 2006), pp. 15–31; M. Schultz, M. J. Hatch, and F. Ciccolella, "Brand Life in Symbols and Artifacts: The LEGO Company," in *Artifacts and Organizations*, edited by A. Rafaeli and M. Pratt (Mahwah, N.J.: Erlbaum, 2006), pp. 141–160. We are also indebted to CEO Jørgen Vig Knudstorp for his extensive comments and help in writing this chapter. All the quotations from Jørgen Vig Knudstorp came from a personal interview conducted by Majken Schultz in Billund, Denmark, April 11, 2007. Thanks also to Iben Eiby Johannesen, former LEGO manager, for her insightful feedback and comments, particularly on LEGO Brand Schools.

5. The strategic intent had been pursued by the LEGO Group from the late 1990s.

6. This process was inspired by LEGO Serious Play, an experiential learning process developed by LEGO and a group of external consultants to stimulate business innovation and enhance

business performance. See www.seriousplay.com. Access date: August 20, 2007.

7. These findings came from internal studies such as the Consumer Understanding Model 2003 and Qualitative Brand Research 2003, as reported to the LEGO Brand Board 2003. The LEGO Brand Board was an advisory board to top management, where Majken Schultz was a member along with the SVP of Global Brand and members of the family that owns LEGO Group.

8. See www.lugnet.com. Access date: August 20, 2007. Similar but country-specific user communities include Germany's "1000 Steine" (1000 Bricks) and Denmark's "Byggepladen" (The Building Plate). The term *brand community* was first coined by A. Muniz and B. O'Guinn in "Brand Community," *Journal of Consumer Research* 27 (2001): 412–432. Chapter Seven includes a full discussion of brand communities. We are grateful for insights into the LEGO brand community provided by Yun Mi Antorini, of Copenhagen Business School. See also Y. M. Antorini, *Brand Community Innovation: An Intrinsic Study of the Adult Fan of LEGO Community* (Copenhagen: Samfundslitteratur, 2007).

9. McKee is no longer with the LEGO Group.

10. This is according to a Global RepTrak study by the Reputation Institute, which used a representative sample of the general public to rank the reputations of the largest two hundred companies in twenty-nine countries. See www.reputationinstitute.com. Access date: August 20, 2007. The study was conducted in 2006 and 2007 by the Reputation Institute and published by Forbes online, November 20, 2006. Available online: www.forbes.com; search for "Global RepTrak 2006." Access date: August 20, 2007.

11. Steve Hassenplug, John Barnes, David Schilling, and Ralph Hempel were all featured in Brendan I. Koerner's cover story, "Geeks in Toyland," about LEGO Group's new development. *Wired Magazine*, February 2006. Available online: www.wired.com/wired/archive/14.02/lego.html. Access date: August 20, 2007.

12. Koerner, "Geeks in Toyland."

13. From a statement by CEO Jørgen Vig Knudstorp, press release, February 2006. Available online: www.lego.com/eng/info/default. asp?page=pressdetail&contentid=18853&countrycode=2057& yearcode=2006&archive=true. Access date: September 20, 2007.

Chapter Nine

1. For a discussion of other kinds of brand organization, see D. Aaker and E. Joachimstahler, *Brand Leadership* (New York: Free Press, 2000).

2. For further elaboration of the strategic process in Novo Nordisk since 2000 and the considerations behind the current brand strategy, see M. Schultz, J. Rubin, M. J. Hatch, and K. Andersen, "Novo Nordisk: Focusing the Corporate Brand," University of Virginia Darden School Foundation, Case #UVA-BC-0192, 2004.

3. As part of our ongoing research on the brand strategy at Novo Nordisk, Majken Schultz interviewed Charlotte Ersbøll, Novo Nordisk VP of corporate branding, four times during 2006 and 2007. Unless otherwise noted, the quotations in this section are from these interviews.

4. Interview with Charlotte Ersbøll, conducted by Majken Schultz, Mary Jo Hatch, and James Rubin in Copenhagen, November 2005.

5. Owen Rankin, J&J's corporate equity VP, made this statement during our discussion at the Corporate Brand Initiative meeting hosted by the University of Virginia, March 2002.

References

Aaker, D. *Managing Brand Equity: Capitalizing on the Value of a Brand Name*. New York: Free Press, 1991.

Aaker, D. *Building Stronger Brands*. New York: Free Press, 1996.

Aaker, D. *Brand Portfolio Strategy*. New York: Free Press, 2004.

Aaker, D., and Joachimstahler, E. *Brand Leadership*. New York: Free Press, 2000.

Anderson, B. *Imagined Community*. London: Verso, 1983.

Antorini, Y. M. *Brand Community Innovation: An Intrinsic Study of the Adult Fan of LEGO Community*. Copenhagen: Samfundslitteratur, 2007.

Atkin, D. *The Culting of Brands*. New York: Portfolio, 2004.

Brown, A. "Narcissism, Identity, and Legitimacy." *Academy of Management Review*, 1997, *22*, 643–686.

Brown, A. D., and Starkey, K. "Organizational Identity and Learning: A Psychodynamic Perspective." *Academy of Management Review*, 2000, *25*, 102–120.

Cohen, A. *The Symbolic Construction of Community*. London: Ellis Harwood, 1985.

Collins, J., and Porras, J. *Built to Last: Successful Habits of Visionary Companies*. New York: Harper Business Essentials, 1994.

Collins, J., and Porras, J. "Building Your Company's Vision." *Harvard Business Review*, Sept.–Oct. 1996, pp. 65–79.

Dutton, J., and Dukerich, J. "Keeping an Eye on the Mirror: Image and Identity in Organizational Adaptation." *Academy of Management Journal*, 1991, *34*, 517–554.

Dyer, G. "A Voice of Experience: An Interview with TRW's Frederick C. Crawford." *Harvard Business Review*, Nov.–Dec. 1991, pp. 115–126.

Fombrun, C., and Rindova, V. "The Road to Transparency: Reputation Management at Royal Dutch Shell." In M. Schultz, M. J. Hatch, and M. H. Larsen (eds.), *The Expressive Organization: Linking Identity, Reputation and the Corporate Brand*. Oxford, U.K.: Oxford University Press, 2000, 77–97.

Fournier, S. "Consumers and Their Brands: Developing Relationship Theory in Consumer Research." *Journal of Consumer Research*, 1998, *24*, 343–373.

Freeman, R. E. *Strategic Management: A Stakeholder Approach*. Boston: Pitman, 1984.

Freeman, R. E., and McVea, J. "A Stakeholder Approach to Strategic Management." In M. A. Hitt, R. E. Freeman, and J. S. Harrison (eds.), *The Blackwell Handbook of Strategic Management*. Oxford, U.K.: Blackwell, 2001.

Greiner, L. "Evolution and Revolution as Organizations Grow." *Harvard Business Review*, 1972, 50, 37–46.

Greyser, S. "Johnson & Johnson: The Tylenol Tragedy." Harvard Business School Case 583-043, 1982.

Guilbert, G.-C. *Madonna as Postmodern Myth: How One Star's Self-Construction Rewrites Sex, Gender, Hollywood and the American Dream*. Jefferson, N.C.: McFarland, 2002.

Gupta, S., and Lehman, D. R. *Managing Customers as Investments: The Strategic Value of Customers in the Long Run*. Boston: Harvard Business School Press, 2005.

Hamilton, D., and Kirby, K. "A New Brand for a New Category: Paint It Orange." *Design Management Journal*, Winter 1999, pp. 41–45.

Hatch, M. J. "The Dynamics of Organizational Culture." *Academy of Management Review*, 1993, 18, 657–693.

Hatch, M. J., and Schultz, M. "Are the Strategic Stars Aligned for Your Corporate Brand?" *Harvard Business Review*, February 2001, pp. 128–134.

Hatch, M. J., and Schultz, M. "The Dynamics of Organizational Identity." *Human Relations*, 2002, 55(8), 989–1017.

Hatch, M. J., and Schultz, M. "Bringing the Corporation into Corporate Branding." *European Journal of Marketing*, 2003, 37(7/8), 1041–1064.

Hatch, M. J., and Schultz, M. *Reader on Organizational Identity*. Oxford, U.K.: Oxford University Press, 2004.

Holt, D. *How Brands Become Icons*. Boston: Harvard Business School Press, 2004.

Hofstede, G. *Culture and Organizations: Software of the Mind*. London: McGraw-Hill, 1991.

Interbrand. *Uncommon Practice: People Who Deliver a Great Brand Experience*. Harlow, U.K.: Pearson Education, 2002.

Ind, N. *Living the Brand*. London: Kogan Page, 2001.

Karmark, E. *Organizational Identity in a Dualistic Subculture: A Case Study of the Organizational Identity Formation in the LEGO Media International*. Copenhagen: Copenhagen Business School Press, 2002.

Kozinets, R. V. "Can Consumers Escape the Market? Emancipatory Illuminations from Burning Man." *Journal of Consumer Research*, 2002, 29, 20–38.

Levine, J. *Pfizer Global Health Fellows: Expanding Access to Healthcare Through Cross-Sector Partnerships*. Boston: Boston College Center for Corporate Citizenship, Oct. 14, 2004.

Levy, S. J., "Symbols for Sale." *Harvard Business Review*, July–Aug. 1959, pp. 117–124.

Levy, S. J., and Rook, D. W. (eds.). *Brands, Consumers, Symbols and Research: Sydney J. Levy on Marketing*. Thousand Oaks, Calif.: Sage, 1999.

Linares, J. "Leading Change: An Interview with the Executive Chairman of Telefónica Espana." *McKinsey Quarterly*, Aug. 2005. Available online: www.mckinseyquarterly.com/Leading_change_An_interview_with_the_executive_chairman_of_Telefonica_de_Espana_1654_abstract. Access date: Sept. 20, 2007.

Magretta, J. "The Power of Virtual Integration: An Interview with Dell Computer's Michael Dell." *Harvard Business Review*, Mar.–Apr. 1998, pp. 73–84.

Moon, Y. "Inside Intel Inside." Harvard Business School Case 9-502-083, 2005.

Morsing, M., and Schultz, M. "Corporate Social Responsibility Communication: Stakeholder Information, Response and Involvement Strategies." *Business Ethics: A European Review*, 2006, *15*(4), 323–338.

Muniz, A., and O'Guinn, B. "Brand Community." *Journal of Consumer Research*, 2001, *27*, 412–432.

Olins, W. *Corporate Identity: Making Business Strategy Visible Through Design*. Boston: Harvard Business School Press, 1989.

Olins, W. *On Brand*. London: Thames & Hudson, 2003.

Ravasi, D., and Schultz, M. "Organizational Culture and Identity at Bang & Olufsen." In L. Lerpold and others (eds.), *Practicing Identity*. London: Routledge, 2007.

Ravasi, D., and Schultz, M. "Responding to Organizational Identity Threats: Exploring the Role of Organizational Culture." *Academy of Management Journal*, 2006, 46, 433–458.

Schein, E. *Organizational Culture and Leadership*. (3rd. ed.) San Francisco: Jossey-Bass, 2004.

Sigurdsson, M. Interview in *Designmatters*, Feb. 2007, *2*, 14. (A publication of the Danish Design Centre, Copenhagen.) Available online: http://www.ddc.dk/DESIGNVIDEN/designmatters/designmatters_no2_2007. Access date: Sept. 28, 2007.

Schultz, M., and Hatch, M. J. "The Cycles of Corporate Branding: The Case of LEGO Company." *California Management Review*, 2003, 46(1), 6–26.

Schultz, M., and Hatch, M. J. "A Cultural Perspective on Corporate Branding: The Case of LEGO Group." In Jonathan Schroeder and Miriam Salzer-Mörling (eds.), *Brand Culture*. London: Routledge, 2006.

Schultz, M., Hatch, M. J., and Ciccolella, F. "Brand Life in Symbols and Artifacts: The LEGO Company." In A. Rafaeli and M. Pratt (eds.), *Artifacts and Organizations*. Mahwah, N.J.: Erlbaum, 2006.

Schultz, M., Rubin, J., Hatch, M. J., and Andersen, K. "Novo Nordisk: Focusing the Corporate Brand." University of Virginia Darden School Foundation, Case #UVA-BC-0192, 2004.

Søderberg, A. M., and Vaara, E. *Merging Across Borders: People, Cultures and Politics*. Copenhagen: Copenhagen Business School Press, 2003.

Van Riel, C., and Fombrun, C. *Essentials of Corporate Communication*. London: Routledge, 2007.

The Authors

Mary Jo Hatch, professor emerita of the University of Virginia, is an adjunct and visiting professor at the Copenhagen Business School. She is the author of *Organization Theory: Modern, Symbolic and Postmodern Perspectives*, now in its second edition (with Ann Cunliffe), and *The Three Faces of Leadership: Manager, Artist, Priest* (with Monika Kostera and Andrzej Kozminski). Her articles on corporate branding, organizational culture, and organizational identity appear in *Harvard Business Review, California Management Review, European Journal of Marketing, Journal of Brand Management, Human Relations, Academy of Management Review, Administrative Science Quarterly,* and *Organization Studies.* Contact Hatch at mjhatch@virginia.edu.

Majken Schultz is a professor of management at Copenhagen Business School and a partner in the Reputation Institute. She is coeditor of *Corporate Branding: Purpose, People, Process* (with Yun Mi Antorini and Fabian Csaba) and author of *On Studying Organizational Cultures: Diagnosis and Understanding.* Her articles on corporate branding, organizational culture, identity, and reputation management appear in *Harvard Business Review, California Management Review, Corporate Reputation Review, European Journal of Marketing, Human Relations, Academy of Management Review, Academy of Management Journal, Journal of Management Inquiry,* and *Organization Studies.* (Visit www.majkenschultz.com.)

Together Hatch and Schultz have edited two books of potential interest to readers of this one: *The Expressive Organization: Linking Identity, Reputation and the Corporate Brand* (with Mogens Holten Larsen) and *Organizational Identity: A Reader.*

Index